Praise for

THE INVENTION OF
ESSEX

'This is a book about Essex people and how they created one of Britain's best-known and most distinctive counties. Many have moved from London, but once in Essex they have stayed there. Tim Burrows' sympathetic and vivid investigation of Essex's unique social landscape reveals that its historical roots are ancient and very modern: both are equally important. It's an addictive read' **Francis Pryor, author of *The Fens: Discovering England's Ancient Depths***

'"Before Essex was a punchline, it was a dream," writes Tim Burrows, and he shows you the hopes and humanity of a county more often the subject of lazy stereotype. Thoroughly researched yet deeply personal, this book takes in marsh and factory, William Morris and *TOWIE* – all delivered with a friendly panache' **Aditya Chakrabortty**

'An exceptional book by a lucid and sharp-eyed writer with a personal stake in his story. Burrows has a winning way of combining solidarity with critical distance, and an invigorating habit of cutting through the clichés with one sympathetic blast after another. This is Essex for the 21st century but it's also a book about England, and all the better for the fact that it absolutely refuses to be an elegy' **Patrick Wright, author of *The Sea View Has Me Again***

THE INVENTION OF
ESSEX

THE MAKING OF AN ENGLISH COUNTY

TIM BURROWS

P

PROFILE BOOKS

First published in Great Britain in 2023 by
Profile Books Ltd
29 Cloth Fair
London
ECIA 7JQ

www.profilebooks.com

1 3 5 7 9 10 8 6 4 2

Lyric from 'A13, Trunk Road to the Sea' written by Billy Bragg.
Published by Warner Chappell Music. Used with permission.

Lyric from 'Violent Playground'. Written by Nitzer Ebb.
Reprinted by kind permission from Mute Song Limited.

Map produced by Martin Lubikowski, ML Design © 2023

Typeset in Berling Nova Text by MacGuru Ltd
Printed and bound in Great Britain by Clays Ltd, Elcograf S.p.A.

A CIP catalogue record for this book is available from the British Library.

ISBN 978 1 78816 676 8
eISBN 978 1 78283 788 6

FSC
www.fsc.org
MIX
Paper from
responsible sources
FSC® C018072

To Hayley, Greta and Ernest;
and to families Singer, Hevey,
Hatton, Gillman and Burrows.

Contents

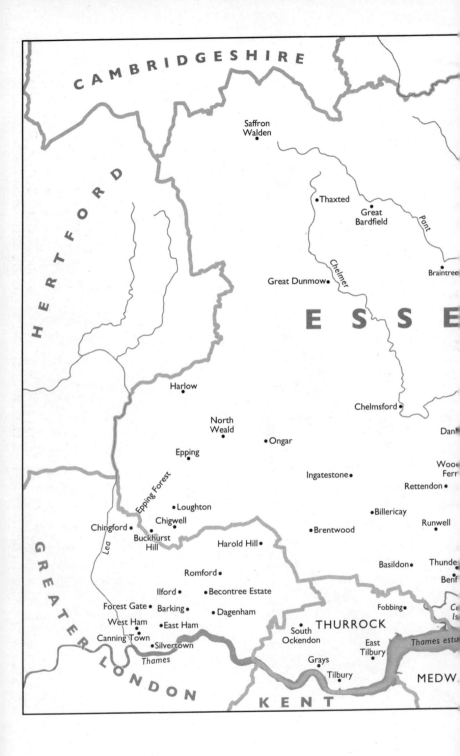

S U F F O L K

Brett

Stour

Dedham •

Manningtree •

Wrabness • Harwich •

Colne

Colchester •

• Coggeshall

Walton-on-the-Naze •

ver End

X

Blackwater

• Great
Braxted

Vitham

St Osyth
Clacton •

*Mersea
Island*

Jaywick •

Tollesbury •

DENGIE PENINSULA

Blackwater

*Osea
Island*

Maldon •

Bradwell •

• Purleigh

Southminster •

uth Woodham Ferrers

• Burnham on Crouch

*Wallasea
Island*

*Foulness
Island*

ayleigh

Barling •

*Rushley
Island*

*Havengore
Island*

Hadleigh

• Great Wakering

SOUTHEND

• Shoeburyness

*Two Tree
Island*

Leigh-on-Sea

N O R T H   S E A

0 1 2 3 4 5 6 7 8 9 10 11 12 miles
0   2   4   6   8   10   12   14   16   18   20 kilometres

Prologue

I was drawn back to Essex after the city had started to squeeze me a little too hard. I was trying to navigate the stresses of a career as a journalist in London while also attempting to figure out why I, a kid from Southend, was even trying to *be* a journalist in London. I lived with my girlfriend, Hayley, in a shared house in Dalston, in the east of the city, which was stuffed full of other escapees from our south Essex homeland. Most of us had met years ago in Southend, either in the haze of secondary school or the stoned interregnum of sixth form. We'd all spent years solidifying our friendships on the streets of Essex, in shelters by the estuary or in the smoke-filled pubs and clubs. The fact we had left it all behind to move to London constituted a historical irony that some elder family members had not been shy of reminding us. It was as if we had betrayed the natural order of things, the trajectory out from the great, swollen city to the open county of Essex. Southend was the destination of all cockneys on a Bank Holiday Monday, and somehow our ancestors had never made it onto the train home.

East London had felt less like home since the runup to the 2012 Olympics sparked a boom in the building of luxury high-rise flats that decanted council tenants to other parts of the UK. Rents were going up. Friends from Europe had to leave as the Conservative Party's austerity programme took hold and they could no longer afford to build their lives there. Living in London had started to feel ever so slightly masochistic, at the mercy of a city that took pleasure in stealing your time and making you beg for each scrap of comfort. Even the things about London I had always loved were turning on me. The relentlessness of its transport systems, timetables and societal pressures – all things that I thought I lived for at the time – had ensnared me slowly and silently the way a boa constrictor does its prey. So I decided to walk back home.

With my friend Adam, I walked from east London to Southend in a couple of days, leaving West Ham at dawn via a path constructed over a gigantic outfall sewer built when the area was still part of Essex. We made it out to the A13, that tarmacked tributary clogged up with vans making the trip into the land of constant development, and then further into hybrid landscapes empty of people, where reclaimed toxic dumps and landfill sites were transformed into wildlife sanctuaries. What really resonated was the sudden feeling of freedom out in the wastes between Barking, Dagenham, Rainham, Tilbury and beyond. In London, each day had become a saga of stress filled with hyper-capitalistic information overloads; these Essex walks, by comparison, were imbued with a sense of possibility and space to breathe.

After the epic walk home, I planned more walks into the edges of Essex, trying to blur the boundaries between the city and home. Despite the fact I hadn't lived in Essex since my late teens, all of a sudden I couldn't stop reading about Essex, walking around Essex, trawling archives for mentions of Essex and talking about Essex. At the same time, I was starting to learn that the act of turning to the open plains and big skies of Essex as a salve for stricken city life was itself a centuries-long tradition of convalescence away from the pressures of urban life.

After a while, it's possible that friends were starting to

question my sanity: why was I spending all my time thinking about the county of my birth? Was I homesick? It was a possibility. Was I obsessed? I preferred to think of it as old-fashioned sleuthing, thanks. I drifted away from reviewing music for broadsheet newspapers and magazines and started to write about Essex. At the same time, Essex seemed to be taking up ever more space in British popular culture. Essex types were filling TV screens as comic staples of reality shows such as *Love Island*, *First Dates*, *Big Brother* and *The X Factor*. One of the biggest entertainment stars working in the UK today, BBC radio and TV presenter Rylan Clark, shot to fame after his outlandishly 'Essex' appearances on *The X Factor* and *Celebrity Big Brother* (the latter show also introduced self-styled Essex girl Chantelle Houghton to the world). Young people from Essex seemed to be everywhere, performing for the camera, as if made in some marshland laboratory to meet the demands of the age of reality TV. These instant celebrities such as Joey Essex or Stacey Solomon served a dual function as heartthrob idols for teenagers to swoon over (and emulate, in the case of the lads copying Joey's distinctive 'fusey' haircut, a shaven-sided and long on top look) and feckless fodder for the chattering classes to laugh at. They were capable of playing it for laughs, while unabashedly upping their desirability through whitened teeth and an array of cosmetic enhancements, creating a look that was simultaneously part of the joke and part of the appeal. It all seemed to confirm a truism first seeded during the brash 1980s that Essex represented an aggressive new way of living for the English lower orders.

My new ventures into Essex reconnected me with the county that I half remembered from my childhood. The solemn cows marooned in the beguilingly alien wasteland of Vange Marsh. Strawberry picking in farms tucked away beyond the arterial roads and suburban adjuncts. St Peter-on-the-Wall, the seventh-century church in Bradwell, the county's oldest church and most sacred spot, which looks to the unsuspecting visitor like little more than an esoteric barn, dwarfed by sky where the Blackwater Estuary meets the North Sea.

Essex seemed to be everywhere and nowhere, unignorable yet unknowable. While quainter areas towards and into the north of the county, such as Maldon, Saffron Walden, Dedham and the Dengie Peninsula, were praised for retaining the Essex character, the new Essex that was predominantly rolled out over the southern reaches of the county in the early part of the twentieth century was singled out for being as hooky as a market trader's wares. The motorised and modernised new British lifestyle meant that the old, rural Essex was being erased from the English story – not that it had even been a major part of it in the first place. No work has been claimed to have represented England during the time of the Great Depression as much as JB Priestley's much celebrated *English Journey*, a travelogue based on the writer's chauffeured schlep around the country. England, according to Priestley's famous sojourn, comprised of Southampton, Bristol, Swindon and the Cotswolds, Coventry, Birmingham and the Black Country; it included Leicester and Nottingham, West Riding, the Potteries, Lancashire and Yorkshire, not to mention the Tyne, East Durham and the Tees, Lincoln and, lastly, Norfolk. What it quite emphatically did not include, however, was Essex. Priestley had seen enough by Norfolk, having grown tired of his journey by the time he was on the home straight back to London. Although he didn't assume there was nothing going on there. 'I would not set foot in Essex. Because Essex begins somewhere among back streets in London's eastern suburbs, some people think it has no mystery, but I know that Essex is a huge mysterious county, with God knows what going on in its remoter valleys. No Essex for me. I was going home, and by the shortest possible route.'

Prologue

In Essex, it can feel like portals to unique historical stories and portentous mysteries are hidden under every A-road. The Prittlewell Prince is another singularly incredible Essex story found by accident during a construction venture in 2003 – the widening of a road in Southend, where the Aldi supermarket now resides – around the corner from the council-terraced house my mum grew up in. Archaeologists, informed by an earlier dig in the 1920s, had expected to find a little something. But what they were presented with was one of the richest Anglo-Saxon burials ever discovered in the UK.

A collapsed burial chamber was unearthed slowly, its features identifiable only through the discoloration of the earth. The fact it sat in free-draining soil meant that everything organic had decayed away to nothing. 'It was essentially a sandpit with stains,' said Sophie Jackson, the director of research at Museum of London Archaeology (MOLA). But the find was nevertheless monumental. Jackson called it the British equivalent of Tutankhamun's tomb. The museum speculated that the individual, presumed male because he was buried with a sword, shield and spears, was not a king, but was definitely a 'high-status individual' judging by his material wealth and his possessions. He was laid in a coffin of iron fittings, again only detectable as darkened soil. The body had completely decomposed aside from tooth enamel. Two small and thin gold foil crosses were found next to each other and were assumed to have been placed over the eyes. Gold crosses, gold coins and a gold belt buckle were also found. The find gave headline writers a field day, riffing on Essex's reputation by naming the unknown notable 'the King of Bling'.

The Saxon connection to Essex had always been known – the clue was in the name: East Seaxe; Essex. But this was something else: the most lavishly expensive Saxon Burial to be unearthed in Britain, connecting the Saxons with Christianity as early as the sixth century, and revealing Anglo-Saxon Essex as a dynamic place in constant exchange with countries across the North Sea. The adornment of the grave with goods, fashioned from metals and animal skin, also suggested a high level of technical expertise among the local people. Essex places such as Southend, Basildon, Clacton and Jaywick are often used as shorthand for lower-class concerns, but finds such as the Prittlewell Prince suggested something else entirely: an Essex of hidden histories, undetectable tremors of past societies every bit as lavish as the pyramids. All I wanted to do was try to solve this puzzle that was forming in my head, the mystery of Essex, a place that seemed to sum up something visceral about the new – always new – and throwaway Britain, but which brought into vision hidden depths when you were least expecting to find them. Why had this place featured in so many joke books, comedy routines and reality TV shows? Why had it become a political shorthand, and its own adjective, which was known for miles around? The more I picked at it, the more Essex began to feel like some kind of conspiracy I had to get to the bottom of. Surely, at the very least, there must be a story to be told about Essex.

1

Marsh, Maligned

When Joan Didion was asked by the *Paris Review* what she missed about California during her early days in New York, her answer was, 'Rivers. I was living on the East Side and on the weekend I'd walk over to the Hudson and then I'd walk back to the East River. I kept thinking, All right, they are rivers, but they aren't Californian rivers.' With me, it wasn't rivers – the Thames's grey murk or the dependable River Lea reached me when I needed them. What I missed most were the marshes of Essex, which felt akin to its soul.

As I travelled through London, I would often notice that road names such as Lower Marsh in Waterloo would only hint at the soggy past of areas that had long ago been drained and concreted, and go on to house some of the most expensive property in the western world. These places felt too well defined and over-designed and had me yearning for the salt marsh: uncategorisable plains of spongy vegetation that seemed menacing in the right light, with reeds and samphire sprouting from a dark yet glistening mud that more often than not served as a promenade for wading migrant birds on the lookout for food.

These spongy vistas were just the landscapes of home to me. Grassy sea walls. Reclaimed munitions dumps. Flat fields with pillboxes and all that mud. But I found that absence had made marshes more present, until a mind's eye landscape would form whenever someone mentioned my home county, of low-lying, porous fringes, a terrain sliced by creeks, accented by sluices and characterised by a great gloop that can remind folk that they are never as far from the primordial as they think they are.

Historically, Essex marsh has been considered wasteland, only fit for outsiders and criminals and the things that people didn't want in their vicinity, such as rubbish dumps, smoke-spewing factories and oil refineries. (The reputation being further enhanced as a localised form of malaria, the ague [pronounced ag-yoo], was rife here until the late nineteenth century.) According to the late Thurrock historian Randal Bingley, what we call marshland was not considered land at all in medieval times: prior to the Tudor era, 'land' only pertained to grounds higher than the river floodplain. Marshland is still regarded as an ambiguous, amphibious zone found on the literal (and littoral) edges of our lives, pockmarked by routinely rotting boats, driftwood and briny creeks that rise and fall at the whim of the moon. It all adds to the general feeling of dread and unsure footedness these places can inspire in the visitor.

Marshes are often alienating, awkward by definition and bewildering even to the people who have lived beside them for years. Looking at marshes from above, in such places as the village of Tollesbury in the Blackwater Estuary, they can look like HD brain scans. You can make them navigable, as long as you bend with the creeks, inlets and sluices. On walks over the years, plans to follow paths using OS maps often had to be ditched after encountering heavy flooding; instead, we might have to head inland, to skirt around puddles and pools, navigate high-security industrial zones or decommissioned rubbish tips, encountering a knotted terrain that seems to refuse any notion of authenticity. Marshland is less landscape, more state of mind, experience. To lose yourself in marshland is sometimes to lose yourself entirely.

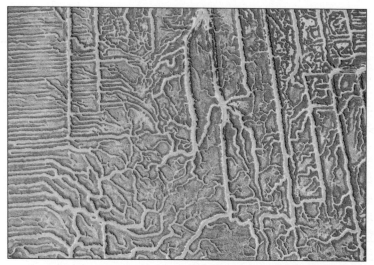

An aerial view of salt marsh on the River Crouch

The marshes were also once hives of activity, filled with people from wildfowlers to shellfish gatherers to sheep farmers tending to their flocks. There was a fishery at Tollesbury in the Domesday Book. The land was often arable and extremely good for grazing livestock. A basic kind of cheese made from sheep's milk was manufactured in Canvey Island, while the abundance of wool provided for towns across the sea in the Low Countries. The dramatic tidal extremes have led to large salt marshes and concentrations of saline pools that have long been exploited to manufacture salt, most famously at Maldon. The marsh acts as a palimpsest built up of silt that is washed down to the sea by the county's many rivers, before being lifted back onto the shore by the tide and left there. The tides bring with them great swells of detritus, including the seeds of salt-loving plants. When the plants grow, the salt marsh builds up. The history of Essex, I came to believe, is characterised quite fundamentally by its marsh, a place where hardy plants and sticky mud speak to a chequered history. In many ways the growth of the Essex marshland mirrors the great migrations of Londoners I'd always heard about growing up. The story of Granddad Burrows who was bombed out of the East End and ended up in a field in Essex, or Hayley's grandfather and grandmother, Ernest and Hannelore Singer, who moved to a new town, where the work was, after the war – two examples of thousands and thousands of families who drifted north and east.

But apart from the implicit historicity within the mud and the reeds, the marshes whispered to me in a more basic way. I just couldn't take my eyes off the marshland if it was ever in view, nor draw myself away from the desire of another marshland walk once I was at a safe distance. I'd stare at the peculiarly ruddy dullness of the thickened bog-brush vegetation and notice the way the light would twinkle from the water, which creeped in at high tide or pinged from the sheen of the mud once the tide had gone. Whether standing on a train platform, viewing from the skate park by the rubbish dump in Leigh where we used to smoke, or from the old ruins of Hadleigh Castle, the beguiling yet uninviting maze that fringed the not-quite sea at this end of the Thames Estuary was an enigma on the edge of our known, suburban world. The marsh posed questions that it seemed none of us who peered out at it from the safety of our residential streets could truly understand, and so it segued into the background, ignored, not to be talked about.

I was starting to feel that the marsh had led to Essex being damned by the self-appointed tastemakers of the British landscape. The writer Ken Worpole has detailed how Essex became the black sheep of English topography through a general 'crisis of representation and exposition in landscape aesthetics' that resulted in *Country Life* magazine awarding Essex zero points for the quality of its landscape. It came in at 30 overall from a possible 36 in the magazine's 2003 survey judging counties and giving scores for schools, pubs, landscape, property prices, wildlife, crime rates and tranquillity. Devon, the picturesque, rocky, coastal county in the south-west of England, came top of the class; second was Gloucestershire, which of course includes the Cotswolds, about which Max Hastings wrote in a *Daily Mail* article on the survey, the 'rolling hills and woodland valleys reflect the English countryside at its most glorious'. Cumbria, home of the Lake District, came fifth.

The Essex landscape has been plagued by negative associations for time immemorial. 'There are few travellers who have not some preconceived idea of the county of Essex,' wrote the travel writer Donald Maxwell in his book *Unknown Essex*, published in 1925. 'All those who go down to the sea in ships, and have business in the great waters of London, have at least a nodding acquaintance with "those cursed Essexian plains", and imagine that a somehow uneventful landscape continues without change to the confines of Hertfordshire, Cambridge and Suffolk.'

It isn't just the Essex landscape that has been historically denigrated; its people have been viewed with as much condescension as parts of its flat-ish topography. The art historian Nikolaus Pevsner once suggested that the county's image problem predated the Roman invasion: 'The Saxon forebears of Essex, envied possessors of an unattractive domain, seem to have been awarded the inferior social status of their Iron Age forebears, the Trinovantes.' The thoughts of the clergyman and writer James Brome were published in his 1700 travelogue *Travels Over England, Scotland, and Wales.* His opinion of late-seventeenth-century Essex described 'Rusticks' who made 'massy and ponderous' cheeses. The 'courtly and affable' were praised, 'but for them who live in the Hundreds (as they call that part of the County which lying more low and flat, and near to the Sea, is full of Marshes and Bogs) they are Persons of so abject and sordid a Temper, that they seem almost to have undergone poor Nebuchad-nezzar's Fate, and by conversing continually with the Beasts to have learn'd their Manners.'

It seems that at some point in its development, Essex's landscape and its people became interchangeable from one another, entwined in a fatalistic and apparently doomed rela-tionship. A collection of 'drolleries', or humorous texts, from the seventeenth century speculated that Essex's landscape had imbued its people with a characteristic that set them apart from the rest of the country, so much so that they were considered as a breed apart. 'We do not understand whence it cometh that the most bitter non-conformity and un-Christian crazes of enthusiasm seem always to have thriven in Essex and the adjacent Eastern coast-counties, so far as Lincolnshire, but the fact is undeniable,' it read. 'Whether this proceeded from their being low-lying, damp, dreary, and dismal, with agues prevalent, and hypochondria welcome as an amusement, we leave others to determine.' The 'plain' people were described as thinking too much of themselves, and were compared unfavourably to people who dwelt on higher geological plains. 'Mountaineers may often hold superstitions, but of the elemental forces and higher worship. They possess moreover a patriotic love of their native hills, which makes them loth to quit, and eager to revisit them, with all their guardian powers: the nostalgia and amor patriæ are strongest in Highlanders, Switzers, Spanish muleteers, and even Welsh milkmaids. It was from flat-coasted Essex that most of the "peevish Puritans" emigrated to Holland, and thence to America, when discontented with every thing at home.'

*

Something about Essex marsh country encouraged the zeal-ousness of religious non-conformism. The Peculiar People evangelical sect was indeed peculiar to Essex, and was set up by a reformed alcoholic in Rochford in the 1830s, who at the sect's mid-twentieth-century height wouldn't allow doctors to treat their families. Sarah Perry, author of *The Essex Serpent*, the bewitching novel set in the Victorian era and inspired by a 1669 pamphlet, entitled 'The Flying Serpent, or, Strange News Out of Essex', grew up in a family that was devoted to a strict Baptist sect. 'I would never have been going to a disco in my white stiletto heels because I didn't know what pop music was,' she told me. She instead channelled an older Essex that was literally unearthed by her father in their garden. 'Dad would be digging over Essex clay, which was notoriously difficult to dig over. It would turn up some Roman pottery because it was so populated by the Romans.

'There is a feeling about Essex which to me is like a micro-cosm of the British consciousness, which is this idea that there is something out there and you have to define yourself against it,' she said. 'If you drill down into Essex communi-ties, you get places like Mersea Island, places like Jaywick, and the knowledge that one is considered to be unsightly or unromantic drives forward a kind of perverse pride. People are very proud of Jaywick, but it's a perverse pride, people are very proud of coming from somewhere that is considered to be unliterary, unbeautiful, unartistic, and forcing forward a confrontation with the literary, the beautiful, the ancient, the myth.'

Though only a few miles away from London, rural Essex folk were for centuries reported as backward by their neigh-bours in the capital – poor, poorly educated, clinging to superstitions long discarded by their urban counterparts. When set against the dominance of the city, there are ele-ments of Essex that still today retain the backwater feeling of centuries past. The family of my nan, Doreen Gillman, were from a long line of agricultural stock in Hadleigh, near Southend. Less than a hundred years before Doreen was born in 1928, locals still relied on a witch doctor, known as a 'cunning man', whenever illness or misfortune should strike. 'In Elizabethan Essex no one lived more than ten miles from a known cunning man,' wrote Keith Thomas in *Religion and the Decline of Magic*. 'If allowance is made for the numerous wizards who must have succeeded in keeping their names out of the law courts, we get an even more striking impression of their ubiquity.' In the yard of the church where Doreen's parents married is the grave of James Murrell, the last cunning man of Hadleigh, who was famous in his day and was said to be able to fly. 'Hadleigh, thirty-seven miles from London by road, was a century away in thought and manners,' wrote Epping-based writer Arthur Morrison (famed for *A Child of the Jago*, his Victorian novel on the London poor) in *Cunning Murrell*, a fictionalised account of his subject's life. Morrison's Murrell was a short man of less than five feet in a worn blue frock coat carrying a gingham umbrella, who was 'alert of movement, keen of eye, and sharp of face'. He would collect plants aided by the light of the moon and carry them home hanging from his umbrella. It's not clear whether it was through intellectual sleight of hand or pure magic that the real-life Murrell cast his spell over the area, but talk of his powers for healing, astrology and clairvoyance spread far and wide. The wealthy from London, Suffolk and Kent would come to ask Murrell to ward off hexes or heal livestock. When Murrell died in 1860, this superstitious Essex was already being lost as the railways and later the car brought the modernising logic of London closer and closer. Still, Essex was held up as proof that England was not succumbing to reason as quickly as many in the city thought. 'Superstition is dying throughout England,' wrote Herbert

W Tompkins in *Marsh Country Rambles*, his train-propelled 1904 travelogue into the south-east English low country via Fenchurch Street, 'but dying more slowly than it is supposed.'

This superstitious, supernatural Essex seems to have made it to the modern day; if anyone wants to see an example, drive past the Anne Boleyn pub on the way to Southend airport and take a look at the adverts for psychics and clairvoyant shows. An air of pseudo-mysticism has been known to hang over England, creating a hazy environment where 'auras' and 'fate' are taken seriously and tabloid superstition often out-weighs empiricism. When Hayley and I were redecorating our new home in Southend after moving back to Essex, we scraped off the wallpaper to find that whoever had decorated the place last had filled the holes in the wall with tightly rolled up pages ripped out of a 1983 copy of the *Sun*, the year our respective mothers were pregnant with us. I unrolled one of the sheets and could make out a familiar lexicon.

HANG 'EM

VICKI ORGY TAPES IN THEFT MYSTERY

STEEL LOSES £1M A DAY

It reminded me of a surreal childhood memory: the time I realised a werewolf lived across the road from me. Bill, the seemingly mild-mannered flat-capped neighbour my mum used to post Christmas cards to each year, made the front page of the *Sun* in the summer of 1987 as the subject of one of its more memorably ludicrous headlines: 'Werewolf Seized in Southend'. The story described a bestial altercation at South-end police station, during which Bill was taken in by officers and reportedly fell into a 'lycanthropic state', snarling, curling back his lips like a mad dog and threatening to kill. In all the commotion he apparently hurled 14-stone officer Terry Fisher across the car park and pinned him to the ground.

It was reported that Bill had to be sedated by a doctor, requiring a dose nearly three times the average strength, to calm him, while five officers held him down before they were able to lock him in the cell. 'I've never seen anything like it before or since, to see a human being doing things like that,' PC Tony Belford told the *Sun*. The fire brigade had to be called to cut him out of the cell door. He was taken to the local mental hospital in Runwell, where he stayed for twenty-eight days. Psychiatrists were unable to explain Bill's behaviour – 'They discovered irregular brain waves but couldn't find a solution,' Bill told the *Sunday People* in 1989 – but it has since been speculated he suffered from a rare psychiatric syndrome, clinical lycanthropy, in which people believe they are an animal. The concept of lycanthropy, in which the afflicted subject shapeshifts into a werewolf, dates back to antiquity.

These fragments of magical memory are easy to retrieve if you grew up around here. I read that Runwell, where Bill was taken to, was the site of an ancient Running Well, which led it to double as a sacred place for magic and witchcraft, while one of the pubs I used to work at in Leigh was named after an infamous local nineteenth-century 'witch', Sarah Moore, who legend had it used to sit by the river in the old town and bless sailors as they arrived. The writer Syd Moore has researched the life of her namesake Sarah, confirming her existence as a widow, which was common for women accused of witchcraft, and also her rather more prosaic profession as a mangler, which may have given her the bent back depicted in the sign on the pub. Hers was a tragic life – Moore's sons died of cholera and she sank into alcoholism. She was blamed for the cholera deaths of other children in Leigh after she made a makeshift potion to try to save them, which did not work. The plight of witches in Essex is well known. Everyone used to say the flats by the bowling alley round the corner from the Broadway on Leigh Road were built on the site of a former 'drowning pool', where witches were tied up and thrown in to test if they were innocent (they'd drown) or guilty (they'd survive to be tortured). In Manningtree and its surrounds in north Essex in the 1600s, the notorious Witch-finder General, Matthew Hopkins, rounded up 'strange' ladies who in truth were often people simply succumbing to the hardships of village life. Rumour and gossip could lead to accusations of wrongdoing by a supposed witch. 'The victims of these trials were villagers of the poor and drab sort,' wrote C Henry Warren in 1950, 'likely to confess to anything under such torture as they were subjected to.' Typical was the case of Eliza Gooding, who asked a local grocer to 'trust her' half a pound of cheese. After he refused, the grocer's horse became ill and died, and Gooding was blamed, an assertion backed up by another witch. Women of precarious means or status used witchcraft accusations as a way of navigating fears and anxieties about their position within the village they lived in, pitting themselves against neighbours and attempting to lift themselves up to their rivals' detriment.

As much as they illuminated the darker customs of Essex village life, often these stories of the fantastical in the every-day betrayed an impatience or ignorance on the part of the visitor making such observations. '[T]he Essex peasants were dull, shy, reserved and suspicious,' wrote Sabine Baring-Gould, member of the Barings Bank family and author of the evocative novel *Mehalah: A Story of the Salt Marshes* (1880), of his ten years as rector on the isolated eastern outpost Mersea Island: 'I cannot say I either liked the place or became attached to the people . . . I never managed to understand them, nor they to understand me.' Baring-Gould surmised that ague and rheumatism and the inaccessibility of the island to the mainland because of the tidal River Blackwater had stunted the locals somehow. 'The Essex folk are fond of picking a big word and mispronouncing it,' he wrote. 'A woman asked me one day whether I had observed the elephant over the house on the preceding evening. She meant the element, when there had been an Aurora Borealis.'

I remember noticing as a child growing up in the 1980s and 90s in Southend that people on the television would often laugh at the word 'Essex'. Many nations have an Essex: a much-mocked place that has grown up in the shadow of a major city to become the supposed spiritual homeland of the nouveau riche. Often ridiculed as they are, these places can come to symbolise something quite fundamental to the country that named them. They are often viewed as the nation's id, its rawest and truest essence, but they are also shamed for being thought of as too loud, too vulgar, too much. In India, the sudden metamorphosis of Gurugram, an old, low-lying farming town just south of Delhi, into a Dubai-like city of skyscrapers and flyovers, has made it cultural shorthand for unabashed vulgarity. The US, of course, has New Jersey – home of straight-talking TV gangsters and the reality series *Jersey Shore*. Like Essex, New Jersey has an industrially abused marshland that doesn't feature on many postcards. When watching *The Sopranos*, the epic American television series about the familial travails of a New Jersey Italian-American crime syndicate, I kept feeling disoriented and unmoored by the flashes of freeways on stilts across ruddy green and brown marsh, flat horizons enlivened by the accoutrements of industry. They could just as easily have been the environs of my south Essex home as Newark.

'Much maligned' is a phrase that has permeated through the ages when it comes to Essex. The earliest instance I could find for the phrase that has become a kind of motto or short-hand for the county was in *The Saturday Review* in 1878, from a piece about country walks: 'even Essex, much maligned as it is, has singularly enchanting nooks and corners.' By the time naturalist and writer Brian Vesey-Fitzgerald wrote about Essex in London-based publication *The Sphere* in 1964 the phrase came in quote marks: '"Much maligned", Essex is usually dismissed out of hand, by those who merely pass through, as flat and featureless.' By the 1990s, it was echoing in the chamber of the House of Commons, when Teresa Gorman, the Conservative MP for Billericay, said in 1996: 'The City relies on the talent and enterprise of that much-maligned person – Essex man and Essex woman.'

Ultimately, Essex was maligned to the point it was effectively ejected from the elite set of English regions that make up the so-called Home Counties. A 2019 YouGov survey showed that only 36 per cent of those polled identified Essex as a Home County, behind Buckinghamshire (55 per cent), Surrey (52 per cent), Berkshire (50 per cent), Hertfordshire (44 per cent) and Kent (42 per cent). In a sense it spoke of a crisis in class terminology – not to mention class itself; by the Second World War the concept of the Home Counties had become a fraught one. It is a 'term we all constantly employ but one we should find it hard clearly to define,' wrote Norah Richardson in a book review of *The Home Counties* by SPB Mais for the *Journal of the Royal Society of Arts* in 1944. Mais had the Home Counties as 'the five counties around London County – Middlesex, Hertfordshire, Essex, Kent and Surrey. Berkshire seems to have muscled in at some point since the war, probably after it was deemed a royal county by the Queen, while unfortunate Middlesex was swallowed up by the endless development north of London and disappeared – the 'death by a thousand developments' fate that Essex has been wary of ever since.

By the time I had finished secondary school at the turn

of the millennium, Essex had been well and truly demoted from the exclusive south-east English club. 'What's the real difference between an Essex home and a Surrey home? The price,' began a piece about the hidden property gems of Essex by the *Daily Mail* journalist Rosanna Spero in 1999. 'But this much-maligned [that phrase again] part of Britain has much more to offer than you may think. Contrary to its hard, urban, white-stiletto and car-dealership image, Essex is a largely undiscovered, mostly rural area with gentle rolling hills and delightfully quaint villages – and compared to the Home Counties it's relatively cheap to live there.' The Home Counties had become a members' club you might get kicked out of if your face didn't quite fit any more, mutating to become a byword for a comfortably middle-class south-east English commuter belt. But Essex was never officially extinguished as a Home County in the way that Middlesex was. Never taken out the back and bumped off. Instead, it was just quietly retired to an out of the way corner, like a luckless employee who returns from holiday to find his desk had moved from next to the boss's office to some back room on the fourth floor.

Talk to people who didn't grow up on the island of Great Britain about how, to paraphrase Wu-Tang, class rules everything around me, and you often get a response somewhere between confusion and shock. It isn't that other countries do not have heavily stratified class systems and grossly unfair imbalances. But there is definitely something particularly intense about the UK variety, and the glee that is felt in finding the demographic butt of the joke.

By the early 1990s, the negative commentary from the rest of the nation reached a delirious zenith. It was captured for posterity during its height in 1991, in a song created for ITV's satirical puppet show *Spitting Image*. Unequivocally titled 'Essex Is Crap', the song came with lyrics that followed the title's lead: 'Essex, Essex, Essex is crap, it's an absolute abomination,' went the gleeful chorus. 'Essex, may it fall off the map, it's a boil on the bum of the nation.' At the end of the song, a rubber puppet depiction of the late game show host Bruce Forsyth listed the supposed ills of the consumer age – shell suits, camcorders, leather sofas, dodgy motors, karaoke, coal-effect fires – and in doing so explicitly attributed them to Essex.

'If you did this ['Essex is Crap'] now, I think you'd be accused of punching down, if not financially then intellectually,' the song's co-writer and chief lyricist, Steve Brown, told me in 2019. He said he felt a little sheepish that I'd tracked him down about a song that he said was more of a contractual obligation than anything approaching his best work. Brown's own history had seen his family move out from Lewisham in south-east London to leafier Bromley in Kent, an outward shift replayed over and over again in the story of suburbia. So why was Essex picked on rather than, say, Kent? 'It felt like fair game because it was and it still is a political barometer,' he said, referring to the fact that the new town of Basildon has been seen as a key indicator of the way the country will vote since the constituency's defection to the Tories heralded Margaret Thatcher's success in 1979. The song, he added, had a double function, satirising the awfulness of the Essex consumerist caricature while also letting it off the hook – celebrating it against the elitism of a sneering establishment. 'The thinking behind it was: you don't have to come from Essex to be an Essex man,' Brown said. 'It was just a joyful stereotype.'

The show that most greatly re-energised the stereotype was *The Only Way Is Essex*, or *Towie*, which followed a rolling cast of tanned and toned twentysomethings as they acted out relationship breakups and holiday romances on screen. *Towie* led to a surge in popularity of fake tan and 'vajazzles' (the latter entering the lexicon as a female genital decoration involving hair removal wax and adhesive diamante gems). The show helped propel Essex to global fame – in 2014, the Oscar-winning American actor Jennifer Lawrence declared herself addicted – and refined the Essex caricature into an extravagantly vapid parody of itself.

The stereotypes on which *Towie* drew so successfully had first emerged in the 1980s. In 1988, the comedian Harry Enfield had reached No. 4 in the pop charts with a single in the persona of Loadsamoney, his self-made geezer from the London–Essex borders, waving fistfuls of £50 notes. In 1990, the term 'Essex man' was coined by the *Sunday Telegraph* journalist Simon Heffer, to describe a new type of voter: a 'young, industrious, mildly brutish and culturally barren' worker in London's financial centre, whose roots lay in east London, and whose political views were 'breathtakingly right-wing'. Essex's place in the canon of British class representations did not occur by accident. Its role in the migration of Londoners into new settlements, whether ad hoc plotland bungalows, or post-war new towns or later even privately built towns such as South Woodham Ferrers, brought upwardly mobile working-class Londoners out of the city. It was a turn of events that was looked upon in horror by vested interests, the landed gentry, but ended up being useful in perpetuating their rule though ensuring the continuing success of the Tory Party in a county that houses pockets of the highest home-ownership levels in the country. Seen as a favourable place for Conservative politicians to project man-of-the-people fantasies, Essex was simultaneously celebrated as home to an authentic England and scorned as the crudest, stupidest symbol of Englishness. Politicians who saw Essex as a way to connect with England embraced its apparently no-nonsense and 'real' people – former British prime minister David Cameron hired the controversial former *News of the World* editor (and ex-*Basildon Echo* reporter) Andy Coulson as his head of communications while at No. 10. But Essex was also mocked for these same qualities, often by the very same political classes who praise its authenticity.

Essex man voted Conservative, but many Conservatives viewed him with the same mixture of fear and horror as other 'refined' commentators have for centuries. To some it seemed as if a new kind of English person was taking over – and his rapid ascent, bypassing the traditional requirements of public-school education and deference to hierarchy, seemed to threaten the very fabric of the establishment. In 1992, the British society publication *Harpers & Queen* despaired at how 'Essex manners stalked the streets'. Essex man, the magazine noted, embodied a vulgar capitalism that had 'eaten into the confidence of the old ruling class and invaded its most sacred enclaves'.

Essex girl was permitted even fewer redeeming features than her male counterpart. 'If Essex man and Loadsamoney are monstrous figures of entrepreneurial money-making and boom economics,' wrote the University of Roehampton's Heather Nunn and Anita Biressi in their book *Class and Contemporary British Culture*, 'then the Essex girl is a monstrous figure of consumption.' The right-wing journalist Richard Littlejohn wrote an Essex girl joke book with his friend Mitch Symonds, published under the pseudonymous pairing of Ray Leigh and Brent Wood, which featured such jokes as:

'What's the difference between an Essex girl and a supermarket trolley?

A supermarket trolley has a mind of its own.'

Reading the book from today's vantage point feels like a walk through the worst excesses of mainstream misogyny. The relentlessness of the vulgarity – a vulgarity someone like

Littlejohn might accuse Essex girl of – is overpowering. But worse was the licence the jokes seemed to give journalists to pry into the sex lives of very young, even underage girls. 'Q: What do you get if you cross 2 Essex girls with New Kids? A: Sex All Night,' ran a headline from the *Sun* atop a story written by Piers Morgan about two 16-year-old groupies who had a liaison with the popular boy band New Kids on the Block. Published with a bosom-heavy and pouting picture of the pair of pop fans from Essex across the two-page spread, the article gleefully told of how they were 'lured back to a hotel for an orgy' with the entertainers (the highest paid in the world according to *Forbes*) and breathlessly described how the girls were 'both just 16'.

A few years ago, Hayley crossed the border into Albania from Montenegro while travelling with an old friend, Sacha, from Canvey Island. The border guard asked where they were from – and when they told him, his response was quickfire: 'I've heard a lot about Essex girls,' he said. 'But I'm sure you are not like that.' Thousands of kilometres from Essex, the border guard had not only heard of this county in south-east England, but even knew what it had come to signify: a land of crass consumerism, populated by perma-tanned chancers and loose women with more front than Clacton-on-Sea. Essex might on one level have been the personification of a moral panic that was decades in the making, since the arrival of the pill and the possibility of promiscuity among British women, which in turn fed into violently lustful and misogynist male fantasies that were afforded space in some of the biggest selling newspapers in Britain. But it was also just another chapter in the centuries-old story of projecting the London-based tale-teller's worst assumptions onto their conveniently placed neighbours. Strange news out of Essex.

Essex's over-representation as the butt of the joke even informs political policy. In 2022, Essex County Council announced it was going to invest more than £300,000 to put its best face on and 'challenge people's preconceived ideas of how they see Essex on TV'. Council bosses wanted to banish thoughts of the fake tan and fast cars synonymous with the south of the county, replacing them with the Constable-country vistas, windmills and nice thatched cottages of north Essex. The council's drive to combat the Essex stereotype was almost as old as the aggressive tabloid stereotype itself. In 1997, moves to improve the county's image were reported in the national press, and it has since thrown hundreds of thousands of pounds of taxpayers' money into the effort. 'Difficulties arise,' said the head of the Essex Economic Partnership, Terry Conder, 'when overseas investors come to the UK, go to competitor locations, and hear jokes about Essex girls having more shoes than books.' Not for the first time, nor the last, Essex was caught up in the churn of a country that was always struggling to come to terms with itself.

2

Under the Water's Spell

Water – its threat, its bounding qualities, its enabling qualities, its qualities of obstruction but also protection – has had a defining influence on Essex, and the way it is perceived. It is here where south-east England starts fragmenting, solid ground disintegrating into islands and marsh. 'Essex has the most torn and untidy coast,' wrote William Addison in his 1949 account of seventeenth-century life of the county, *Essex Heyday*. 'It is in shreds and patches from the Thames to the Stour. The Colne, the Blackwater, the Crouch, the Roach, with their creeks and marshes, the lovely islands and treacherous mudbanks, give it a character that attracts some and repels others.'

When Hayley and I realised after thirteen years in London we could no longer afford to live there, for a time we tried to repel the inevitability of returning home. But, as sure as the moon pulls the tide, we found our way back to Essex. In 2019, we decided to move back with our two young children, Greta and Ernest, in tow. We found a house opposite a park replete with cricket pitch where Essex used to play, boating lake and rose gardens and a minute's walk away from the beach in Southchurch. One of a number of ancient parishes subsumed within Southend-on-Sea, Southchurch was once a marshy area characterised by lagoons comprising of 'an area of 1,879 acres of land and 1,292 acres of water', according to a slim historical book published in 1949, which I picked up shortly after moving to the area (original price one shilling). It was a rural parish until around the time our house was built a few years after the turn of the century, the 'beach walk a cart track, waving corn fields stretched to the brink of the sea'.

The aqueous affiliations of our new home were revealed to us in mysterious ways, such as when dozens of eels were found dead in the park over the road, a 10,000km migration from their breeding ground in the Sargasso Sea to an Essex boating lake depleted by a lack of rainfall, with hundreds more rescued by volunteers. Viewed from the middle of the park, you notice, from the way the shape of the roofs arc up to a certain height all around, that this area is a basin that isn't much higher than sea level. Southchurch's marshy history isn't something that comes up all that much during doorstep chats with neighbours, but I read that it could at one time be described as a 'prehistoric lake village'. Living in an area once known as a prehistoric lake village might seem awfully quaint but it doesn't sound all that future-proofed against the sea-level rises predicted by climate scientists. On one crisp and bright morning I received a text message from Floodline. This was the national flood alert service Hayley and I decided to subscribe to once we knew we were moving into, if not a floodplain (perhaps we were still in the denial stage), then definitely a place that was au fait with the odd awkwardly large puddle. The message told us in block capitals that there was a chance of flooding; further investigation revealed an unusually large spring tide was threatening the Essex coast, the moon conspiring with the intrusions of the tidal estuary to make us sit up in our bed wondering whether we should have sourced some sandbags after all.

Essex's watery associations have helped to characterise it as somewhere voracious, extreme and nonsensical. Much of Essex's land has been claimed and reclaimed from the sea by the enterprising spirit of its inhabitants, while those same people have been engaged in a pitched battle with the fate of the tides and the weather for centuries. Marshland folk in Essex lived under the guidance of the 1210 'law of the marsh', which stipulated that each man must contribute to the upkeep of flood defences to protect the portion of marshland they benefited from. It has been said that the high tides that flooded Essex in 1376 helped add to the depth of feeling that inspired the 1381 rebellion among agricultural workers, which took fire in Brentwood and is commonly known as the Peasant's Revolt.

After receiving the Floodline message, I walked around the corner to see the sea-facing restaurants on the beach were inches away from being flooded. I looked out at the fulsome swell, innocently reflecting the bright blue sky as people walked by in their long padded coats and bobble hats, taking in this highest of high tides. It was as if it was some friendly occurrence that had little impact on our lives, but the more I marvelled at it the more I began to see it as something more portentous, potentially disastrous. I looked at the water and then over at the sloping street that ran downhill to our neighbourhood. The swell appeared to the naked eye far higher than the Edwardian park and the neat rows of houses that somehow looked serene, as if politely accepting that if this mass of water picked a fight, they knew it would win. I left the beach, and thanked not God but the local authority powers that allowed the building of such a high and, so far, protective concrete wall, and the maintenance of a high ridge of sand and stone, which defend us against inundation.

Spending a length of time walking into and out of Essex creeks at low tide can feel as much of an effort as scaling a tricky section of mountain. You have to be patient, to be ready to let your feet sink in and have the strength of mind to pull them out again without panicking. They say England is sinking, and I sometimes daydream when out walking at low tide that it is being sucked down into estuarial Essex, a spoiled country succumbing to the revenge of some merciless gloop.

If you can visualise the map of mainland Britain as a wild-haired angry monster shouting at Ireland, then Essex rests above its rectum, the Thames Estuary. A diagonal line drawn from the south-west of the county to the north-east would measure 55 miles in length, although the fractal nature of the creeks and inlets on its eastern side make the Essex coastline 400 miles long. Its shore is home to more than forty islands – although no one can quite agree on exactly how many – with grimly exotic names such as Lower Horse, Cindery and Foulness. Some are not much more than a lump of hardy grass protruding from a river; others, such as Canvey and Mersea, are inhabited by thousands of people. I sometimes think of Essex itself as an island, separated from the county of Kent to its south and Suffolk to its north by the rivers Thames and Stour; from Hertfordshire to its west by the M11; and from London, loosely, by the M25 that skirts the south-west of the county. And, as with most islands, it has always been easy for those looking in to assume that they know exactly what happens there.

My childhood trips to the seafront at Southend were characterised by explosions: ballistic experiments and bomb disposals that occurred on Foulness Island at the northern lip of the Thames Estuary, a military testing site since the middle of the nineteenth century. Now we had moved back I was reacquainting myself with the sonorous booms that regularly sounded from the island. The house we had bought was a few miles away from Foulness but level along the flat coastline. On some days the explosions sounded like someone repeatedly shutting a town-sized car boot. THAWOOMP. On others, a lower frequency gave the day a menacing undertow, vibrating the ground and making the window frames click and my desk gently shake.

The development of Foulness as a British military testing site meant that the island received an access road in 1922, but for centuries before that, there was only one way onto it, via the ancient Broomway path, which provided a route on and off Foulness over the mudflats at low tide. The Broomway was once a functional route marked by sticks with shrubs tied to them (the brooms) stuck into the mud, which were placed thirty paces apart along its six-mile length. In recent years it has become a kind of celebrity; Google it and you will read mention after mention of it being the country's most dangerous path. Set off at the wrong time or in bad conditions, fail to study the route, or just get complacent, and you could be done for. Islanders have died in their scores over the years when they have misjudged the tide or simply lost their way. But then the thrill of dicing with disaster is part of the attraction. The nineteenth-century writer Philip Benton, in his history of the Rochford Hundred, suggested some islanders relished the inherent risk the route posed to those who travelled it. 'It is extremely perilous for any stranger to attempt the passage to or from this island without a guide, but the dangers attending it have been a pleasurable excitement to many. Some farmers would stay to the last, and then race the tide, and swim the creeks.'

A few years back, when Hayley was pregnant with Greta, we decided it was time to experience the thrill personally. We joined up with a group of similarly curious friends and were taken out by a local guide, Brian Dawson, setting off from Wakering Stairs in the village of Great Wakering for Asplin's

Head on Foulness. As we left the land behind, following the tide as it receded, Brian pointed out Southend, small clusters of tall buildings several miles away, and the wind turbines over Herne Bay and the Isle of Sheppey in Kent. 'I'm glad the flag isn't flying,' he said as we started off. 'Because the website is down and I am reluctant to phone them up as I am not particularly popular. They don't want us down here.' On the way out, our party kept noticing discarded bits of shell embedded in the grey-brown mud. Brian joked constantly about the fear of the tide turning. The first part of the journey, as we edged out onto the flats, felt the most daring, but as time went on, our wellingtons slapping over a muddy sheen, we felt anything but imperilled. With Brian, our trip out to England's most dangerous (yet strangely firm) path felt more like passing into an alternate reality, with three miles of slime and nothingness between us and our sandwiches.

More than anything, perhaps, a walk along the Broomway confirms the relentlessness of estuary conditions. I recorded the trip on my dictaphone so I could recount what Brian told us with some accuracy, but the further we went out the more the constant wind from the mouth of the estuary engulfed the recording. Brian's well-rehearsed recollection-filled patter was overlaid with screeching blasts that made it sound like I was suddenly thrashing around in a nylon sleeping bag. You could just about make out Brian pointing out the Isle of Grain power station over on the Kent side of the estuary, which was set to be demolished a few months later, and telling us it was 800 feet tall, as tall as the viewing area on the Shard. We eventually reached Asplin's Head, stopped for our sandwiches and took pictures of the many terms and conditions the MoD had left displayed to make it clear they were not responsible for our deaths at the hands of discarded weaponry, should they occur. After dawdling and digesting, we turned and headed back to the Broomway, the chase of the tide now adding a little more urgency. It was only later when we sat down for our pints at the Railway pub in Southend that we realised our pinkened, slightly sunburned hue, despite the overcast conditions, proving that out on the estuary, if the tide didn't get you, another kind of exposure would.

The relatively uninhabited 'Essex archipelago' contains the islands of Wallasea, Potton, New England, Havengore, Foulness and Rushley. John Harriott, a notable seafarer from Great Stambridge who set up the Marine Police Force (today known as the Marine Policing Unit, part of London's Met police), was obsessed with Rushley after he kept noticing a sunken island while out on his boat, 'containing between two and three hundred acres of land, dry at low water and covered at half tide'. After it was put up for auction in the 1780s, Harriott bought it for £40 with a plan to grow crops there (a local farmer told me the low-lying Essex islands such as Foulness are still prized for the richness of their soil). He recruited men from as high up the English east coast as the Fens of Lincolnshire to help reclaim it, erecting a building on a high point of the island to provide shelter from the whipping estuary storms. Harriott even employed someone to supply employees 'with good London porter' from a booth on the island. The effort began in the summer of 1781, but progress was halted again and again by the power of the tide. Harriott later wrote that he entered into a fight with his contractors, who asked for more money to get the job done and refused his advice to use timber. In the end he felled scores of trees to construct a cofferdam to shut the sea out. By December, a sloping wall that was eight-feet high and two-and-a-half miles long was built, surrounding and in theory protecting the island from the tide. When January came, the month the tides were usually at their highest, the wall held, and so Harriott got on with ploughing the land.

Harriott's endeavour at Rushley, however, was destined to

make him the Sisyphus of the sump. While the water was kept at bay, it was years until the rains desalinated the soil, for so long swamped by the sea, enough to allow crops to be grown. His second wife died, leaving him three children, and he added three more offspring after he quickly married again. In 1790, his farmhouse and offices were destroyed by fire, before his greatest fear was finally realised in 1791 when the sea eventually found a way over the wall. 'In this situation of my affairs, the second of this month [February] produced a tide on this coast, higher by a foot than was remembered by the oldest man living,' he wrote. 'My island fell a victim to its ravages; above one fourth of the wall of bank, had settled nearly a foot more than the rest. This was intended to have been raised eighteen inches last summer, if my loss by fire had not obliged me to defer it.'

Water flowed over the reinforced wall and flooded the entire island, destroying crops and taking Harriott's desalination process back to square one. He drained the water, set about repairing and heightening the sea wall but in the end he could not face going through the tedious process again only for the sea to put paid to the project once more. Harriott's project tells of the constancy of Essex's fight against the sea. 'The conflict is perennial – claim and reclaim, challenge and counter-challenge,' wrote the Essex Record Office's archivist and chronicler Hilda Grieve. Although his creditors were kind and let him off some of the money he owed them, he could see no future on Rushley. He sold up and fled for America, where he again sought island life, trying to set up farms in Rhode Island and Long Island, where he was reportedly accused of being a spy.

The water is not just a boundary, a moat, but also a road, a getaway. It connects us to elsewhere and the implicit promise of escape is often intoxicating and inviting. I remember my dad parking the car on the desolate eastern edge of Mersea

Island and tuning into Dutch radio as my sister, Sophie, and me excitedly tried to make out strange new words through static. The south Essex fringes have the help of settlers to thank for their continued survival, most importantly the enterprising seventeenth-century Dutch engineers led by Cornelius Vermuyden. The Southend-born, Netherlands-based poet Lucia Dove has quoted an old saying that helps explain the can-do mentality that has fed into lowland culture over time: 'God created the world, but the Dutch created the Netherlands.' The Dutch helped create some of Essex too, the country's drainage technology making its islands inhabitable.

In *The Oaken Heart*, her memoir of rural Essex during wartime in the Blackwater Estuary, Margery Allingham wrote of how the enormous guns used during the unsuccessful defence of the Netherlands against the Nazis made the windows of her home 'rattle faintly in their frames', as they had done when she was a little girl during the First World War. Allingham wrote of feeling an affinity with the defeated Dutch, a sense of kinship at the apparent feeling of the drab and the unexotic: 'They, like us, are not primarily charming and entertaining like most foreigners.' She suggested that the Dutch had left more than a legacy of engineering along the estuary coast, pointing to local names such as the DeWitts and the DeMussets, in addition to the local character: 'Much of the local severity, staunch independence, and hard bargaining powers come from the Lowlands.' Women were known to wear Dutch costume on Foulness as late as the First World War, and there have been suggestions that people on the island even spoke Dutch until the twentieth century.

History unfolds through surprising means and accidental reactions. I happened across a popular seventeenth-century ballad that seemed to suggest that the Puritans did not escape Essex for the New World across the Atlantic for reasons of religious persecution as is often cited, but because their beloved creeks were drained by the visiting Dutch engineers.

The upland people are full of thoughts,
And do despair of after rain;
Now the sun is robbed of his morning draughts,
They're afraid they shall never have shower again.

Our smaller rivers are now dry land,
The eels are turned to serpents there;

And if Old Father Thames play not the man,
Then farewell to all good English beer.
Why should we stay then and perish with thirst?
To the New World i' the moon then away let us go;
For if the Dutch colony get there first,
'Tis a thousand to one that they'll drain that too.

If Essex's low-lying inhospitable coast felt to many like a cursed place, it's because it was – by a malarial disease that was rife in its copious marshlands to such a degree it was known as the 'Essex ague'. In his travelogue *A Tour Thro' the Whole Island of Great Britain*, published in the 1720s, Daniel Defoe wrote that the wildfowl-shooting day-trippers from London would sometimes pay a substantial price for their visits, often returning with a 'heavy ague on their backs, which they find a heavier load than the fowls they have shot'. Essex is reported by Defoe as home to a marsh-dwelling breed of people who exist outside civilisation, beyond the prying eyes of their betters. He wrote of meeting some hardy sheep farmers on Canvey Island who had married multiple women they had taken from the 'uplands'. But the men weren't part of some sexually liberated polyamorous Essex sect; it was just that every time one of the men brought a new wife home, the unfortunate women succumbed to the 'fogs and damps . . . got an Ague or two', wrote Defoe. He recounted meeting a farmer who said he was on his twenty-fifth wife, while his son was on his fourteenth despite being only 35 years old. What if their new wives perished? 'We go to the uplands again, and fetch another.'

I have known this story for as long as I have read about Essex, and long suspected that Defoe, who admitted in the account that he thought one of the marsh men might have been lying, was himself accentuating the grotesqueries of a supposedly diseased breed of Englishmen. But the ague was real and it really did plague Essex marshland for centuries. Carried by mosquitoes, symptoms were said to include hot and cold fits, vomiting, and, perhaps most unpleasantly, a swollen spleen that sufferers called 'ague cake'. In the late eighteenth-century, infant mortality was much higher on the Essex coast than further inland, with 80 per cent of marshland parishes recording more burials than baptisms between 1626 and 1646; the corresponding figure in non-marshland parishes was only 11 per cent. These excess burials charac-terised the marshland, wrote historian of medicine Dr Mary Dobson. They suffered 'without parallel in other rural com-munities of south-east England during the early modern era'. Even when contracting the ague didn't kill them, it severely weakened the marshlanders, leaving them vulnerable to other mortal threats such as typhoid or smallpox. When thirty local people were asked by the eighteenth-century travel writer and agriculturalist Arthur Young whether they had ever had the ague they all 'answered in the affirmative, in a tone and manner that marked sufficiently how common and universal they were'.

In the seventeenth century, people did not know the ague was transmitted by mosquitoes; it was instead assumed to be an outcome of the stagnant water of the marshes, which had somehow poisoned the air. (The word malaria – malaria, literally meaning 'bad air' – was imported from Venice by Horace Walpole.) The mosquitoes' effect was hidden in plain sight, and they thrived in the perfect conditions of the warmer than average Essex summer, hibernating in dark and damp thatched marshland cottage roofs during the winter months.

The threat of ague ensured that marshland parishes were solitary places, the mortal danger of living in them contributing to their lower-than-average population figures. Dobson wrote that the average density of the Essex coastal and Thames marsh parishes was 42 persons per square mile, while it was 63 per square mile for other agricultural and rural regions in Essex, and 240 for the textile district in the north of the county. It seems that these marshes were visited only under financial or spiritual duress. A diary quoted in the *Essex Review*, this time by the artist Joseph Farington, suggested that, in the early nineteenth century, servants were paid more than in other parts of the country to be persuaded to work there. Priests, rectors and other men of piety were often sent to these parts of Essex only grudgingly. The south Essex area close to the Thames containing villages such as Laindon and Fobbing was so ill-reputed by clergymen it was known as 'killpriest country'.

Marsh fever led to a geographical disparity or inequality in Essex and arguably laid the parameters for future faultlines of poverty. Essex's ague contributed to its damnation in the received wisdom of the land, with its low-lying parishes quite literally avoided like the plague. The county's islands and marshy villages were described as extreme places outside of the norms of laws and agreed-upon customs, consistent with the Essex character which was viewed as obstinate and aggressive in periodicals of the time. Foulness, for example, in the windswept Essex badlands, had men outnumbering women almost 2–1. They had often made it to the island to escape the long arm of the law, keeping unkempt beards and filthy manners, and sleeping in dormitories, marauding in large gangs, entertaining themselves with bouts of bare-knuckle boxing, and vanishing upon mention of 'the constable'. The historian Benton wrote how open carts full of daytime drinkers travelled from Foulness to the mainland and created 'scenes [that were] most offensive to decency'. Booze frequently made its way into home-made remedies to ward off the ague, with many self-medicating with copious servings of opium and beer. The Great Leighs farmer Thomas Beadle's pocket book from 1746 recommended making a hole in an onion and placing a large nutmeg inside it, roasting it in the fire until the nutmeg went soft and then putting it in a quart of strong beer mixed with a large glass of brandy.

The Essex coast was so rife with the ague that it might in hindsight seem inevitable it would contribute to the scientific research around curing it. Robert Talbor, a quack doctor who did not complete his studies at Cambridge, instead becoming apprentice to an apothecary, was compelled to research the 'Quartan Ague' after he had come down with it. Finding that little progress had been made in terms of treatment, he decided to try and have a go himself. '[T]here was no other way to satisfie my desire, but by that good old way, observation and experiment: to this purpose I planted myself in Essex near to the sea side, in a place where Agues are the epidemical diseases . . . where you will find but few persons who either are or have been afflicted with a tedious Quartan'. It was in Essex, while treating a French officer who had contracted the ague while fighting the Dutch in Flanders, that Talbor proved quinine from the bark of cinchona trees was an effective remedy for malaria, leading him to being made a knight of the realm.

By the nineteenth century, the ague had started to subside in Essex, but it still lingered in pockets even after the modernisation of the industrial age. A 1919 study of malaria in the previous century said soldiers at Tilbury Fort were relieved every six months as the ague was so rife; in 1872 there were 34 admissions for ague among 103 men. A 12-year-old girl from the East End was admitted to the London Hospital (now Royal London Hospital) in Whitechapel in 1923 after returning home from a Girl Guides' camp in a barn at a 'lonely spot in the marshes' in Pitsea. 'The farmer of the nearby farm said that in his youth "everyone" on the marsh had "ague",' wrote Neville M Goodman in the *British Medical Journal*, 'and he himself had had two attacks, one as a boy and one as a young man, some thirty years ago.' In 1938, a year before the Second World War was declared, another *British Medical Journal* reported testimony from Burnham-on-Crouch by Dr WHM Wilson describing 'a generation of men and women [living in the area] who can remember malaria in England. The ague, they call it.' A map sent to the British director of hygiene in 1942 to help stop any rise of malaria in war-torn UK detailed three at-risk categories. Category C, which covered most of London, much of inland East Anglia and coastal Lincolnshire up to Yorkshire was designated a 'potentially dangerous area', while most of coastal Essex and Suffolk and the south coast of England was designated B, a dangerous area. A small ring looped around the Thames Estuary area of the country (including islands Canvey and Foulness and the area of Southend we live in now) was category A – a 'very dangerous area'.

Historical evidence suggests the ague was eradicated, not by some collective concerted effort focused on the disease itself, but by a number of factors linked to the modernisation of the marshes. Drainage might have helped move breeding grounds of mosquitos elsewhere; Dobson suggested the fact we live in modern houses and not thatched barn-style dwellings as the marsh folk once did has probably helped, as has improved general health and better nutrition.

Or the strain could simply have changed, which leaves open the fear that the ague could one day return to Essex. Clouds of mosquitoes descended during our first full summer in Southchurch, taking over the parks and back gardens of our sunken terrain and forming stagnant murmurations that did not budge for months. Giant lumps appeared all over Greta's skin. People complained on the local Facebook pages that they had never seen it this bad. It was the first lock-down summer and I became prone to idly wondering if the ague could ever come back. It didn't take much to extend the already present feeling of shared dystopian dread to imagine the feverish disease one day making a return.

Essex's coastal fringes tell their own damp, geological story. Around 8,000 years ago, Doggerland, the lost landmass that once joined the east side of the UK to mainland Europe, was submerged under newly melted waters released by the end of the last glacial period. Eventually named the North Sea, the sudden influx of water isolated a collection of hills, valleys and plains, and created what is now the ninth largest island in the world, Great Britain. Dutch ships first found evidence of the vanished plain of Doggerland at the bottom of the sea 150 years ago, uncovering tusks and remains of woolly rhinos and other beasts that can appear fantastical to mod-ern day observers. In 1985, human remains from a burial site were brought back to shore by fishermen. Radiocarbon dat-ing pinned this unknown hunter-gatherer to the Mesolithic period 9,500 years ago. This gargantuan geological divorce has set the tone for the United Kingdom's isolationist quirks ever since, with Essex seemingly at the sharp end of the split as much then as it is now.

A lot is spoken about the north–south divide, but an east–west divide exists too. After all, the former UK prime minister David Cameron's yearly seaside excursion was to the beaches of Cornwall, not Canvey Island. Essex's geology is derided unfairly, wrote one of the foremost authorities on the Essex landscape, John Hunter, who was Assistant County Planner at Essex County Council. 'Compared with the ancient rocks of our western shores, displayed for example in the cliff formations of Pembrokeshire and Cornwall, the geology of Essex may seem unexciting and, in terms of geological time, very recent. But in this lies its interest.'

On the way back from a holiday in Wales and Glouces-tershire, sloping back down to the south-east, the destiny of Essex's geography felt stark. We had spent time in the Brecon Beacons, which so bewitched the Romantic poets, before camping on a hillside in the dramatic valleys of the western Cotswolds around Stroud, all endless green hills bountiful with dairy cows and daisy-fringed stone walls, with devel-opment kept largely contained in urban enclaves so as not to disturb the stunning natural aspect. As we made our way out of the Cotswolds, traffic was slowed by some Glouces-ter cattle, who meandered lugubriously onto the road with a nonchalance that reminded me of the 'Old England' beloved of the nostalgic JB Priestley. 'But we all know this England, which at its best cannot be improved upon in this world. That is, as a country to lounge about in . . . It has few luxuries, but nevertheless it is a luxury country.' The drive back home felt like one long slide down into the swamp. As we made our scheduled descent to Essex along the M25, I could suddenly see the place I had always taken for granted in a way similar to that which has shocked other visitors. The sharp flatness of the landscape as you approach the Lea Valley and Epping Forest on the M25 was a mere prelude to the wastes of my south Essex swampland of curvilinear flyovers over marsh-land pools.

In its geology, as elsewhere, Essex seems to simultaneously be the receiver of great fortune and great damnation in equal measure. 'No county in England, and probably no district in the world, has a climate better suited than that of Essex for corn-growing,' wrote William E Bear in 1892. 'It is the costli-ness of cultivating the clay soils of that county which has driven the poorest of the land out of cultivation.' The extent of clay might have become exaggerated in the geological understanding of Essex, but it is dominant in the south of the county, and has come to represent something of the place. 'I have a theory that the Essex countryman's character owes at least something of its quality to the nature of his land-scape,' wrote the author and broadcaster C. Henry Warren in his book *Essex In 1950*. 'Clay and sky are all – the heavy clay that tears the soles off a man's boots and the wide open sky where he hears the larks singing. And my theory is that just this combination helps to give the Essex countryman his odd mixture of harsh realism and tender poetry.'

And yet while clay might have been considered by Warren a fundamental material in terms of forming the Essex psyche, it also made Essex eminently exploitable during the building boom in London and the south-east. Before much of South-church and wider south Essex was built, acres and acres of land were used for brickfields, with bricks made and dried before being shipped to London via the Thames; before the capital ate into Essex and the wider Thames Estuary in terms of borders and administration, it took its coastline. Aggregate was also taken, from the Essex seabed where it was turned into cement in the Medway region of Kent and sent up to London on barges. Vast quantities of cementstone were dredged up between Harwich at the top of the county's coastline down to the mouth of the Thames outside Southend. Stucco was needed to build London in the eighteenth century and a new product was on the market – 'Parkers Roman Cement', which was so popular it contributed to the erosion of the clay cliffs at Harwich.

The extraction of the Essex seabed just adds to the feeling that that county is particularly exposed by its proximity to so much water. During our first winter back in Southend we sheltered inside as we listened to a series of violent storms do their worst. Walking along the prom in the aftermath, we saw that the high spring tides had broken up beach huts, spilling detritus across the beach and dragging some of it out to sea. The tempestuous attentions of the North Sea can eat whole swathes of land away. Near Harwich in the north of the county is the Naze, a bit of land sticking out between the North Sea to the east and the marshland of Hamford Water to the west. It used to stretch miles further out to sea than it does today, before its farms and churches succumbed to the coastal erosion the clay cliffs are now unfortunately famed for.

The fear of instant annihilation, total wipe-out, at the hands of erosion or flood in the age of climate crisis is of course not exclusive to Essex. Whole villages such as Happisburgh in Norfolk are at the mercy of erosion at an unforgiving pace, and the oft-told story of the lost medieval port town of Dunwich in Suffolk suggests that no one has ever truly been safe on England's east coast. The old estuary Essex village of Creekmouth, west up the Thames near Barking, was wiped out by the North Sea flood of 1953. A few years ago, at the open day of a large new housing estate, Barking Riverside, which had been built near to where Creekmouth once stood, I talked to a member of the Creek-mouth Preservation Society. (Not that there was much to preserve of Creekmouth aside from the memories of former residents.) Shirley told me how her family tried to stop the water coming into their house during the flood by blocking the doorways. 'All of a sudden Mum said, "Oh look, it's coming in the front door as well!", as if it shouldn't. Fancy using the front door!' The residents of Creekmouth never returned to their damp cottages, which were pulled down as the village eventually got turned over to heavy industrial purposes that would soon populate the Essex estuary. The old village school became a company called Squibb Demolition, which has had a hand in much development around the south-east of England – development that can at times feel akin to a force majeure of its own.

The North Sea flood killed 307 in England, 120 of them in Essex: 58 people on Canvey died and 35 in the similarly threatened Jaywick in the north of the county. Our new house was one of thousands that were flooded in 1953 (on Canvey, 13,000 people were displaced from their homes). Shortly after we moved to Southend, when we were stripping the hallway wallpaper before we moved in, we noticed a line of thicker plaster, which must have been slapped haphazardly over the original wall after the inundation. When a damp specialist came to survey the house, he told us with some relish that the floodwater had made it to the seventh step. Our street wasn't the only one affected: 600 houses east of Southend pier were flooded up to 4 feet. Steve, our next-door neighbour whose great-grandparents bought the house when it was newly built, said the floodwater filled up the nearby gasworks like a swimming pool, before unleashing a mini-tsunami towards our street. The water came up through the floorboards and brought with it coal dust and rubbish. Steve said he was still finding bits of old coke from the yard of the gasworks scattered around his garden until fairly recently.

More than 1,800 people in the Netherlands perished in the flood. While it left more of a scar there, in Essex it has at times felt like something that is only remembered on a need-to-know basis. Published in 1959, *The Great Tide*, Hilda Grieve's intricately detailed and masterfully told account of the days surrounding the disaster, was an effort to memorialise the event, and it is a truly epic account of Essex's experience of the flood over 900 large pages of small type, based on impeccable research gleaned from emergency service log books. Grieve wrote that although Essex was 1,528 square miles in size (this was some years before the borders of Greater London swallowed up its metropolitan fringes), it was never more than 34 miles from tidal water. On the night of the floods there was a tidal surge two metres higher than usual. Homes were destroyed and many people drowned but some also died while waiting in vain for the emergency services to rescue them. 'Children died quietly of exposure in their parents' arms as they tried to hold them, hour after hour, above the water,' wrote Grieve. Tens of thousands of farm animals perished. The rescue effort was a gargantuan undertaking. On Canvey Island, sea scouts dragged people to safety, despite treacherous conditions and the fact that some of those trying to save lives couldn't even swim.

People living in Great Wakering in Nissen huts left over from the war perished after falling into the water from the roofs they had attempted to take shelter on. Two on Foulness and one on neighbouring Havengore died during the flood. High winds delayed the rescue operation for two days, meaning villagers had to live in the upper sections of their houses. Rabbits sat up in tree branches like cats. Vessels, such as an oyster dredger skippered by a veteran of the Dunkirk evacuation, braved the five miles of choppy sea that now separated the Foulness village of Churchend from the mainland, and 362 islanders were brought north-west to Burnham-on-Crouch, most carrying all the money they had in the world, as there was no bank on Foulness. Old boys brought biscuit tins full of their pay packets from before the war into the

Cows on a ruined farmhouse during the 1953 flood, Foulness

post office at Great Wakering after they had been evacuated, and sockfuls of gold sovereigns that had ceased to be legal tender around the First World War. On the mainland, helpers were on hand to offer food – 'joint' and vegetables, apple pie and custard, and tea – and hot baths, reported Grieve. 'Two or three old men refused to change or bathe – they seemed more afraid of baths than floods.'

We had started to settle into life in Southend when we were given our first reminder that the water is always ready to interrupt our daily lives. I had returned home late from London to a flooded street. A sewer had collapsed nearby under pressure from a torrential downpour, and the drains couldn't handle the amount of water coming downhill towards us, so a mix of rainwater and raw sewage was sent in the other direction and out of the drains. While I was on the train home, Hayley had sent me anxious updates and pictures of the water edging up our driveway and filling our back garden. A newly formed stream ran down the road, collecting and bubbling outside the house, the swell getting closer and closer. I feared that if this storm kept increasing, maybe the swell of the sea would even come this way as it had done in 1953. After wading through a newly formed pond to get to my front door and cleaning myself up inside, I called the council's emergency line ('Nothing we can do, it's Anglian Water'), before trying and failing to sleep as the rain started again.

We were lucky that, while there was a steady wind, there was not a storm to send spring-tide waves over the edge of the sea wall, and woke up to streets drying with the greyish tinge of raw sewage, and a strange-smelling shed. What lingered longer was the feeling of impermanence, that the community we were part of could be upended at any moment, and without as heavy a presence of volunteer groups and state organisations on hand to bail us out as they had done in post-war Essex. Medieval chroniclers saw the great storms and tides that would beset them as judgements on the wickedness of men, and considered them portents of things to come. What troubled me about the phoned and texted flood warnings that were often followed by a completely dry day was that nobody seemed to see them as a sign for anything.

3

'These Children of Nature'

'Oh ye! Who have your eye-balls vex'd and tir'd,
Feast them upon the wideness of the Sea'
John Keats, 'On the Sea'

The tide has drained slowly away to reveal a breathtaking expanse of mudflats. Some tourists wander over the slop, but most have pitched up on the beach or are taking a walk along the promenade. Kids squeal as they run through the water fountains, while a small group of teenagers throw fun snaps, those little paper explosives that look like screwed-up cigarette papers, in a disinterested fashion. Ice cream varieties – strawberry, bubblegum, chocolate, rum and raisin, in soft scoop or whippy, cone or tub – are carried to waiting friends and family. Cigarette smoke hangs around the pubs opposite the beach, mingling with air made sweet by the proximity of candyfloss and the sour spike of vinegar evaporating from bags of chips. I breathed in fondly this scent I had known all my life. It was noon and the sun was high, but the amusement arcades, palaces of discombobulation that face the estuary with generic names such as Happidrome, Las Vegas and Monte Carlo, remain dark caverns (albeit ones that fizz with electric light). Inside, a chorus of coin-operated games from different decades flash for attention as a cacophony of incessant jingles and random catchphrases whirl around like a flurry of intrusive thoughts. Outside the arcade nearest the pier, a group of young men with their tops off take it in turns to test their strength by punching a boxing machine as hard as they can, while the rest of them whoop and cheer.

It is an evergreen scene that could be any sunny bank holiday in the last couple of decades. But it occurred during the first Covid summer of 2020, during which news helicopters hovered above our house to capture images of the throngs suddenly packing the beaches. The front page of the *Daily Mail* used press photographs taken on Southend beach that day to illustrate an England gone mad. But what I saw in the lines of flip flops and bikinis, trunks and bare torsos, passing my window on the way to the beach was Essex casually readopting its role as a place in which it is possible to escape into instant, accessible frivolity.

Southend wasn't planned to be the populous place it is today. But it ballooned when London's working classes visited and liked what they saw – the cockles, the drink, the fairgrounds and the escape. It has long offered up open-skied excursions via the medium of cheap train travel, a place where the capital's certainties begin to waver. The widescreen estuary affords enough space for a vista of purple-grey clouds punctured by brilliant white gaps of sunlight. It is a part of the world that grew up as a promised land for the working poor, including migrants like the parents of my mum, Margaret, who came here from Ireland before starting a family in the Essex seaside town.

I have a deep love for Southend on a packed bank holiday, its noise and unpredictability, its competing odours and culture clashes. That said, there is a thrill when the fog arrives. Sometimes it can creep in so thick you are barely able

Holidaymakers at Canvey Island, August, 1935

to see the shoreline, let alone the other side of the estuary. On a particular morning before breakfast, I found myself drawn to the estuary's edge at low tide, peering into a void of soft-focus cotton-wool air, the lack of visibility accentuating the angles of the things that I could just about see – the strange poles that stood to attention out of the mud, the shack-like beach cafe, the jetty and the rectangular pool that captures tidal water so that children can swim, whether the tide is in or out. Not that the fog upsets many people around here. Southenders love it when they are no longer reminded they are just a settlement (albeit one that recently became a city) on the north side of an estuary. On a good day, you can't see Kent.

Southend's identity has long had a listless and intangible air similar to that fog. Growing up here, I never really thought about just how anonymously named it was. 'South end', the casual name for the coastal part of Prittlewell, the old settlement complete with ancient priory, which faded into obscurity as the southern resort boomed. Southend rose to prominence as a bathing resort during the Victorian era, and its status in England's collective unconscious has since been built from cameos in the BBC soap *Eastenders*, cockney nostalgia, and the lure of a good time by the sea. There is something beautifully pointless about Southend pier, the mile-and-a-third road to nowhere that constitutes its most famous landmark. (Its importance to the seaside settlement was brusquely summed up by Betjeman's celebrated line: 'the Pier is Southend, Southend is the Pier'.) The iron-built curiosity is the longest pleasure pier on earth, which was built largely during Victoria's reign and has been in danger ever since (several major fires and boat crashes attest to that).

If you turned the pier on its side, it would be the tallest building on earth by some distance, but instead of going up to the heavens it penetrates the mouth of the Thames. It was built for paddlesteamers to bring trippers to and from this burgeoning Essex town, so boat passengers did not have to rely on it being high tide to visit Southend. The pier was the work of local entrepreneurs, suggests Jim Worsdale, who were 'frustrated and annoyed that passing trade was doing exactly that: passing Southend on new-fangled passenger-carrying steamers.' The pier was first built in 1830 and extended in the 1840s. In 1889, a new, sturdier iron pier opened, which could now accommodate more steam ships and pedestrians. But by then it wasn't the only way to get to Southend. When the first railway arrived in 1856, it revolutionised travel to the seaside resort, making it more accessible for working-class Londoners. The train fare was more affordable than the steamboat, and it was quicker too.

The structure hasn't had much of a practical purpose

Tim and Hayley on their wedding day
at Southend Pier, July, 2014

since, but still survives, a monument to the gnomic surreal-
ism of Southend. So many cafes, chip shops and pubs have
met their ends due to the pier's many fires. The puny RNLI
Museum offered only keyrings and disappointment, and
the fortune teller knew long ago that the game was up. The
pointlessness of the pier has always appealed to Hayley and
me; so much so that we got married at the end of it. On our
wedding day the weather was a little odd even for an English
July. It wasn't quite raining but there was a fine mist that
obscured the industrial towers over at the Isle of Sheppey
across the estuary. I met her at the shore to walk to the end
of what had now transformed into the longest aisle in the
world, into a haze that seemed charged with the dreamlike
innocence of Southend's early days.

The boom of seaside resorts drew outsiders towards Essex.
Before the Victorian eruption in seaside holidays, the north

Essex destinations of Clacton, Frinton and Walton were sleepy places for farming and fishing. The coast itself was thought of more as a place for defending the realm against the French than a place of mass leisure, as the Martello towers dotted along the northern shoreline of Essex could testify to. But the Essex seaside's allure has always reflected the needs of the burgeoning population of London, and sea air was thought to be the answer to complications arising from over-exposure to the smog-filled city. Some even thought drinking a pint of saltwater a day was good for you. As time marched on into the twentieth century, seasides became places to play, to perform, and Essex's were the nearest to the industrially overripe East End. Clacton, with its history of Pierrot troupes and minstrels, still houses the West Cliff Theatre, which boasts the longest running summer season in the country. Cliff Richard, for a time England's answer to Elvis Presley, started off at Clacton Butlins. (South African entrepreneur Billy Butlin's dream began in Skegness; Clacton was his second venture. Despite being closed down almost immediately by the outbreak of the Second World War it opened afresh in 1946 and seemed to kickstart a boomtime in holiday camps.)

The reaction to this influx of the unwashed to seasides such as Southend and Clacton was predictably fierce. Those looking to keep Southend better-heeled were aghast at its accelerating cockneyfication. Local businessmen fretted about 'excursionists', as they were known, threatening the tranquillity of the well-to-do inhabitants and 'visitors' of Southend. 'Visitors' were recognised as respectable, middle-class individuals who came for the bathing waters and the cliffside gardens. 'Excursionists', on the other hand, were perceived as a mass invasion from the East End slums who dared to jig to street bands and who spent what money they had at bawdy auctions, fruit and seafood stalls, or one of the many new taverns cropping up. A fairground opposite the pier, with its aerial railways, shooting galleries, swings, roundabouts and coconut shies, was, according to an outraged letter-writer to a local paper, 'disgraceful and debased to the level of an East End pandemonium'.

After the Bank Holidays Act of 1871 the majority of people coming to Southend were excursionists on day trips. A cartoon from the *Southend and Westcliff Graphic* depicted a well-fed couple, Mr and Mrs London, with their hundreds of children snaking in a queue as far as the eye could see behind them. Another depiction in this publication showed 'A Whitechapel Wonderland', with people clapping and dancing their cares away, self-evidently presented as the worst thing in the world. The town acquired such a bad name that Robert Arthur Jones, the local jewellery store owner, wrote an open letter to the people of Southend suggesting that it change its name to Thamesmouth: 'How many of them are ashamed of the acquaintance? It has been so long associated as "Sarfend" where the trippers go to eat cockles and shrimps.'

Improvements to the railways only increased the flow of excursionists into Southend. Some hotels banned trippers. There was an apparent riot in Southend by a group of excursionists from a Plaistow timber works – the army were called from Shoebury to deal with them, although the local paper said the vast majority of excursionists were 'very well-behaved'. Thomas Arnold, a farmer from the eastern end of town, wrote 'if east London is to be let loose and 30,000 of its number poured into Southend from the first Monday in August from this year forward, then something must be done for the protection of property in this district . . . Southend has become the playground of the lower classes of excursionists.'

Around this time there was a feeling from the gaggle of entrepreneurs, businessmen, masons and the like who passed for the establishment in the young seaside town that enough was enough. In reaction to this invasion of impropriety, Southend started to split along class lines, using the pier as its checkpoint. Alderman Brightwell, the owner of a high-end draper's in the town, suggested the area to the west of the pier, a suburb with some prettified corners and landscaped gardens overlooking the estuary known as Westcliff-on-Sea, should be reserved for the respectable visiting families and locals. The east should be for the excursionists 'where they are catered for' by the The Kursaal (the largest amusement park in the south of England) and the seasonal entertainers. Alderman Brightwell wanted to enshrine the division in law somehow, disallowing lower-class people from travelling west of the pier. But there wasn't much point. Such zoning of class had already occurred, through punitive charges enforced at the entrance to the pleasure gardens along the western cliffs, a move that deterred the trippers.

Despite the misgivings of the town's top brass, Southend allowed the East Ender to throw off the chains, toil and drudgery of the working week. Thrill-seekers came to cajole their souls out of the stupor of daily life and feel a sudden sense of escape from the eyes of the boss and the dank oppressiveness of the narrow, pestilent streets. The Victorian writer Walter Besant described the mass exodus to Southend on Whitsun bank holiday: 'Above all, at Southend he will find all the delights that endear the seaside to him; there is the tea with shrimps – countless shrimps, quarts and gallons of shrimps; he is among his own kind; there is no one to scoff when, to the music of the concertina, he takes out his companion to dance in the road; he sings his music hall ditties unchecked; he bawls the cry of the day, and it is counted unto him for infinite humor.'

Besant seemed to approve of the East Enders' revitalising trips to the seaside in general. 'These children of nature, if they feel happy, instinctively laugh and shout to proclaim their happiness,' he wrote. Although, like many genteel onlookers, he was shocked by some of the behaviour of the underclass suddenly released from the confines of London, he was sympathetic to their need for escapism. 'They would like the bystanders to share it with them; they cannot understand the calm, cold and unsympathetic faces which gaze upon them as they go bawling on their way. They would like a friendly chorus, a fraternal hand upon the shoulder, an invitation to a drink. Let us put ourselves in their place and have patience with them.'

Besant was one of many Victorian writers responding to the plight of the East End, along with others such as Henry Mayhew, who wrote obsessively about the many faces of poverty in nineteenth-century London. Mayhew introduced the public to figures such as the 'pure-finders', who sought out discarded dog shit from the filthy streets, which they would sell for next to nothing to the tan yards where it would be used to 'purify' leather, or else as a drying agent for book-binding leather. The main protagonists of Mayhew's searing account of the city's endemic poverty, *London Labour and the London Poor*, were the costermongers (more commonly referred to as barrow boys today), a type of Londoner he painted as an echo of premodern 'wandering tribes', a rough, outlaw band without any airs and graces to speak of. 'All more or less distinguished for their high cheekbones and protruding jaws – for their use of slang language – for their general improvidence – their repugnance to continuous labour – their disregard of female honour – their love of cruelty – their pugnacity – and their want of religion.' Mayhew's profiles of London types often veered into the cartoonish, but his findings painted Victorian working-class London as a place existing outside the received wisdom about British sensibility, instead illuminating the repressed, resourceful and repetitive nature of life for thousands and thousands of people in the biggest city on Earth. His analysis, too, seemed to explain the appeal of seaside Essex to Londoners seeking desperate solace in boozy trips away from the city: '[M]orality on £5,000 a year in Belgrave Square is a very different thing to morality on slop wages in Bethnal Green.'

And yet east London was also burgeoning with new skills and crafts imported by impoverished workers from overseas, while its industries attracted migrants looking for employment from across the country. These arrivals worked in newly built factories by day and squeezed into East End slum accommodation with their families at night. The silk weavers of Spitalfields descended from Huguenots who had come to London as refugees fleeing persecution in France due to their status as protestants. By the mid-nineteenth century, their industry suffering due to free trade that knocked tariffs off the French imported silks, the silk manufacturers looked to Essex, where workers could be employed for cheaper wages than in London, leading to the industrialisation of north Essex towns such as Coggeshall.

The growth of industry in London helped give rise to perhaps the most familiar trope connected with the East End. Today, the word 'cockney' is both a global brand (most famously depicted by Dick Van Dyke during his boundlessly chirpy yet not at all convincing performance as Bert in *Mary Poppins*) and a shorthand for white working-class London, personified in the shape of pearly kings and market traders. People say cockney when they mean anyone from the southeast of England who might be a bit rough around the edges. Often Essex and cockney caricatures are interchangeable.

The cockney was born out of an ever-changing, and arguably ever-empowering, London that had sucked out the fat of the old, rural ways of immigrants to the metropolis, leaving behind the sinew of a new way of living. They exuded an 'air of levity and indifference', wrote the essayist William Hazlitt, which contrasted with the 'harshness, a moroseness, and disagreeable restraint' of countryfolk. 'A real cockney is the poorest creature in the world, the most literal, the most mechanical, and yet he too lives in a world of performance – a fairy land of his own.' Hazlitt posited that the cockney had grown to be like this due to the dominance of the city in comparison to other metropolises around the world. 'There are now more people in London than anywhere else; and though a dwarf in stature, his person swells out and expands into ideal importance and borrowed magnitude.'

And yet a distinction must be made between the trippers that so irked Southend's top brass and the cockney that so obsessed Hazlitt. The latter wasn't the downtrodden factory worker, costermonger, mudlark or petty criminal you might find in one of Dickens's novels or Mayhew's social taxonomies. His crime was to be of clerk class, the lower-middle, the most petit of bourgeois. But something happened to the cockney as east London industrialised and was filled with low-paid workers and their families. Arriving on the scene as a figure of social mobility, he 'gradually starts to slip down the social scale, moving down into the London working class, and also to change its valency in the process,' wrote Professor Gregory Dart. 'No longer a term of abuse, it became more and more a term of affection; no longer a synonym for social ambition, it referred increasingly to those who, like Sam Weller in Dickens's *Pickwick Papers* (1837), seemed strangely content to remain low. The word changed, in short, from being a way of worrying about the petite bourgeoisie to being a way of reassuring oneself about the urban proletariat. Cockneyism had finally found a home.'

Traces of London are still present in Essex seaside towns thanks to the connections made in the nineteenth century. Fans in short-sleeved West Ham shirts stand stoically on the platform at Clacton-on-Sea station on cold weekend mornings, waiting to make the journey to the London Stadium in east London's Olympic park. 'Kings Cross born and bred,' said the man outside the social club during one of my visits to Jaywick, when someone asked where he was originally from. Elsewhere in Jaywick, a retired beachsider with stiffly swept-back white hair told me he used to sing in the pubs and clubs of the East End of London, 'and the singers these days just don't cut it.'

The connection between Essex and east London can often feel ritualistic, even showy. I once saw souvenir posters of the Kray twins in Pitsea Market, and on the way to the toilets in a pub in a rural Essex village not far from Rochford I walked past a sort of makeshift shrine to the gangsters. But it has deep and wide roots. I met Joel Friedman, who helped to move an Orthodox Jewish community, his family included, from north London's Stamford Hill to Canvey Island, spurred on by London's housing shortage and the hope of better air quality for their children. Friedman told me the community had wondered whether they would be welcome on the island but was relieved to tell me they had been and suggested this could have had something to do with Canvey's East End heritage. 'I was surprised at the history of people on Canvey: a) so many are from London, and b) so many people I speak to say they have connections to the Jewish community from the East End. They all know about the bagels and the fish. They know more about the Jewish community than our old neighbours in London did.'

Although not strictly kosher, seafood helps to replenish the connection between London and Essex. When I lived in Hackney, some of the pubs we drank in were visited by men who brought in cockles and whelks gathered from the mouth of the Thames and hidden illicitly in a cold-storage box, ducking in and out of the pubs that still let them trade. Tubby Isaacs' 'world famous' jellied eels stall closed in Aldgate but there is one that still bears the name in Clacton. When I was a boy, my dad tried to turn me on to whelks, thrusting a polystyrene tray full of the rubbery specimens at my sister and me during trips down to the old town in Leigh-on-Sea, where East Enders still make summer day trips for crayfish, cockles and pints. The cockle, owing to its two-hinged shell, is a bivalve (as are the mussel and the oyster) and so is much more pleasant to eat; the whelks required too much endurance. But then the cockle, admittedly, is not exempt from the complaints of visiting tourists unready for the odd bit of grit cracking between their teeth when sampling the estuary delicacy.

Southend has always seemed to be slightly unsure of itself, a quality that could have been attributed to its feeling of inadequacy next to London, which at once sustains it in terms of endless job opportunities and cultural injections, but also deprives it in other, less quantifiable ways in terms of its self image, its identity. 'Southend is a cheaper Brighton,' wrote John Betjeman, which, while it sounds like a kind of slight, an affected put-down of the type that came easy to the eventual poet laureate of the United Kingdom, ended up being quite an accurate description. 'Southend is twentieth century,' wrote the Irish novelist Kate O'Brien. 'It has set to face its future, and has run through the dangers, crudities and mistakes, which are the lot of the courageous and the outgoing. It has decided to be a place of pleasure and a home from home.' O'Brien seemed fascinated by Southend because of its 'designlessness' that came from its inherent newness. Not for this town the architectural coherence of more established R&R destinations, such as Bath – no stone for a start. It had no real respect for any particular architectural tradition, and no real need for it: 'There is at least no truck in this town with "Ye Olde" nonsense. If anything is old, it is so by accident, and no one thinks the worse of it for being so – but nothing else is dressed up to humour it.'

The house we moved into in Southend was built in 1910, at the apex of Southend's population boom (the town's population more than doubled to 70,000 in the 10 years up to its construction) and formed part of a brand new, relatively upmarket housing project, the Riviera Estate. By the time our street was built, Southend was welcoming 100,000 people each August bank holiday. People frolicking in front of the bandstand, horses and carriages bumper to bumper. The estate had been built in an attempt to civilise the end of Southend east of the pier that the excursionist rabble were pushed towards, but it couldn't keep a lid on the desires of the working classes. Our next-door neighbour Steve said his family had come from the East End to chase the opportunities Southend had in abundance, running excursions from the end of the pier and, later on, an illegal bookie's. Steve told me of how he had found scores of telephone wires in the upstairs of the house, which would have been manned by operators ready to take people's bets. The promise of crowds and, therefore, custom, has long helped Southend draw out an enterprising spirit in its inhabitants. My uncles used to take squirrel monkeys down to the seafront, asking day-trippers if they wanted to be photographed with one. When these monkeys weren't going down the prom for their day's work, my nan had to look after them, dressing them in nappies to preserve the carpets.

Some of Essex's seasides have resisted this kind of ad hoc spirit. I talked to a Frinton woman, Beverley, who I met at the counter of a bookshop she worked in on the seaside town's main drag, Connaught Avenue. She said there used to be a saying: 'You don't have any Flash Harrys in Frinton.' Unlike nearby Walton or Clacton, the day-tripping cockney was not to be catered for here. A late developer as far as English seaside resorts go, Frinton was conceived by Sir Richard Powell Cooper in the 1890s, who made sure he built the reserved nature for which Frinton is famous into its very fabric: no amusements, no pier, no shorts at the golf club and certainly no public houses.

Frinton today is retired stockbroker nirvana: they built the golf course before anything else. It grew in prominence during the twentieth century, until it became known as 'the Bond Street of Essex'. Part of the Clacton constituency, its MP for a time was Ukip's famous former Tory, Douglas Carswell, a man who liked to take BBC Radio 4 news presenters to Wimpy in Clacton for lunch to prove himself to the common man (there is no Wimpy in Frinton). There was a public spat when the first chip shop opened there in 1992 and the town centre was famously pub-less until 2000. One of two Indian restaurants politely justifies itself with its cosily colonial title, British India, and when I visited there was a golliwog toy in the window of one of the bric-a-brac shops. 'There is a strong trend of keeping things as they are, so it's a battle between being welcoming and contemporary without losing the values that made Frinton,' said Beverley in the bookshop.

The modern seaside town often tells a political story. From Frinton to Clacton to Jaywick, aspiration falls into abandonment like a tumbling Alka-Seltzer. Jaywick is a sprawl of plotland bungalow developments, built in the 1930s for east Londoners to holiday and retire in. Much as the Victorian ruin-seekers visited the lost East Anglian town of Dunwich in search of medieval scenes of decay as it fell into the sea, Jaywick's dilapidation has long fascinated artists and writers. In the 1980s, Paul Theroux likened it to a seaside slum in Argentina or Mexico. In 2013 it was pronounced the most deprived place in the UK, which encouraged a further slew of photographers and writers to document the dilapidation. When I first visited Jaywick, just being there as a journalist felt like a gauche enterprise, but as a poster child of decline, it lived up to type: I arrived to a drunken daytime altercation between a man and a woman, with a small crowd gathered round. It was a low-key display of the despair and division that the politics of the last decade have tapped into, but certainly not one that is unique to Jaywick. This ad hoc Essex settlement of unshowy properties at risk from flooding was exempt from Thatcher's miracle of pulling people up by their bootstraps by giving them all mortgages and watching house prices go up and up. Talking to residents, who bemoaned the stagnant wages of this seaside economy but who looked out for each other, I realised that the place could be simply described – as might Essex – by the name of its charming pub on the edge of the North Sea: Never Say Die.

4

A Curious Frontier

The best time to walk in Essex is that point when October suddenly rushes into November. At this time of year there is a real clarity to the light, which I was told is because there are fewer dissolved water particles in the air than during the heat of the summer. And here I was again, out beside a narrow strip of water fringed by marsh in a baleful autumn light. Look one way past the blonde grasses bent back by the wind on the sea wall and you notice the tiny pockmarks of the village of Tollesbury; look the other and you see the grey blocks of Bradwell's decommissioned nuclear power station, which somehow looks computer generated, an uncanny placement against the greens and the browns of the marshes. Although there can often be something timeless about the Essex coast, these flat landscapes can tell us much about the march of modernity, like the nuclear power station, the oil refinery at Canvey, the huge QE2 suspension bridge at Thurrock, the gigantic cranes at the great ports at Tilbury and Corringham, and the enormous Chappel Viaduct that crosses the River Colne near Colchester. Seen at a distance, these engineered interventions into the warp and weft of estuarial Essex can seem to segue into the reeds and the grasses, but come up close and you can be caught unawares by an alarming sublimity and grandeur.

I started coming to this area of the Blackwater Estuary and the Dengie Peninsula when I still lived in London to leave the madness of city life temporarily behind. It's a place where one can feel a sense of eerie seclusion, of being suddenly and decisively outside of things, despite the close proximity to one of the biggest and most teeming cities in the world. At such places as Rainham Marshes or the oddly barren paths by the River Roding between the London boroughs of Red-bridge and Newham you can fall into a state of such silence and seclusion that time itself seems to flatline. I lost count of the amount of times when I still lived in London and trav-elled on a train out to an open field or marsh, only to feel this particular feeling, so much so that I gave it a name, 'the Essex solitary', a condition that describes the eeriness of a sudden disappearance of urban markers, an escape from the overload of London, so far yet so near.

Out here in these places of biting arctic winds, creeks, bucolic villages and farms that can be viewed from the M25, it is still possible to plug into an old Essex quality, one of muteness or silence. 'Essex is a queer country,' wrote H Cranmer-Byng, a compiler of old Essex folk stories in the early twentieth century. 'A famous writer who once lived for some time on the fringe of Roding country once said to me he had a curious feeling that Essex was completely deaf. I recall that he could not explain it. It was just a feeling, a sudden personal insight into something too subtle for anal-ysis or explanation.' Walter Besant, the chronicler of late Victorian London, tapped into an idea similar to the Essex solitary in his 1901-published study, *East London*. He took the train to Barking when it was still described as an 'ancient village . . . on the little river Roding' and not the built-up commuter hub of Greater London it is in the twenty-first century. After reaching the Thames and walking along the wall protecting Barking from inundation, he declared shock at his sudden change in surroundings. 'No one ever walks upon this wall; once beyond the chemical works we are in the most lonely spot in the whole of England . . . you may see no one in the meadows protected by the wall; you may walk mile after mile in a solitude most strange and most mysterious . . . If one were to tell a murder, this would be a fitting place for the crime.'

This sense of isolation remains in parts of Essex, but it is easily punctured. A farmer from Foulness, John Burroughs, told me about how one evening he was looking at some migratory birds wading over the flats. He caught sight of a visitor in luminous attire on a nearby island, Wallasea. John, completely alone watching across the River Roach from Foulness, said he was almost counting the seconds knowing this one person in a yellow jacket, a bright dot in the marsh landscape, would make these hundreds of birds fling themselves into the air in a great cloud of life. And, just like that, they did.

I had driven to Tollesbury to meet a local man of the marsh, Flavian Capes, to talk to him about what it's like to live on the edge of some of the most isolated wetland in Essex. I arrived frazzled and a little late after contending with heavy traffic out of Southend (Essex's convoluted nature is dictated by the waterways, but the fact that it takes an age to get anywhere thanks to so many rivers that don't have bridges over them is one of its great strengths). Capes looked at me with a smile that was almost apologetic. He didn't own a car himself, he said; in fact, he lived out here to get away from them. He told me he saw the marshes as 'the last freedom' away from all the maniacal movement and development that characterised much of Essex and the south-east of England.

Capes has lived alone on his boat, a 1960s-built fishing vessel from Normandy moored up in a creek at Tollesbury Marshes, for several decades. His dad was a fisherman and was born here, while his mother came from Sudbury just over the Suffolk border. But they still weren't considered an original village family. The Capeses first came here in the Victorian era because it was an appealing place to holiday. There used to be a railway in Tollesbury, with a pier, which attracted tourists. The fact that the railway was closed in 1951 has given Tollesbury an out of the way feel, but Capes said that the village used to be much livelier, situated at the end of a swath of common land that attracted Gypsy travellers and Huguenots. 'It was a settling ground for people who don't fit in, which is why I think I fit in.'

In the marsh, things stay there until they degrade and disappear into the mud. In addition to the two big boats he owns, Capes has accumulated a host of dinghies that had been abandoned in the mud. He has found Roman, Iron Age and medieval pottery (as well as plenty of degrading electric batteries) during low-tide explorations. Capes said he knew where there was an eighteenth-century cannon from a ship, a frigate built during the early years of George III's reign. Upturned duck punt wrecks, too, which people once used to catch fowl by shooting them from their boats back when these marshes were teeming with ducks, teal and widgeon. Capes had even found coal from an old sunken barge. 'I actually mined it for a couple of winters. It was good to use after a day.'

At times Capes has lived off the marsh itself. He pointed out sea spinach that he had boiled up and eaten. For two years most of his diet consisted of anything he could hunt, pick, fish, forage or rake up from the mud. And the Blackwater did provide: Capes lived off an enviable diet of oysters, mussels, winkles, cockles, whelks, shore crabs (although they are a little bit bitter, he said), scallops and occasionally, if he was lucky, lobsters. 'I walk right down to the middle of the river [to catch them]. Or I use lobster pots, my dad had lobster pots, but they are more of a seasonal thing.' He fell out of full-time foraging but does it still 'as a treat'. In the end he found he

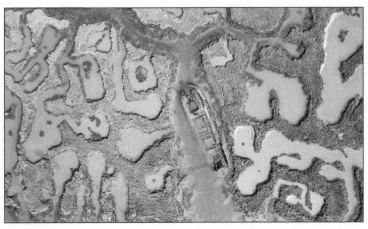

A wreck in the mud

was missing things he liked too much. 'I don't think there are many people queueing up to do what I do,' he said. 'A friend of mine once said he heard the nature reserve weren't keen on me living on the marshes, because of the wildlife, and my friend said to me, "But you *are* the wildlife."'

Capes told me he had done thirty-five winters on his boat, but it was his second winter on the marshes in the late 1980s that was the worst he has experienced here by far, when the snow was 3-feet deep on land. Drifts as high as 15 feet blocked the way out of the village, completely cutting it off from the outside world. Supply deliveries were dropped off in the square by helicopter. Ice a couple of inches thick covered the creek for the best part of a week. 'I put my thermometer outside and it was below minus 20 for five nights.' He said the frozen water would come down on the marshes and break up and fill all the gullies and creeks as the tide came in before doing the same again the next night, and the next day.

Miniature icebergs formed and ploughed into his boat in the middle of the night.

Capes took me to dig some Roman pottery directly out of the mud. He told me that the local tribe, the Trinovantes, who occupied Colchester and this area, paid auxiliary troops working for the Roman army in salt to try and slow down its conquest. The Romans' arrival in Colchester marked the successful end of an invasion begun almost 100 years earlier by Julius Caesar and was accompanied by a show of pomp like Essex had never seen. Historical hearsay describes the victorious Emperor Claudius arriving in Colchester on an elephant in AD43. Claudius revelled in the victory but didn't stay long, leaving after barely two weeks (his entire voyage to Britain and back is said to have taken six months) but the Roman legacy lives on in the roads and the coins and the walls they left behind – and of course, their pottery. After five minutes of searching in the mud, Capes helped me find a fragment of a Roman vase and the handle from a jug. The Romans made Colchester, or Camuladolum as it was, the first British city, and veteran soldiers moved to idyllic spots by water, and had olives and other Mediterranean delicacies delivered to them. While they were here the Romans made oysters a desirable foodstuff, Capes said; it was initially a poor man's food and after they left it returned to being so again, only revived in the Tudor Renaissance.

Others had different plans, however. Colchester was razed to the ground by the courageous, furious efforts of the Iceni queen Boudica and her tribe from neighbouring East Anglia. The rebellion began when the Romans attempted to seize their lands, flogged Boudica and raped her daughters, after the death of Boudica's husband Prasutagus. London was also sacked by the Iceni (as was Verulamium, modern-day St Albans), but after the defeat of the revolt it would win out over Colchester as capital city because it was positioned on the mightier Thames, a waterway more able to sustain cargo than the Colne in Colchester.

Some have speculated that the Roman presence never entirely left. The Rev Sabine Baring-Gould, the rector for Mersea Island, wrote in the nineteenth century of the local belief that a Roman centurion was patrolling the Strood, the causeway linking Mersea to the mainland. Some witnesses claimed to have seen the officer clashing with anyone who might have had the courage to approach him. In 1926, the landlady of the nearby Peldon Rose said she had encountered the centurion on the Strood, although she could only hear his presence marching beside her as she navigated the causeway. 'I could see no one, yet the feet were close beside me, as near as I could have touched him,' she said. In the 1960s, two naval officers were reported to have had an encounter with the centurion while driving across the Strood, seeing the silhouetted figure with a helmet in the glare of the headlights. Coming to a hurried stop, they got out of the car – only to be greeted by no one at all.

Tales of hauntings apply narrative to the general eeriness of these solitary Essex places. And yet, as the nineteenth century gathered pace, the feeling of relative emptiness in the parts of Essex nearer London came to feel ever more fragile. The county's absences offered an opportunity to the kinds of Victorians who were born to speculate and accumulate, and their actions brought with them an abundance of presence, in the form of factories and the people drawn to them for work.

If you could pinpoint the exact historical moment that led to the creation of the busy county we know today, it would be found in West Ham on the historical border of London and Essex, the River Lea. In the latter half of the nineteenth century, this represented the extreme end of London's industrial and suburban expansion. Downwind from the city and outside the jurisdiction of governance of London itself, the River Lea provided the perfect environment to industrialise, not least as the cost of transporting coal by land was prohibitively expensive. Instead, factories were built next to rivers and creeks where coal could be delivered by boat, making the location ideal for industry.

Of all England's counties during the decade that fell between 1881 and 1891, Essex had the greatest population increase: 36.3 per cent compared to 20.5 per cent in Surrey, which had also experienced London overspill, but not to the extremes that West Ham did. In 1801, there were 6,500 people living in West Ham. In 1851, this had risen to 18,817, but by 1901 had increased by 1,321 per cent, swelling to 267,358 and matching the population of twenty-first-century Stoke. It was an alarming pace of development even when set against the dramatic consequences of nineteenth-century industrialisation. The metropolitan Essex districts of West Ham, East Ham, Walthamstow and Leyton were utterly transformed to welcome industry and accommodate workers. In 1886, West Ham was incorporated as a municipal borough and by 1931, there were 294,278 people there. Jobs such as dockwork, engineering and construction, and work in the chemical, food, textiles and leather industries, all attracted people to an area that was characterised by quieter agricultural ways half a century before. Between 1860 and 1919, around 290 manufacturing businesses established premises in West Ham. Workers were also attracted to railway engineering works at Stratford, or the Victoria Docks on Plaistow Marshes or shipbuilding at Thames Ironworks. The HMS *Warrior*, the first ironclad ship made in Britain, and the HMS *Thunderer*, a huge warship, were built at the shipyard.

A never-ending East End was being created, a place built

up so fast it was not quite London but not quite Essex, with factories rubbing shoulders with farmland. 'Really there is no limit to London,' wrote Henry Morley after visiting West Ham for Charles Dickens's *Household Words* magazine in 1857, and writing an article that coined a quietly infamous term, 'Londoners over the Border'. Morley pointed out that this suburb on the edge of the Essex marshes was cut off from some of the controls that industry on the other side of the Lea was required to adhere to. The polluted sub-metropolitan border country around the River Lea therefore represented an illicit opportunity for less scrupulous business owners thanks to it being outside the area governed by the Metropolitan Buildings Act 1844, which stipulated that dwelling houses were required to be built at a distance from 'offensive business' such as oil boiling, varnish making or chemical works, with no such rules in West Ham.

The Lower Lea therefore became a 'hybrid creation of the natural flow of water and human efforts to manipulate that flow', according to the Canadian professor Jim Clifford, who has extensively researched the effects of the industrialisation of West Ham's marshland. The burgeoning population of West Ham led to an intense environmental burden, not least thanks to the infrastructure suddenly required to turn marshland into an industrial city. A hybrid hydrologic system was installed that formalised the water into a network of pipes, sewers, canals and natural rivers. Tall towers came to dominate the marshes, the factories they were attached to bringing workers, their sewage and, by extension, disease.

As in the better-known slums of the inner East End, density of living was married with a paucity of the infrastructural elements that might have staved off local health disasters. Sickness reigned, with West Ham residents often succumbing to illnesses that those in the better parts of London thought had long been eradicated. As with the malarial marshland of previous centuries, the perilous risks of living in West Ham set it apart and cemented the disparity between this far-East End and more comfortable suburbs closer to London's centre. Morley wrote of 'ghostly little children' succumbing to the filthy air of a 'pestilential ditch'. Alfred Dickens, the brother of Charles, made public the scale of the problem in West Ham. The Victorian novelist's younger sibling was a civil engineer, asked to highlight the calamitous housing situation as the parish's biggest issue in his government report. Residents would go to the toilet in privies, which were emptied into ditches that gave off awful smells. There was so much sewage it couldn't all be washed away by the tide, and so it polluted the River Lea and sometimes even the water that residents were forced to drink, as they were not connected to the local waterworks.

In West Ham, fates were decided by whether you lived on low or high ground. The poorest lived on the marsh in the south and west, which was characterised by low-quality rental accommodation. The Northern Outfall Sewer, designed by Joseph Bazalgette after the great stink of 1858 and still surviving today, stood higher than the houses that resided by it and served to split West Ham in two, wrote Jim Clifford, while 'Canning Town was laid out in a haphazard web, originally determined by drainage ditches'. Forest Gate and northern Stratford were 'more orderly and spacious' than these disorganised, dishevelled marshland streets, home to some of the poorest people in London. Clifford's research paints the typical working-class house in Canning Town as damp with wallpaper peeling off the walls and liable to flood. One of the most notorious streets, Hermit Road, was reputedly built on a marsh without adequate foundations, and so found to be 'subsiding in the soil'. The dampness of the dwellings combined with the heavy industry of the area characterised Canning Town as a tough place of 'smoke, sewage, and other contaminants'. A malt manufacturer reported that the water of the Lea was so polluted it could not be used. Reports on the area blamed the people who lived there, terming them as 'the lowest class of loafers', for their plight, but it was clear that in West Ham, societal and environmental problems buffered up against one another like boats moored up in the waves. Plenty drowned trying to ride the dramatic tides of industry, or else were stuck in the mud after fortunes had receded.

As time went on, Essex's destiny started to be bunched together with that of the industrial East End. 'The great home county of Essex is less explored by tourists than almost any other part of England,' wrote the Stratford-born Jesuit poet Gerard Manley Hopkins in literary magazine *Once a Week* in 1860. 'Seen from the Thames, it must be owned that its margin is not inviting, and the road to it, through Spitalfields, Mile End and Stratford, is so dull, flat and poverty-stricken, that few visitors care to pass along it.' In 1928, the New Survey of London Life and Labour said 14.5 per cent of West Ham's inhabitants were living in poverty; the degradation of the nineteenth century cast a long shadow over the area, both in terms of a deprivation that still exists, or the inhabitants' exodus in search of better lives. The same survey described Canning Town and Silvertown as 'perhaps the largest area of unbroken depression in east London', and the parts of Essex just outside the borders of London were looked upon with horror by commentators and seemed to be influencing the way Essex men of letters started to talk about their own county. 'It has often been said that there is less county pride in Essex than probably any other British county,' began the first editorial of the *Essex Review* in January 1892. 'This is, perhaps, correct with respect to the metropolitan portion, but in the county generally is certainly more apparent than real.'

Worse still were the people arriving to make their home in Essex. In 1902, Perry Clark wrote an article-length jeremiad

against the development along the south of the Thames ema-
nating from West Ham and eastwards past Tilbury Docks and
into Thurrock and beyond. These were 'serried rows of small
suburban erections, all built like card-boxes, as if turned out
of the same mould, examples of poorer Whitechapel and
Stepney dumped down among the Thurrock Marshes'. Clark
bemoaned that a 'richer class' of London emigre was choosing
Kent over Essex. The settlers, he wrote, came 'from a poorer
stock' and were building homes 'reared with scant regard to
the principles of art, or any aesthetic feeling. Herein lies the
crux of the whole matter, and hence the peculiar danger with
which the Essex countryside is threatened.'

When the railways arrived like pugilistic insertions into
Essex in the second half of the nineteenth century, they
utterly transformed it. What must the small farming com-
munities and clusters of artisans or fishermen surrounded
by arable fields and marsh have made of the sudden arrival
of steam trains, these great groaning ogres that whistled,
shunted and ached, and which appeared like ghostly appari-
tions in the peripheral vision of farm labourers or country
squires? Romford was once known for its country market:
droves of cattle blocked roads during the midsummer cattle
fair, wives of farmers sold milk and eggs and butter, while
rabbits and pheasants were hawked. Its population of 3,000
in 1803 had swelled to 115,600 by the time it was subsumed
into the London borough of Havering in 1965 with its easy
access to London by train.

The late nineteenth and early twentieth century expansion of London's residential and industrial boundaries
transformed the physical and socio-economic character of
many of the districts of south-west Essex by the 1930s. Many
became more accessible due to improved transport facilities and acquired a 'suburban' character, housing London's
expanding urban working population. The development of

Essex into a collection of different-hued suburbs for wanta-way Londoners did not just constitute ecological destruction, the swapping of fields and hedgerows for cement and tarmac, but also a reminder of how diminished an entity the English gentry had become. Essex in particular had for centuries been a bolthole for inherited wealth, home to wealthy elites from the Boleyns to Robert Rich, the Earl of Warwick. Great estates and hunting lodges were built on the fringes of London, such as the Queen Elizabeth Hunting Lodge on the edge of Epping Forest, and further afield, in places such as Layer Marney, where a large Tudor estate is now a visitor's attraction.

By the 1920s, lord of the manor no longer carried with it rights over land. In truth, rural Essex villages had been stagnating for a while, the remnants of a decaying feudal tradition of dividing the county into different 'Hundreds' that stretched back to the Saxon times of 'free peasants' living in allotted 'hides'. Manorial estates around Essex were being portioned off and sold along with the abandoned farm-land, to the chagrin of antiquarians and aristocrats alike. The rector of Runwell St Mary's church near Wickford, John Edward Bazille-Corbin, wrote that building work had flowed from the corner opposite the church and up the lane from the 1910s after Southend's Land Company, headed by a man named Frederick Francis Ramuz, purchased plots of an old manorial estate. 'With the steady decay of the Manorial System of land tenure which had commenced by the middle of the fourteenth century, the several farms constituted the main units of sub-division,' he wrote. 'The sole people of social prominence – and their prominence was purely local – were the family who lived at the Manor House, Flemings Manor . . .' Bazille-Corbin mourned that from the eighteenth century there was no prominent family in Runwell.

If the established rural gentry were struggling by the late

nineteenth century, then their working-class counterparts were drowning. The countryside, far from being the idyllic rural paradise it was sometimes painted as by city-folk, was in crisis. 'Substandard housing, inadequate sanitary provision, lack of educational opportunity and a rigid class system – which in many places was almost feudal – were common,' wrote Essex-based social historian Ted Woodgate, who had grown up in a farming community in north Essex before moving down to Basildon to accept a job as a teacher when the new town was built. Woodgate told me of an organisation called the National Agricultural Labourers' Union (NALU) in Essex, which unfortunately did not enjoy the collective heft of the industrial unions, such as the highly skilled and politicised workers in metropolitan Essex, whose presence ultimately gave rise to the dawn of the Labour Party when its founder Keir Hardie became MP for the emboldened constituency of West Ham. While the unions of east London were fighting for better wages and conditions, the NALU was seen as deeply suspicious by those with opinions that mattered in innately Conservative rural Essex. Colonel AW Ruggles-Brise, Maldon's Tory MP, described them as 'nothing less than Communism and contrary to Scripture'.

Many parts of rural Essex were experiencing the opposite issue to West Ham's over-abundance of people. As London became a magnet for those seeking work, population levels in declining agricultural and textile districts in the north of the county such as Braintree, Dunmow and Saffron Walden dropped off a cliff. Essex's role as the breadbasket of England, a place that helped keep London in cow's milk and corn, was in a state of turmoil by the nineteenth century. Farms were going bankrupt due to cheap US grain imports driving down crop prices and bad weather ruining harvests. Many south Essex farms were led to ruin, their once-grazed fields turning to a scrubland wilderness.

*

The wider agricultural situation in Britain was so dire (with Essex bearing the brunt more than any other county) that the prime minister, Benjamin Disraeli, instigated a Royal Commission in 1879. The depression meant that a surplus of land was for sale. Again, geology seems to have sealed Essex's fate. A new wave of developers took advantage of the sudden availability of the less coveted 'three horse land' – so called because that's how many nags it would take to plough it – that became available as much of it was of the thankless heavy clay type. The Royal Commission quoted a Dengie farmer describing his soil as 'stiff, tough, numb, dumb, and impervious'. Wheat was the only crop that could be relied upon to grow and even then, it was a slog. As imports grew cheaper, the land fell into disuse, becoming rough scrub. Farms were sold under the duress of bankruptcy. Whole estates were bought up at once, often by single developers such as Ramuz.

Land in estuarial areas such as Canvey in south-east Essex and Jaywick in the north-east near Clacton were available due to a different – yet still familiar – problem, the perpetual risk of flooding. Canvey Island was reclaimed by the Dutch and later built on by Londoners trying their luck, freehold by freehold. In 1866, Canvey was home to just 111 inhabitants; today it's pushing 40,000.

Canvey is easily the most 'Essex' of all the islands and it wears the hope it has offered Londoners for generations on its sleeve. The paucity of holidaying options for the poor in London during the lean old nineteenth century brought them to Canvey for a day out, and once they were here, many wanted to stay over, stop a while. In the intervening years, East End pioneers moved to the island to begin new lives. Entrepreneur Frederick Hester divided up farmland he'd bought during the agricultural depression into plots, marketing them as a place to holiday, supplying 'murky London with yet another lung'. (One islander, whose family has been there for the best part of the last century, told me doctors used to actually prescribe a visit to Canvey to remedy the ills of the dense city.) Hester became a kind of godfather of Canvey, building a monorail and exotic winter gardens, and planning to turn creeks into grand, Venetian-style canals. His desire to transform the island into a dream destination was so strong he overstretched his finances, filing for bankruptcy in 1905.

Canvey, the nearest island to where I grew up, has always summed up for me the way people in Essex seem to speak their minds, unafraid of cracking a joke or five as if styling out their county's fate as a national punchline. The paranoiacally high sea wall, built as part of a huge sea defence project after the deadly 1953 flood, has meant there has been no repeat of the disaster on the island since, even if it seems to give it an insularity that has concentrated its character. As a result of Canvey's relative security from the elements, the island has become a chequerboard of different housing styles. Sturdy gaffs with faux Doric columns, Beverly Hills-style bonanzas replete with swimming pools, stolid bungalows, the odd seventeenth-century Dutch survival. That this area has fostered some of the highest levels of property ownership in the UK despite the rising tides is one of countless ironies of this coastal landscape. Canvey is safe from the sea for now, but the tide has risen through the centuries, with some Essex islands being slowly swallowed up until they are often only visible as smears of vegetation atop a swollen pool. I started to recognise an intrinsic feeling of accentuation when it came to Essex, between sparseness and density, bucolic abandonment and oncoming modernity, realism and poetry, country and city, rich and poor – buzzing dichotomies that meant that, as hard as I tried to pin Essex's story down, it always somehow slipped away. And yet, learning the tales of historical extremity that begat the great movement from London into Essex eventually illuminated the county I had moved back to, revealing it as a place built through a stubborn belief in the promise of survival.

In the autumn of 1922 an ambiguous wooden figure was discovered by workmen digging up the land to prepare it for its new industrial usage. The wooden figure with asymmetrical eyes and a horizontal mouth was found at a depth of about nine feet. It must have seemed like an old wooden doll, perhaps discarded by a careless child. But it was dated to around 2,250 BC, the cusp of the Bronze Age, the late Neolithic period. It was eventually nicknamed 'the Dagenham Idol'.

The Idol's oldness accentuated the sudden newness of its surroundings, its discovery somehow heralding the dawn of modern Essex – only nobody knew where to put it. Metropolitan Essex was not the kind of place to keep such treasures of antiquity and so it was whisked 50 miles away in the north of the county to be housed at Colchester Castle Museum. Today, the Idol hovers behind glass in the Valence House Museum, inside a former manor house within a park in the Becontree Estate in Dagenham: an 18-inch-tall figure with two legs but no arms. Glanced at from the front, it could be holding them behind its back, as if quickly concealing something incriminating. It withholds its gender, too. Perhaps it was part of some kind of ritual or ceremony: the skeleton of a deer was also supposed to have been found in the peaty soil around 30 yards away but was lost after it was dug up. But, whatever the meaning of its initial burial, its discovery marked Essex as a place at a crossroads, between an ancient past and a searing present.

5

The Better Life

William Morris grew up on the edge of Epping Forest in Essex. When Hayley and I lived a short walk away from his childhood home in Walthamstow, we'd go for walks around the grounds that would have once felt like a calming gateway to the greatness of the forest, with its glum and gnarly common oaks and hornbeams stretching 12 miles from London into Essex. It is easy to mock Morris as just another socialist son of a stockbroker but, while he may have been wealthy and educated at Marlborough and Oxford, he was also serious about his life's work, which sought to promote the idea that all workers should have the same life of 'refinement and education' as he had.

His novelistic vision of utopia, *News from Nowhere*, however, was of a high-handed strand of radicalism, flying in the face of the working-class experience. Morris's utopia was a sylvan fantasy where people only worked in jobs they loved, and the burgeoning subtopia of suburban London was destroyed for a dramatic campaign of rewilding. Instead of working fingers to the bone as a cog in one of the many industries that had appeared in the past few decades, he envisioned an England where pollution-spewing factories were pulled down, along with London suburbs and the railways. This was prompted in part by Morris's shock at what had happened to his beloved Essex idyll, singling out the sprawl of Canning Town for a particularly unsavoury fantasy of 'de-cockneyfication'. And Morris wasn't the only one projecting this idealistic fervour onto the county.

Before Essex was a punchline, it was a dream. Its availability in the nineteenth century thanks to the agricultural depression and its proximity to London saw it become the answer to a thousand questions posed by social reformers and radical dabblers who sketched out alternative ways of living, whether they were adherent or heretical, communal or individual, fantastical or mundane. There was Moonella in Wickford, the UK's first nudist colony, which was established in 1924; the grand garden experiment of Mayland on the Dengie Peninsula (where the American soap heir Joseph Fels attempted to turn England into 'an agricultural country again'); the vegetarian colony in Stanford-Le-Hope and the pacifist community at Frating Hall Farm on the Tendring Peninsula (these stories and more have been told brilliantly over time by Ken Worpole, the indefatigable godfather of Essex's social, going on socialist, history). Collective artistic engagement flooded into the gaps, too. Composer Gustav Holst's regular four-day Whitsun music festival at Thaxted Church in the 1910s has been described by the music writer Rob Young as 'the moment English music lost its inhibitions'. The work of the Great Bardfield artist group, whose leading figures were Eric Ravilious, Tirzah Garwood and Edward Bawden, seemed imbued with a domesticating urge that saw them transform Brick House from a dilapidated dwelling with no gas, electricity or running water into a thriving colony in the 1930s. Essex became a screen for desires to be projected onto.

The Purleigh Brotherhood Colony, established in 1896 and influenced by the teachings of Tolstoy, was a typical example. Members set about digging heavy loam all winter, before they could go ahead with planting, putting up fences, building sheds and greenhouses, acquiring bees and keeping chickens for eggs come the longer days. The Purleigh pioneers hadn't much training in this kind of survivalist experience: they were of bank clerk stock in search of meaning, who existed on 'cold porridge and an occasional onion to take the taste away', as their biographer, the historian Victor Gray, wrote. One of those who had seen the light was William Sudbury Protheroe, heir to an antiques business in east London. 'The time had come when I must choose between God and Mammon,' he wrote. The colony failed, Gray suggested, as it could not reconcile its inherent anarchism with the decision-making required by a fragile yet ambitious community that sought to provide alternatives to the scourge of poverty while welcoming all comers. Arguments over principles, lustful affairs and the corrupting influence of money all contributed, but Gray settled on the fact that 'there were as many different versions of "the better life" and how to achieve it as there were colonists' as the deciding factor in the Purleigh Brotherhood's capitulation.

Essex in the nineteenth century set about bettering itself through moral rather than material uplift. Companies organised excursions for the very poor to visit Southend during its day-tripper heyday, followed by the inevitable complaints about the unruliness of the visiting rabble. A reply to one such letter found by local Southend historian Ken Crowe said, poignantly, that Southend was 'the only seaside resort that the very poorest of our London factory hands and matchbox girls can be brought to and taken home again for one and sixpence, a special excursion fare organised by firms in London for their workers.' In 1893, the inmates of the West Ham workhouse were given an excursion to Southend. General William Booth, the Methodist who founded the Salvation Army along with his wife Catherine (and had already started a farm colony in Hadleigh near the ruined castle), brought 5,000 people there on a visit, from his Christian mission.

Frederick Charrington, who inherited the fortunes of the old East End brewery firm that bore his surname, instead decided to dedicate his life to fighting alcoholism after seeing a drunk man punch his wife outside one of his family's pubs, after she had asked him for some money. It spurred him to set up a charity to help people dependent on alcohol and drugs (the Tower Hamlets Mission, which survives in the East End to this day). In 1903, Charrington bought Osea Island for a relatively cheap fee, and had grand plans to set up an experimental temperance colony for 'inebriates' in the style of a similar scheme in New York. The sale, manufacture and consumption of alcohol was prohibited. The temporary guests of the island would come via train to Maldon and from there by steamboat, thereby avoiding any temptation for debauchery en route.

Charrington brought kangaroos and emus onto the island and started a zoo to help distract the drinkers, but it couldn't soften the fact that the crux of the exercise was the notion that hard work and few comforts were the solution to the ills of addiction. Men slept on bunk beds in wooden huts through stormy weather and ate in a communal tent. Money earned from their toil on the island went back to wives and families; one newspaper reported how a worker who told his wife he was coming home was begged to stay as she finally had the money to buy their children's clothes back from the pawn shop. An April 1904 edition of the *East London Observer* carried a story about an occasion during which 250 men who had worked at Osea over the winter and their wives were entertained by Charrington and the Mansion House committee for the unemployed. 'They had proved they were not loafers and were men willing to work,' the article read. But the men had less luck continuing in such an industrious vein after returning to the East End. One of them asked the Mansion House delegates to send them back to the island, if only for a few weeks. 'In words full of sadness, he said it was hard . . . to go out morning after morning to find no work and come back to the children who were crying for bread they could not give them.' But the committee said they did not have sufficient funds to do so, and Charrington's experiment, like all true utopias, was doomed to failure. Financing the feeding, transporting and improving of all these men coming to the Essex island was hard enough, but how do you account for scheming boatmen selling smuggled booze to the island's inhabitants by night, as was reported to have happened on a regular basis? In the end, the island was requisitioned during the First World War to be used as a torpedo boat base, yet another Essex experiment fading into fragments.

There was, however, an unexpected renaissance in Osea's status as a refuge for those with addictions. Nigel Frieda, the press-shy record producer famous for launching Sugababes, has owned Osea Island since 2000. After Frieda bought the island, he and psychiatric nurse Brendan Quinn tried to revive its role as a rehab centre, whose clients included Amy Winehouse. After a notorious incident involving the suicide of a Channel 4 executive, the island became known as 'showbiz Alcatraz' in the press, and so Nigel gave up trying to assume the role of Osea's twenty-first-century Charrington and concentrated on turning it into a destination for high-end holidays, band recordings, TV productions and corporate events, which feature everything from axe-throwing contests to cross-country Segway courses for different clients.

At the turn of the twentieth century, Essex was thus already a petri dish for the experiments of modernity, meaning it became as much a place for people looking for new ways to profit from the burgeoning, and increasingly globalising, capitalist system as it did to find new, alternative ways of living. Kynochtown, a few miles west of Southend, was built to house workers who made gunpowder and cartridges during the First World War at the Kynoch explosives factory down-river, which then became Coryton when an oil storage depot and refinery took over the site. In 1922, Marconi established the first regular radio broadcasting company in the world on Valentine's Day in a hut in Writtle, near Chelmsford. In Southend, in 1926, Eric Cole set up EKCO, to manufacture radio devices with cutting-edge techniques and rounded, modernist Bakelite design (created by the architect Wells Coates) that were exported around the world.

Visitors to East Tilbury in Thurrock, halfway from South-end to London as you travel west along the Thames, might today marvel at its juxtapositions: the concrete grids and clean-lined modernist houses appear like mirages in the bewitching marsh landscape. The Bata estate, an innovative workers' village that was modelled on a Czechoslovakian city, still stands out against the ragged nature of the post-industrial bucolic surroundings today. The houses themselves feel both self-contained and spacious, cosy and civilising, although one resident, May Rippingale, told me that they had their detractors. 'A couple of years ago,' she said, 'I had a group of twenty architects visit. They went round the house and told me what was wrong with it! That the bannister was dangerous for children and the balcony wouldn't be allowed [today].' May bought her childhood home in the 1980s when the estate was put up for sale. The estate it was part of was built by Bata Shoe Company in the 1930s, as housing for their employees.

The arrival of Ford's huge car manufacturing plant, a few miles away at Dagenham, in 1931 had provided thousands of jobs, and became the starting pistol for a great wave of indus-trial and residential development breaking away from Essex's metropolitan fringe. As an entrepreneur, the Czech Tomáš Baťa, the founder of the Bata Shoe Company, mimicked Henry Ford's conveyor-belt system in his shoe factories. He

The old Bata factory, East Tilbury, 2017

was against communism – his son wrote that he once fought off communists with a shotgun in their original home of Zlín – but his footwear Fordism was allied with a utopian vision of community living. Though Baťa died in a plane crash in Switzerland just months after buying the land in Essex, he had left explicit instructions as to how the project should be executed.

Construction began in 1933. As well as the chequerboard of workers' houses, there was a Bata supermarket, a Bata shoe shop and a Bata farm that supplied bacon, eggs and milk for guests' breakfasts at the Bata hotel. There were tennis and netball courts, a swimming pool and full-size football pitches provided for workers' leisure (West Ham United trained here and played an annual charity match against Bata's team, which Bata once won, I have been told, although I am yet to find the match report). Scooters and motorbikes lined up outside the espresso bar, which opened in 1963, complete with a coffee machine and jukebox.

These days, the purpose-built cinema is used as a village hall, while the hotel ballroom, where Tom Jones once played, has been transformed into the post office, its original parquet floor almost worn down to the bitumen. East Tilbury library, tucked away round the back of the old hotel on the edge of the largely intact estate, doubles as the Bata Heritage Centre.

East Tilbury, like all Bata towns, followed the blueprint of the industrial garden city of Zlín, a fully realised 45,000-strong worker town with a 16-storey-high HQ as its centrepiece. It was designed by a pupil of Le Corbusier, František Lydie Gahura, and by Vladimír Karfík, who had worked for Frank Lloyd Wright. 'Under this rational mechanism,' said Le Corbusier on a visit to Zlín, 'I perceived a much more valued and effective factor – the human heart.' The same sentiment echoes around accounts of East Tilbury in its heyday.

Mick Pinion grew up on the Bata estate. His father already worked at the factory when he became an apprentice engineer straight out of school in 1966. 'You were dropped in at the deep end – you had to learn on the job,' said Pinion. 'If you had a Bata apprenticeship, you could get a job anywhere.' The Essex factory employed 3,000 people at its peak in the 1960s and 70s. Czech management moved there, as well as immigrants from all over the world. Rubber was supplied by Nigeria, leather from a tannery in Leicester. Some elements of the Bata way might seem intrusive by today's standards. 'People knew if their garden was overgrown they would be pulled into the office and asked politely to sort it out,' said former employee Graham Sutcliffe. 'It made them respect the town a bit more.' The creators of this new, gleaming and hopeful town on the Thames Estuary had hoped to provide, through meticulous design, order and security enough to achieve a functional goal – the creation of a new town that looked after its inhabitants, while encouraging them to, quite naturally, become a cog in a machine in pursuit of profit.

Further north in Essex, similarly industrious plans were afoot. When Crittall Windows, run by the philanthropist Francis Henry Crittall, expanded from Braintree to an unpopulated area on the way to Witham in the 1920s, Silver End welcomed a new vista of white-painted and flat-roofed modernist homes on wide, tree-lined streets over 220 acres of farmland. 'Modernism began in Essex,' wrote the Essex-born architect and essayist Charles Holland of the Crittall-commissioned buildings that predated Silver End in nearby Braintree. 'In the context of the early twentieth century this was boldly innovative stuff'. The estate's buildings were designed by Thomas S Tait, whose roster included pylons for the Sydney Harbour Bridge, and his assistant, Frederick Mac-Manus. As with East Tilbury, the communitarian nature of the exercise only went so far, with two streets of terraces built for workers while management were moved into detached houses rendered in white and boasting the art deco detailing of the period, and wide and spacious gardens. People flocked to Silver End to such a degree that it had the lowest death rate and highest birth rate in England for its first decade under the management of Crittall. During the Second World War the factory put Crittall windows into sea forts and manufactured parts for Bailey Bridges to be erected around Europe, and after the war was over, the company employed injured veterans.

Silver End was built to work in an even more self-sufficient manner than Bata's town, to the point where people never needed to leave. The village hall, which still remains a working community space, was and still is the biggest in Essex. Residents grew produce on their allotments and there were flower shows. There was a print works and newspaper, a dancehall and a cinema, and the pride of the village, the Silver End department store. The store had two entrances, with pillars and big windows that displayed furniture and drapery. It housed chemists, offices, a post office, a bakery counter, a sweet counter, a tobacco counter, provisions, a grocer's, a greengrocer's and a butchery. It was destroyed by a fire in 1952, steel girders reportedly twisting 'like putty'. Crittall still makes windows today in nearby Witham, but its architectural traces survive in Silver End. Preservation orders keep the village largely in architectural check; I am told not everyone wants to keep their Crittall windows, but are forced to by an Article 4 Direction from the government, which keeps its status as an uncanny relic of an overlooked era of English architecture.

'It would have been here, I am sure of it,' Dad said, as we searched for the place where Nan's bungalow used to be. We walked past an area of wood and scrub that he said was filled with the noise of playing when he was a boy, but was characterised by the churn and scrape and burn and whirr of power tools when we visited. This used to be one of many sites of self-built developments, today known as 'plotlands', which were settled by some of the earliest migrants from the East End, travelling what is now a well-worn path in search of a better life. Whether their new houses were rectangular DIY bungalows or reclaimed railway carriages or buses, padded out with asbestos or corrugated iron sheeting, Londoners moved out in great numbers in pursuit of freedom, or at least a bit of respite. We stood next to a hoarding, shouting over the noise, before my dad stopped and fixed his gaze in front of us. 'I remember seeing my first glow-worm, just there,' he said, pointing to a spot in front of the builders' Portaloo.

We were exploring the old plotland patch of Essex where my nan grew up, once a series of shoe-box-shaped, low-rise bungalows in a wooded glade but now covered in tall five-bed houses in various stages of composition, promising to maximise value from the site. The family of my nan, Doreen Gillman, settled in Thundersley near Southend in the mid-1920s, when they built their own bungalow. Thundersley was a south Essex frontier village if ever there was one, the early days of its development seeing a sea of pebble-dashed rectangular bungalows flow on to the wooded and hilly rural landscape to add to the more established weatherboarded cottages, which count for traditional architecture in these parts.

The myth of the plotland bungalows has grown in stature the more the actual buildings have been torn down or have rotted away into the landscape. They were built all over the country, often in coastal areas from Grimsby in north-east Lincolnshire to the Gower Peninsula in Wales, but in Essex they have taken on a foundational role in its collective history. The bungalows represent the material reality of what chasing paradise in Essex actually looked like for thousands of people. Moral, utopian gestures were integral to Essex's growth, but the plotlands represented something more accessible and enduring and without the need for complex philosophical theorising; a contiguity of modest hopes of all shapes and sizes.

I spoke to Barry Howard, an Essex-based 'full-time outdoor educator', about the plotlands. He had been helping lead learning trips with schoolchildren near Basildon when he and the kids started finding bits of old rusty metal, wall tiles, bricks and pottery buried in the scrub of what they had assumed was an ancient woodland floor. When they found what looked like walls of old houses, Howard thought perhaps it was something worth investigating further. He asked the children to tell him straight away if they had made a discovery. 'You'd hear this scream from 100 metres away: "Mr Howard, we found some guttering!"' The kids found pick-axe heads, marmalade jars, candle holders, milk bottles, smashed up bits of china and porcelain crockery and various other fragments of past lives.

What Howard and the children had stumbled upon felt like Essex's secret history, and the project led him to delve into his own past. The home Howard was born in was built by his grandfather and was called the Haven (one of the most common names for a plotland dwelling, for obvious reasons). At the plotlands, dwellings often had names, not numbers. It reflected a newfound sense of ownership of not just property, but of lives and dreams as people allowed their imaginations to wander a little more than they might usually. You could call it what you liked, and people did. Take your pick from Joylands, the Limes, the Nook, Jessie Cottage, Eastney, David-stan, Lil Fantana, Baradine, Avalon, Toulon, June, Ernden, St. Olafs, the Trees, Dilkusha, Somerleyton, Rowarl, the Laurels, Kilcan, the Maples, Homeland . . .

The concept of neighbourliness often has a zeal of comforting nostalgia, but at the plotlands it was usually for the sake of survival. 'All the guys round there worked on each other's houses,' said Dad of the house his grandfather Charles built with the aid of his brand-new neighbours. 'One was a bricklayer, Granddad was a carpenter, someone else was a roofer.' In Laindon, people often had to carry all the materials they needed to build their houses using a wheelbarrow they had bought from a builder's merchants on the high street. Barry Howard went on one of the last dog-sledge-led polar expeditions in the 1970s, but he still singled out the effort of the plotlanders for sheer endurance. 'They would do two-, three- or four-hundred carries of wheelbarrows of stuff up into the woods to where their plot was to build their house.' Huge trees had to be chopped down to build makeshift roads, a big task for these people fresh off the train who had started off with the deeds for a single plot but had been brought together in collective effort. There was often no gas, no electricity, no running water, no sewerage. Howard said the first years of his life were hit by excessively cold winters, with four feet of snow during the first month after he was born. 'It was real backwoods, pioneer stuff. It would have been tough.' People used cesspits to dump their waste and water was collected in rain butts. Howard's father worked for the electricity board and pushed the council to lay on electricity, which was switched on during the last year of their stay, in 1956.

Henry George's *Progress and Poverty*, first published in 1880, was a hugely popular book that reflected the fact that land and housing were the issues of the day. George's treatise began with a section simply titled 'The Problem', which introduced his central thesis: 'The present century has been marked by a prodigious increase in wealth-producing power,' he wrote. 'At the beginning of this marvellous era it was natural to expect, and it was expected, that labour-saving intentions would lighten the toil and improve the condition of the labourer; that the enormous increase in the power of producing wealth would make real poverty a thing of the past.' George linked the diminishing returns for the urbanised, industrialised working class to the paucity of their access to land.

Though George wrote *Progress and Poverty* in San Francisco, it struck a chord in Britain, which was a nation of tenants at the turn of the century, with 90 per cent of households renting the roof over their heads. In Essex, land was a particularly pertinent question. From dark age serfdom through to the land enclosures, which denied access to common land in England from the seventeenth century, Essex folk had long lived under the whims of their betters. In the eighteenth and nineteenth centuries, before the decline of agriculture, rents rose sharply in some parts of Essex. The Du Cane family came to Essex from the Low Countries in the latter part of the sixteenth century, via Jean du Quesne, a Huguenot refugee from Flanders, who fled persecution in 1568 and ended up, like many families from across the water, in the Coggeshall wool trade. By the eighteenth century it was clear the Du Cane family had done well out of the association: Peter Du Cane, the director of the East India Company, owned 500 acres at Coggeshall before buying more than 2,000 acres at a nearby estate, the Great Braxted Lodge. He played a prominent role in establishing the Bank of England and the East India Company, as well as in British politics. But despite the Du Caneses' humble origins, 200 years of wealth eroded any sense of solidarity with the less-well-off, especially when it might get in the way of profit: from 1755–99, the rent on the seven farms located on his land at Great Braxted rose by 36 per cent.

Proprietors were sitting on land that was appreciating in value without them having to lift a finger. George speculated that the great cause of the inequality of the age was 'not in the relations of capital against labour' nor 'the pressure of population against subsistence'. Instead, he wrote, inequality in wealth distribution went hand in hand with inequality in the ownership of land. Ownership was, he wrote, 'the great fundamental fact which ultimately determines the social, the political, and consequently the intellectual and moral condition of a people'. When material conditions improved, when industry boomed, when more money than ever was made, it resulted in land becoming ever scarcer, because, as is the case today, the people with the most money were buying it up as an investment. The solution, for George, was obvious. Equal rights to the land would need to be secured. The only just way to solve this moral dilemma was to declare all land public property, nationalising land and freeing it up to be used by 'whoever could procure the most out of it', valuing it by its potential rather than by simply what it was currently used for.

The work of Henry George influenced George Lansbury, the reforming socialist Labour head of Poplar Council in east

London and later Labour leader, who started a number of colonies for the unemployed in the Essex countryside. It also inspired William Morris, and Ebenezer Howard, the father of the garden city movement that was to influence the Essex new towns. George appealed to these figures and the many others who sought to find solutions to poverty in London and Essex. It prompted the proposal of a revolutionary future for the working class in England, which combined collectivism with self-sufficiency, imparting the idea that no social progress could occur unless people had access to the land. As with today's tussles with large corporations reluctant to cough up, one of the big issues was getting landowners, many of whom were waiting to sell to developers, to pay their fair share of tax. George's plan to nationalise land was predicated around forcing politicians to increase tax on the rents received from their tenants and also on the value of the land itself. It became increasingly common to argue that land belonged to the community that toiled or lived within it, and anyone earning wealth from it should be taxed for the benefit of the whole community. George's book was hugely influential and sold millions of copies around the world. It provoked a great campaign for land reform in the latter half of the nineteenth century.

Someone who acutely understood the allure of land nationalisation was Frederick Francis Ramuz, who was in no way an adherent of George's tenet that land must be nationalised, but made a lot of money under its premise. Better known as FF Ramuz in the thousands if not hundreds of thousands of advertisements, flyers, plans, auction announcements and posters (that often promised land nationalisation is coming) aimed at wantaway Londoners that were printed in the late nineteenth and early twentieth centuries, Ramuz pops up everywhere when you delve into the story of the growth of housing in London and its eastern and northern and then southern fringes. According to his obituary in the *Southend Standard*, Ramuz sold more than 50,000 acres in his lifetime. (He also built the Grand Hotel in Leigh-on-Sea, the pub where one day Dr Feelgood's hard drinking Lee Brilleaux would prop up the bar and where I bought my first pints, saw my first gigs and had my first grown-up job.) Witnessing evidence of the voracious nature of Ramuz's land purchasing is like seeing rapacious Essex being made in front of your eyes, report by report. Here he is selling off swathes of farmland to potential landowners. There he is buying portions of Southend seafront to make the most of the boom in day-tripping. It was Ramuz who bought up the land where the council-built terrace I grew up in in Leigh-on-Sea in the borough of Southend was eventually built, marking a new neighbourhood out plot by plot for resale. The reams of posters, plans and articles say little more than where the land is, what the freehold deposit should be, and what time the train left Fenchurch Street, always with the constant: APPLY FF RAMUZ.

Curiously for such an integral figure in the growth of the ideal of home ownership (at least in Essex), there is no biography or autobiography of Ramuz. He might have become a kind of hero to a suddenly burgeoning Southend – he eventually became the mayor of the town – but what he wasn't, even judging by what little we know, was a saint. The *London Evening Standard* reported that Ramuz, 'a builder', was summoned to the East Ham Local Board 'for allowing the house, 23 Ranelagh Road, East Ham, to be occupied without previously having obtained a certificate from the Board that there was a proper and sufficient supply of water', contrary to the Water Act. Ramuz did not appear but was prosecuted – he had previously been fined for a similar offence. He was ordered to pay 5 shillings and costs or fourteen days imprisonment.

Ramuz was not alone in seeking wealth through the resale of land. In July 1891, *The Pall Mall Gazette*, the precursor to the *London Evening Standard*, ran a story on how 200 men and women with 'an air of business' assembled at Fenchurch Street on the invitation of a man named Robert Varty, a 'statesman' of Cumberland and a radical liberal who stood for Parliament in 1892 and almost unseated a Tory MP when he ran in the north Essex port constituency of Harwich. Varty had been 'buying land in Essex and selling it in small plots to cockneys and others', and proposed selling larger plots to small farmers with the desire of starting a co-operative scheme where the produce of their efforts would be sold to the markets in London.

His was a pursuit that, perhaps on the face of it, was closer to George's idea of land nationalisation than Ramuz's. But if this was socialism, it was socialism that was always guaranteed to turn a profit. *The Gazette* reported that Varty was 'a shrewd man' who usually did well out of the land he sold, and he wasn't the only one. 'Rich men are buying land in Essex as a speculation and selling it in small plots. Syndicates are being formed for the same purpose.' To get bums on train seats, the plotland auctioneers laid on a substantial lunch. Varty, for example, promised prospective buyers a feast of cold beef, ham, pies, cheese, salad, beer and, to wash it all down, a drop of whisky. Some 300 plots were sold in Benfleet, near to where my nan grew up, on the day *The Gazette* accompanied the trip, and another 200 in Hadleigh; 500 patches of Essex sold to excited (and sometimes beer-goggled) East Enders in a matter of hours. It seemed like even more of a bargain when you considered the return ticket and lunch were free to all purchasers, but a fee of two shillings was required from those opting not to buy, 'in order to keep out idlers and roughs'.

Prices for Varty's 20ft by 150ft plots ranged from £3 15s to £10 or £12 on the main road, or about £300 up to almost £1,000 in today's money. Plots were often bought using hard-earned savings and the purchase was unquestionably an act of small-scale class mobility, a stride forward and away from life on the lower rung. *The Gazette* report listed the eclectic range of careers held by the purchasers who came from all parts of London, though the majority were from the East End: 'Licensed victuallers, pawnbrokers, publicans, housekeepers and care-takers, chemists, small tradesmen, engravers, fish porters, ivory turners, tennis-bat makers, and others.'

The plots brought with them huge benefits, adding colour to lives in the city and giving people a renewed sense of purpose. 'It gives a man some reason for saving,' said one purchaser, a cabinet maker, 'especially when one can get possession by paying a 10 per cent deposit, and the balance by sixteen quarterly instalments, for one scarcely feels the money leaving one's pocket.' Policemen were keen buyers of plots, the report suggested, with one commuting to south Essex to grow plums so he could take them back to London to try his hand at making jam while his wife was away. Some even built properties to rent to workers in return for a profit, but the sense of betterment wasn't only achieved through material gains. Health was a concern too, and Varty said tee-totallers were keen purchasers of plots.

The plotland explosion started Essex's love affair with property, answering the left's clarion call of land nationali-sation with the very modern, capitalistic right-wing answer of property ownership. The 1906 catalogue of Ramuz's Land Company reads like a manual in sturdy Conservatism: 'Land is the basis for all wealth. Even an acre leads to independence.' And the suburbs that eventually appeared cemented whole swathes of property ownership in an ever-densifying Essex. The plotland pioneers were 'proud to own their own plot of English soil' through a 'lifetime of abstinence and thrift', said Bernard Braine, the erstwhile MP for Castle Point between 1955 and 1992. Far from installing a socialist utopia, as George and his legions of followers might have wished, in the success of the plotlands you can see the seeds of Thatcher's famous Right to Buy policy, suggesting that, a century before the 1980 Housing Act, the yearning to own your own patch of England was a very real and growing desire. 'So, quietly, almost without notice,' the *Gazette* reported, 'cockneys are establishing themselves as small land-owners in Essex.'

For Dad, the memories of the bungalow are of an Edenic childhood prelude to an adolescence of confusion and shame when his father left the family.

Walking through the wooded area where the Prittle Brook watercourse rises from the ground and runs all the way to the River Roach in Rochford, we stumbled over the foundations of a long-destroyed house. Only a discarded television and some gardening materials remained of the lives that once filled the now exposed space. Dad spotted a cavity dug into the ground he identified as a 'soakaway' (a rubble-filled hole into which wastewater was drained to literally soak away, rather than being channelled into sewers). The plotlands were a human-scale answer to an industrially made problem – what to do with all these people concentrated in London after the industrial revolution? – and they retained their sense of a compromise solution: somewhere between speculation and depreciation, between the ad hoc and the prescribed, between the unmade roads and the main arteries from London. Although humble in design and implementation, the plotland bungalows offered something wild and different, which did not thrill everyone who viewed them. Descriptions of the plotlands often use the vernacular of the United States, their farmsteads and their towns made from nothing, and not always in a good way. The first plotland settlers to Woodham Ferrers in the late nineteenth century, for example, were deemed squatters whose chosen way of living was queried in *The Essex Weekly News* in March 1898 that it 'might do in the Australian bush or the American backwoods but is hardly what one might expect in the highly civilised county of Essex'.

The late Colin Ward, the closest thing the plotlands has ever had to a biographer, wrote that many plotland dwellings had been worked upon to such a degree you wouldn't recognise them against the suburban housing that surrounded them. 'Today in the exploding cities of Latin America, what begins as a straw shack becomes in about fifteen years a fully serviced suburban house, through the efforts of its occupier, who, starting with nothing, invests his own energy, income and ingenuity in his home,' he wrote. 'I could take you to Essex plotlands started before such efforts were ruled out of court by our building regulations, public health and planning legislation, where exactly the same phenomenon could be seen.'

Dad and I stopped at another rectangular bungalow. There was a woman kneeling down outside the front of it scraping weeds out from the gaps between her paving. She told us her name was Louise and that she was retired. She seemed keen to speak about the history of the community and the changes in the area. 'I like this history, the people who lived here. But the kings and the queens and all that – cross me off. I like real history.' Louise said my great-grandfather Charles had helped to build her home back in the 1920s. 'I think four of them helped each other, and the buildings were all the same. A door in the middle, and a window either side.'

Louise told us how her and her husband used to go to Leigh-on-Sea to get old cockleshells to firm up the path so the children could walk to school over it (although she couldn't stand the smell), and how it was still even now up to the residents to add improvements such as speed bumps and streetlamps. Louise's husband made their own sleeping policemen, but it didn't stop the four-wheel drives bouncing up and down the road as we talked, going to and from their big houses and out to the busy A-roads and shopping complexes of Essex, shooting great clouds of dust into the air as they passed. 'They don't care. They just fly down here like there's no tomorrow.'

The cars seemed to communicate a greater sadness for Louise. The community had always done things for each other – shopping, errands and the like. 'When there was snow, whoever went out would knock on the door and say, do you want anything, a pint of milk or whatever. But now, you can drop dead and nobody would know.' The new people faceless inside their luxury transport represented the absence of community. 'They look down on you like you're a piece of dirt. It's progress, I'm afraid. But it's not progress for me.'

In the weeks after our visit, I started to see plotland survivals everywhere I looked. On the corner at the end of my mum and dad's road. On the way into Runwell under the roaring A130. Of course, they can't have known, but the plotland people, who built the original bungalow properties, set in motion a chain of events that led to the whirring and the pummelling and the erecting of gates, the bumbling of the Land Rovers and Qashqais over the still-unmade roads and the bitterness felt by those not keeping pace with the detached Essex dream. The plotlands were at one time the apex of modern living in Essex, or at least the closest most could get to it, but aside from some that survive unnoticed they were either gone or hidden under a thousand modernisations and additions by generations of builders. 'It may be argued that the modern character of the southern half of Essex was moulded by the aspirational migration in the first half of the last century from some of the most deprived parts of London,' wrote Marcus C Granath, a Basildon-born writer and teacher. 'Like the Diggers on St George's Hill, they now owned their own little share of the riches of the earth: a small piece of England.'

The 1953 flood brought Hayley's family to Essex. Her grand-father, Ernest Singer, was working as a welder, commuting from east London to help build the huge Coryton oil refin-ery at Canvey Island. After the swell of the floodwater had receded, mounds of driftwood were left in piles, blocking Ernest's path into work. Attempting to find his way over the debris, he stepped on a rusty stake that went through his boot and into his foot. The resulting septic poisoning meant he was signed off work for six weeks. Recounting the story to us years later, half sunken into his cushion-laden leather sofa, Ernest said he saw the accident as fortuitous. While convalescing in the cramped family home he shared with Hannelore and their two boys in Stratford in metropoli-tan Essex, he noticed an advert for a job in the new town of Basildon.

Ernest was born in 1928 in the village of Chadwell Heath in the old Essex hundred of Becontree, where his father (also called Ernest) had grown up. The 1921 census has his father's family's employment as representative of the area's sudden diversity of opportunity, mixing city and country, sweeping development and agricultural reality, and reflecting a rural Essex poised on the cusp of total transformation. Ernest Sr's 14-year-old brother Leonard was a farm hand at Mays Farm, Chadwell Heath, while his brother-in-law was a ploughman at another local farm. Ernest Sr, however, was working for the other side: he was part of the building effort of a new Essex, a labourer working for Mills and Sons contractors on a new London County Council housing scheme in Chadwell Heath. The project became known as the Becontree Estate, the largest council estate in the world built between the

The Becontree Estate, 1970

First and Second World Wars, where 100,000 people today live.

In 1919, London County Council (LCC) acquired swaths of agricultural land in Essex to rehouse working-class people from London with powers given to them by the Housing and Town Planning Act. The LCC would build five 'out-county' estates in Essex in total, but Becontree dwarfed the rest. As the century progressed it was easy to become blasé about the development and rehousing that occurred not just in Essex but around the country, but looking back from a twenty-first century characterised by a feeling of societal abandonment, it seems a miraculous time indeed.

At the time of its conception the Becontree Estate was a unique project, built in the twentieth-century sweet spot where large-scale ambition met patrician duty. (For the LCC, it was to become a habit.) The result was colossal. Thanks to Becontree, between 1921 and 1931, Dagenham's population grew by 879.1 per cent, from 9,127 to 89,362. The populations of Barking and Ilford, which parts of the estate sprawled into, increased by 44.3 per cent and 53.8 per cent respectively. At the same time, formerly bustling industrial centres in Wales and northern England were in decline; the Rhondda losing 13.1 per cent of its people and Barrow-in-Furness losing 10.6 per cent. The construction of Becontree transformed a once rural idyll of farmsteads and cottages into one of the biggest sites for London overspill. A giant Ford car-manufacturing plant soon arrived, providing thousands of jobs, tempting East Enders further and further east.

Critics pointed out Becontree's centreless character: housing and parks and shops planned to fit together without necessarily creating any meaningful alternative to the sprawl of suburban London – some said it merely stretched the city out. From its initial position as an escape from London, Essex gradually transformed into its shadowy other. The architectural critic Reyner Banham went as far as suggesting places such as Becontree created a monster that 'destroyed' London by inviting it to spill out into the 'formless, inorganic sprawl' of these new estates. 'They were the true twilight zone of London, neither city nor country, village nor town.'

I always felt a sort of kinship with Becontree. The perfunctory brick aesthetic of the houses not slathered in render was similar in design to the terrace I grew up on in Leigh-on-Sea. I was always aware we lived in a brick house built by the council; they were different to the standalone houses and bungalows, to the Edwardian terraces or the cute cottages down in the old town. After I moved to London in my early 20s, I visited Becontree when desiring release from the inner city. I would walk around and marvel at its scale and the way it sits there on the edge of Greater London, sprawling yet self-contained, suburban yet not characterless (evidenced by idiosyncratic flourishes such as the pedestrian cul de sacs known as 'banjos'). As I walked, the place spun past me like a zoetrope of rough-cut render, pargetting, brickwork, pastel painted pebbledash and green, green grass that bounced against the bright sunshine. Straight lines and circular streets, corner pubs and established trees. In Becontree, cars marked their territory everywhere you looked, parked on pavements in spaces marked in white paint, on paved-over front gardens, and sometimes even making the most of the NO BALL GAMES green spaces that no one quite knows what to do in. As in East Tilbury, this was a working-class town built from the bottom up, only this time it was the size of a city, and, architecturally, with a less obviously utopian feel compared to earlier experiments like the Bata town. Whether London County Council built it under a fit of left-wing fervour, or, as has been suggested, out of fear the workers might rise up if they didn't get what they wanted, here was action to meet housing needs on an unprecedented scale.

The Second World War intensified the idea of Essex as escape, its green fields and open skies becoming not only a solution to London's crises of housing and inequality, but also as refuge from the bombs of the Luftwaffe. Places like Benfleet, Wickford and Laindon had built up thanks to the plotland boom, the first time Essex had been identified as a site for a new, aspirational England. But the war seemed to spell the end of the Essex plotlands, extinguishing whatever arcadian sentiment there was left in England by the mid-1940s. Barry Howard's grandfather died shortly after moving the family from the East End to plotland Essex, and his father was called up to fight in the Second World War. When he returned, most of the plotlands had become run down. 'There were some that were so dilapidated – and with people actually living in them – they didn't take much to push over.'

At the start of the post-war period, Clement Attlee's

Labour government proposed the creation of a number of new towns, mainly built in the countryside around London, to answer Britain's housing shortage. Once again, Essex offered hope to working-class Londoners. The new towns were just that – new – but they weren't exactly a complete departure; more a continuation of an ideal that had started in the late nineteenth century with the garden cities inspired by the Arts and Crafts movement. The establishment of Letchworth Garden City and Welwyn Garden City, both in Hertfordshire, in turn led to a new post-war solution to house London escapees. The LCC planned and built other projects, including the Harold Hill Housing Estate in Romford, the largest post-war housing estate in the London area: 7,600 dwellings spanning 630 acres, completed in 1958. The first show home on the Harold Hill Estate that was exhibited to the public was a semi-detached house with three bedrooms, all with central heating. These were working-class homes, a direct hit on the scourge of slum landlords and a solution to Blitzed-out families.

But more was needed, which is where the new towns came in. The new towns were the culmination of years of planning and evolution in the ways the authorities were trying to solve the problem of London; the idea tallied with the sentiments of Morris, too, in the sense that they were a conscious corrective to what was seen as decades of unforgivable centrifugal sprawl away from London. Two of the first wave of new towns, built in the late 1940s and the 50s, were located in Essex: Basildon was to be built on the Thames Estuary, while Harlow was planned to utilise land near North Weald and Epping Forest. The name of Labour's minister for new towns, Lewis Silkin, does not carry the weight of other post-war ministers in the party's third government. Diligent, shy and softly spoken, he was the eldest of seven siblings in a family of Jewish Lithuanian refugees in east London.

He won a scholarship to Oxford University, but came up against an unhelpful intervention from his headmaster, who reputedly wrote in his report to the university, 'this boy will not benefit from a university education', leading him to miss out on an opportunity to study there. Instead, he worked as a tally clerk on London's Docks, later becoming a solicitor before entering politics. These experiences must have contributed to Silkin's feeling of egalitarianism when it came to the new towns. 'I am most anxious that the planning should be such that the different income groups living in the new towns will not be segregated,' he said of the New Towns Bill. 'No doubt they may enjoy common recreational facilities and take part in amateur theatricals, or each play their part in a health centre or community centre. But, when they leave to go home I do not want the better-off people to go to the right and the less well-off to go to the left. I want them to ask each other, "Are you going my way?"'

Unlike many other areas, Billericay District Council jumped at the chance to welcome Basildon new town into south Essex, as it addressed the problem of the spread of anarchic and unsanitary self-built plotland homes, which were coagulating into gigantic settlements. *The News Chronicle*'s Stanley Baron reported in 1947 that the 'extraordinary town of Laindon-Billericay-Pitsea-Wickford' had a population of 40,000 – a population, he noted, equal to Rugby, Dover or Shrewsbury. 'If you stretched out its unmade streets, deep in ore as a medieval cattle track, they would stretch a distance equal to that between London and York.'

Baron suggested the plotland project had failed on its own terms and had created an area woefully under-served by a scant and ragged selection of amenities. There was only one maternity home, which was private, two chain stores and one cinema. There was a bowling green and a football pitch, but no tennis courts, no swimming pool and no laundry. A woman Baron spoke to, Mrs Prager, had to get her coal delivered in the summer 'or not at all' due to the unfitness of the roads in the wetter seasons. Ambulances and refuse carts couldn't make it to their property either. The cost of new roads and amenities such as running water were calculated to be too great an expense for this sporadic and gargantuan group of ad hoc dwellings. The rates would have to increase by 7s 6d (£13 today) if only 55 of the 200 miles of unmade road were modernised. When L Dudley Stamp's *Land Utilisation Survey of Britain* rolled into south Essex, the writer of the Essex volume, NV Scarfe, was not impressed by Laindon. 'Into this poor bramble covered region has penetrated a vast array of tiny bungalows, corrugated iron shanties with dreadful rutted mud roads, reminiscent of the backwoods. Mankind seems to have sought relief from the rush and roar of London in the wilderness of wild nature with a few poultry, goats, rabbits and perhaps cows.' The general landscape of south Essex was criticised for being 'foggy and muddy in winter' and full of 'weedy pastures'. The only hope, wrote Baron, was for 'the mess to be rubbed out'. And rubbed out it soon would be.

The development of the new towns is often viewed with a real rose-tinted disbelief from people of my generation, a shock that something so benevolent and for the public good could be achieved on such a scale. Their arrival, however, wasn't exactly the purist enactment of post-war optimism and benevolent patrician statism that it is often thought to have been when compared to the fractured nature of civic decision-making today. Once it was decided that Basildon must be built, the residents of Langdon Hills, Laindon and other settlements received letters that their houses were to be vacated to make way for the new town. Many residents of the plotlands, such as Howard's grandmother, were happily rehoused in one of the very early flats provided by the Basildon

Development Corporation (BDC), the Whitehall-run body set up by the government to administer the creation of the new town. There was, however, a sizeable portion of people who didn't want to leave their plotland homes, but lacked the financial capability to take the council to court to fight for compensation. Some were conned out of their land by estate agents looking to make a profit. The Canning Town-born first leader of Basildon Council, Joe Morgan, described in his memoir *Eastenders Don't Cry* how an 80-year-old widow who lived in a shack her husband had built visited Morgan to ask whether what one estate agent was offering her for the land – £600 – was a fair deal. After asking to view the books of the development corporation, he found that BDC officials had promised the agent £1,400, meaning the agent and someone at BDC were pocketing the difference.

Some plotland residents refused to leave when commanded to by the authorities, instead staying put in the houses they had built, clinging on to dreams that were disintegrating like the plotland bungalows themselves. A few owners just waited and watched as the JCBs came up the road to destroy their houses. Other residents set fire to everything they owned, lest they allow the corporation to get the better of them. In the end, much of the land in Langdon Hills was never actually developed and some of it is now a nature reserve peppered with hidden foundations and buried bricks, archaeological fragments that hint at the trauma of a lost domesticity.

But however compromised, at its core the building of Basildon and Harlow embodied, through their architecture and planning, an implicit will to improve the conditions and quality of life of the people who moved into the towns, a utopian vision of society. They advanced the cause of housing from the LCC's early efforts that packed them in at scale. If Becontree was an early example of what could be achieved by state housebuilding, the new towns were a kind of corrective to its sprawl. Basildon's creators were adamant they would not make the same mistakes. The point of the new towns was to provide a new urban centre, not a satellite that relied solely on London as its source of culture or income. Manufacturing firms such as Yardley cosmetics factory in Basildon were given grants to set up in the new towns, while Harlow's town centre featured work by the English sculptors Barbara Hepworth and Henry Moore, all of which implied that the future of the UK was to be guided by civic-minded, social democratic ideals. 'I believe we may well produce a new type of citizen,' Lewis Silkin told the House of Commons in May 1948. 'A healthy, self-respecting, dignified person with a sense of beauty, culture and civic pride. In the long run that will be the real test.'

For years I have carried around a battered copy of a 1950s edition of Nikolaus Pevsner's *Buildings of Essex*. Like many who have tried to get to grips with Essex, Pevsner wasn't completely enamoured of the place, damning it by association with its entry point of Liverpool Street station. But, even in the early days of its development, Pevsner saw Harlow as a triumph, growing from the slow gestation of the garden city principles and allying them with something altogether more modernist and European. For him, it proved you could design 'Englishly', in a way that was both functional but not too studious. To Pevsner, the committee-led approach of English urban planning was stultifying. 'In England, the success of a new venture depends on the lucky accident of a man who believes in it, is insistent and can at the same time handle committees,' he said in his lecture, 'The Englishness of English Art'.

Frederick Gibberd, Harlow's so-called master planner,

was one such man. Pevsner called Gibberd's passion project 'an unusual case of cordiality between architect-planner and Corporation'. His vision was to build a town guided by the shapes of the countryside it would be built into. 'The plan for the new town has been evolved around the structure of a very beautiful stretch of Essex landscape,' he outlined in the *Architects' Journal* in 1950. 'Although the plan is a "landscape plan" it breaks away from the character of the traditional garden city or green belt town in that it provides built-up areas in which there is a definite town sense.'

The first thing I noticed about Harlow when I visited for the first time is how green it is. Surrounded by open countryside, the town was carefully designed by the landscape architect Sylvia Crowe who allowed the built environment to breathe by accenting living quarters with lawns, parks and grand swooping tree-lined promenades. I stopped first to look up at The Lawn, a ten-storey 'skyscraper' surrounded by greenery that was the first ever residential tower block built in Britain, created with public funds for council tenants to rent at low cost. Built in sympathy with a large oak tree that still stands today, its 'butterfly' design ensured balconies and living rooms faced south for optimum light. Opposite, a straight terrace of houses with grass lawns out the front completes what Pevsner described as an 'eminently successful' section of Harlow, who went on: 'Generally speaking Harlow has more than any of the other new towns what might be called the new town look, an appearance resulting from urban types of building in a green rural setting. It is a happy look.'

The emblem of Basildon's first residents' association was a pioneer wagon. 'People who came thought there was something to aspire to in Basildon,' said Eric Moonman, the Labour MP for Basildon between 1974 and 1979 (and before then Billericay, between 1966 and 1970). 'They could do more, better and faster. It was like a little bit of America in Essex.' Something like the American dream was materialising in these newly built places in Essex, a dream that spoke to a kind of egalitarianism, which felt reachable in a way that seems fanciful in today's unedifyingly disparate society. 'It was a very mixed community,' Angela Smith, the Labour MP for Basildon between 1997 and 2010 and now the shadow leader of the House of Lords, told me when I visited her in her Westminster office in 2018. 'I recall the person next door to us was a guy who was sports editor of the *Sun* at the time, a journalist. The person next to him was a senior teacher, next to him was a manager at Yardley's. A lot of dockers, a lot of Ford workers, and we all lived together. You met different people. It was quite an exciting time.' For her family and many others who had moved here, Essex was a welcome jolt of modernity, delivering them from often squalid conditions that still characterised much of post-war London. 'When my family moved to Basildon in the 1960s, it was the first time in my life we had a house with a bathroom in it,' said Smith, who moved from a flat above a shop in Hackney to the new town after the firm her father worked for relocated there. 'For us it was a dream come true.'

However, not everyone agreed, with Reyner Banham adding to his dislike of Becontree by positing these new places in Essex as a series of anonymous, displaced Londons. 'People in the new towns are uncertain Londoners, but they remain Londoners. Nevertheless, they are really at the maximum distance at which London is still psychologically real. Modern legislation has moved them out of London; modern transport makes it possible for them to get back in again. But there is a limit to how far this process can go.' In Basildon, there were reports of supreme isolation bordering on existential crisis for some of the first cockneys who had moved out there. The sudden feeling of alienation for those pining for a lost

Basildon town centre, 1969

community was exacerbated when it came to who exactly was in charge of Basildon. Joe Morgan, who moved to Basildon with his wife in 1953, wrote in his memoir how the community, which as yet had no councillors representing them, felt 'disenfranchised and alone' against the centralised Basildon Development Corporation. 'The treatment we received from the powers that be, and the locals' open hostility towards us, made life as deprived as any cockney back street, but without the compensation of East End camaraderie,' wrote Morgan. 'People did not come and chat to you, or sit on their doorsteps. They were inside, the women using their new-fangled washing machines, the men perhaps watching the television if they could afford to rent or buy one.' Morgan complained of there being few amenities in the largely still-being-built new town. There were two pubs in his neighbourhood, one shop, and scant else to do. 'Many people ended up at the doctors, suffering from new town sickness.'

New town sickness was commonly referred to as 'new town blues', the supposed feeling of dislocation indelibly linked to moving to Basildon, Harlow or another of the new settlements. Yet the existence of such a tangible and localised kind of depression was disputed. It might just have been a natural reaction to moving to places that were still being built. A 1964 survey of mental health in Harlow, more than a decade into its stride, found no evidence of new town blues, emphasising that 'nine-tenths of the new population are satisfied with their environment and the one-tenth who are dissatisfied are for the most part constitutionally dissatisfied – that is to say, they would be dissatisfied wherever they were'.

The Cowleys largely fitted into the 90 per cent as described in the report. The father of Jason Cowley, who is today the editor in-chief of the *New Statesman*, the British left-of-centre weekly magazine, was born in Upton Park to a bus-driving father who met his mother at a dance in Chigwell. He told me his mum, who had grown up in the borderlands of Dagenham and east London, was the family's ambitious figure, someone who was keen to see her son 'get up and get out of London'. The Cowleys married young and moved to Harlow in its early days. 'The estates were being built around you back then in the early 50s,' Cowley said. 'It was just like one giant building site . . . Harlow was really green then, it was very rural west Essex. It had the space and the air and the countryside they weren't used to. And after the war, so much of the East End was bombed – there were bombed, ruined streets of dark Victorian terraces.'

His mother and father were part of Harlow's left-wing milieu. 'They believed in the new town as a kind of utopian project,' he said. 'There was a very small, motivated group of what you would call the intelligentsia, the middle class, often they were communists or strong socialists, and they gathered around this theatre called the Playhouse. They were politically motivated, members of the CND. Obviously involved with the Labour Party. This was the new future that the Clement Attlee government had created after the war. And they were living it. They were determined to build this vision of what they called the new Jerusalem.'

Yet the frenziedly independent, home-owning energy ignited in the plotlands was not going to go away; you might also have called the Cowleys upwardly mobile. The desire to own one's own home, to grab your own bit of England that nobody could take away, and to leave past memories of poverty behind for good, were intoxicating. By the time Jason was six, the Cowleys had bought a private house in a cul de sac. 'For Harlow, that was posh. If you lived in a private house, that was quite different because nearly all the estates were either council estates or corporation estates.' By the time of the mid to late 70s, Cowley remembers noticing that for Harlow, the gig might have been up already, the town was sinking into decline. 'You could see that already. The original investment hadn't been repeated.'

For Stan Newens, who eventually became MP for Harlow, memories of the Victorian extremes of East End poverty were alive and well in his household growing up; Newens' great-great-grandfather and his father before him lived in the first slum ever cleared by the LCC, the notorious Old Nichol, with its labyrinthine geography of narrow alleyways between terraces of damp slums, and his grandfather, a policeman, had been transferred to Bethnal Green at the time of the Jack the Ripper murders, which terrorised the East End. When young Stan was growing up, he would be taken to see his great-grandfather, a bearded gentleman born in 1843. He would sit quietly while his Uncle Sam read the bible to the old man, because his great-grandfather had never learned to read. Newens told me looking back he was struck by the fact his elder had just missed out on Gladstone's 1870 Education Act, which effectively meant education for all. As with Lewis Silkin, Newens' politics grew directly out of his early life experiences in the East End.

To the Newenses and thousands like them, Essex offered the chance to break from a generations-long association with London. His father had been in the First World War – 'invalided out' with flu and pneumonia – and was convinced there would be another, so he looked to a bungalow in North Weald for their refuge. They moved in six months before the Second World War broke out, going backwards and forwards to Bethnal Green with their haulage business on behalf of the borough council to salvage what they could from the bombing.

Newens was elected Epping MP with a comfortable majority in 1964 on a tide of support from the unions at places such as the Ford Motor Company at Dagenham. Shop stewards rallied to knock on doors during the campaign. In the Commons he became part of the Labour Party's burgeoning left-wing, and helped form the Tribune group of socialist MPs. He condemned the war in Vietnam and started an early day motion in the Commons, in the knowledge that he would not get a promotion thanks to his 'remaining true to his socialist ideals'.

Newens wasn't the only grammar school pupil from near Epping Forest to enter frontline politics in the post-war years. One of the key architects of Thatcher's revolution, Norman Tebbit, was an Essex boy, or near enough. He was born into a working-class family just over the border from Essex in Ponders End, Enfield. 'Heard a chap on the radio this morning talking with a cockney accent,' the old Etonian Tory prime minister Harold Macmillan said after hearing

Tebbit's voice for the first time. 'They tell me he is one of Her Majesty's ministers.' This aspirational trajectory became Tebbit's brand; he even called his memoirs *Upwardly Mobile*. He turned up regularly on satirical puppet show *Spitting Image*, making a cameo in the routine 'Essex Is Crap', caricatured as Mrs Thatcher's hardened enforcer, the Chingford skinhead, an image he was keen to cultivate and obviously still relishes to this day. Steve Brown, the writer of the infamous *Spitting Image* song 'Essex Is Crap', told me Tebbit had to be included as he was seen as 'the patron saint of Essex man'. He preached the gospel of self-improvement from the beginning of his political career; he was already advocating a free-market agenda when first agitating to become an MP in the 1960s. His 1981 Tory conference speech, delivered in the wake of the race riots in Toxteth and Brixton – with its infamous line that his father, unemployed in the 1930s, 'got on his bike' to look for work instead of rioting – is probably the best-known piece of British political oratory on the much-debated idea of meritocracy.

When Tebbit challenged Newens as the Conservative candidate for Epping in 1970, he did so as his antithesis. He didn't seem to have much chance of winning over Harlow's unionised East End diaspora, many of whom worked in one of the factories in the new town itself, and voted Labour – but the constituency also contained the forest-fringed commuter belt of Chingford, Ongar and Chigwell, whose votes Tebbit sought hardest. Tebbit later said that when campaigning, he had his children cry out 'Enemy coast ahead!" from the back of his car when approaching Harlow. He was offering Thatcherism before Thatcher, arguing that the government should abolish council housing while aggressively attacking Newens for his left-wing values. Two visions of Essex, and perhaps England, were vying for supremacy. One was the escape from one's own class by stealth through capitalist guile; the other was the idea of being aided by the state and moving to a new town; and each position seemed to be personified by the two candidates fighting to represent Epping.

In 1953, a year after the conscientious objector Newens had served his national service down a coal mine in North Staffordshire, Norman Tebbit was proudly doing his at North Weald with the RAF's Middlesex 604 squadron. As Newens refined his socialist commitment to solidarity and workers' rights, Tebbit flew Meteor and Vampire jet planes and got into drunken scrapes with his fellow servicemen. Almost thirty years after the Battle of Britain took place over the skies of Essex, here was the Battle *for* Britain, for the future of a utopian vision, and the right to carry these children of tomorrow into a different world entirely, or one that held up individualism, home ownership and the right to consume as sacred tenets. The latter way of living was in the ascendency and spoiling for a fight. 'I think he would agree with me, he [Tebbit] fought a pretty rough campaign. [He said] that I was a coward who wouldn't fight for my country and all that stuff,' Newens told me during a long phone conversation a few weeks before he died, aged 90. 'The count was very unpleasant in 1970. My wife was in tears.' Tebbit won by 2,575 votes, 51.5 per cent to 48.5 per cent, a relatively narrow result that represented a seismic shift in trajectory (and a remarkably similar percentage to a more recent and much more consequential vote in Britain). A new right-wing was emboldened: if it could win in the constituency of a socialist-built new town, it could win anywhere.

6

We Play for Real

*'The idea is that the man ... must have every second
necessary but not a single unnecessary second'*
Henry Ford, 1922

*'We're going out to play/There's no fun at home/No one
can stop us/We play for real/We play for power'*
Nitzer Ebb, 'Violent Playground'

You could say that the unofficial Essex anthem is Billy Bragg's
'A13, Trunk Road to the Sea':

> 'If you ever have to go to Shoeburyness
> Take the A road, the okay road that's the best
> Go motorin' on the A13'

More so than the more green-fringed A127, the A13, which
runs from Aldgate in London to Shoeburyness at the mouth of
the Thames Estuary, is characterised by the sublime violence
of modern life, offering up an iconography of south Essex:
huge warehouses and industrial zones, subdued greenbelt
farmland, wind turbines, and signs for not one but two freight
ports. Bragg wrote the song in 1977, when he was singing in
his old punk act, Riff Raff. 'I just objected to singing about

these places that I didn't know,' he said in 2006. 'I wanted to put the A13 on level pegging with Route 66, as there's a tradition of driving down the A13 to the glory of Southend. Growing up in Barking, that was the promised land, in quite a Springsteenish way. Later, when I saw where Springsteen is from, the New Jersey Turnpike, it did look a lot like Essex.'

The DJ John Peel once bemoaned the aggressiveness of the Essex driver on the BBC comedy show *Room 101*. He would actively avoid driving through the county from London, despite that being the most direct route to his home in Suffolk. Essex has always been the road out, the road through. Stratford gets its name from 'strata', a Roman road; this one ran all the way to Colchester, and still does, under the guise of the A12. There is something not for the faint of heart about driving in parts of Essex, where the style is firm, fast, some might say impatient. The car is at the heart of both Essex and 'Essex', the place and the myth.

The roar of the M25 motorway is a familiar sound on walks in Epping Forest or along the Thames Estuary and underneath the QE2 bridge. As with much of the country, the dominance of the car in Essex was ensured when Beeching's cuts to railway branch lines came into effect. 'The car was really essential to growing up in Essex,' Darren Hayman, the Brentwood-raised musician who was the frontman of the indie band Hefner, told me. 'You just immediately learned to drive when you were 17, and there were really young drivers around. All my friends would get a car somehow by the time we were 18, because there wasn't much else to do.' For Hayman, 'the car defines Essex. Even the houses, I think, are different, where they're almost built to cater for lots of cars: they have double driveways, two garages.' The new towns of Essex were designed for the car – Basildon didn't have a railway station until 1974 – but judging from how clogged the roads can be their dominance has outgrown planners' expectations.

It wasn't just where you lived, but where you worked. The importance of the Dagenham Ford factory to the identity of south Essex cannot be overstated. Samuel Williams purchased 30 acres of land at Dagenham Breach in 1887, planning to build a new deepwater dock for London. Business prospered, and eventually land was sold to Ford, Union Cable and the LCC, with the area growing into a thriving industrial estate. When Ford opened a factory there in 1931 it installed a 24-hour production line that covered over 600 acres; 50,000 people were employed during the 1950s, producing 4,000 cars per week. Hayman said he remembered how in 1970s Brentwood everyone knew someone who worked at Ford. If you had a relative who worked there, he said, you could get some kind of family discount. Hayman's first vehicles were south Essex rite of passage cars: he started with his dad's old Ford Cortina (retro), before moving on to a Fiesta (inevitable choice) and a Ford Focus (coming of age).

The Ford Capri, the jewel in the Dagenham crown, was mass-market exoticism on four wheels, an achievable slice of the American dream made on the Essex marshes. Ford produced desirable vehicles at a relatively affordable price in an efficient manner by the time-managed methods of Fordist capitalism. But behind the dream was a sharp realism. The assembly line was quick, hard, monotonous work for their thousands of workers. The American managers were an inspiration to modern working practices: bosses were addressed using their first names as opposed to English formalities, an ostensible equality that masked a furious desire for profit. Jobs such as those at the foundry, the biggest in Europe, where huge engines and machines were made, led workers to spend shifts in sweltering and pressurised conditions moulding cars for hours on end. It was not uncommon for staff to suffer mental breakdowns. In an anticipation of the practices of Amazon today, the Ford plant workers weren't allowed to go to the toilet for too long, or their card was marked.

The sea isn't the main draw on Southend seafront – for many people, it's the cars. I can hear the customised sports cars from our bedroom at night, growling and popping like some far-off dragon at play. On balmy summer evenings they vie for vacant parking spaces, proud owners standing outside their souped-up Beemers or retro Fiestas and chatting about mechanical specifics or anything at all. The car cruise subculture is synonymous with the seafront. Excited by the noises I'd hear at night and the sudden arrival of queues of cars as weekend evenings drew in, I started to watch YouTube videos of the cruising scene at its height. Darren Coles used to go cruising down Southend seafront on Saturdays in the mid to late 1980s. His first car was a customised Escort Mark 1: a 1300E with a walnut dash and cloth seats. He exchanged it for a Ford Mustang Mach 1. Still a teenager, he would take his mates down the front, splitting the petrol cost. They would park up on the seafront near the pier, and girls would come and check out the boys' cars as some drivers ripped the roundabouts, smoke rising from the tyres as they attempted to execute the perfect 'burnout' – letting the wheels spin while attempting to keep the car as stationary as possible. Eventually the police got involved, issuing tickets and trying to slow down the boy-racer energy. Nevertheless, Coles tells me that the value of the cars to their owners meant that it was actually a very responsible scene, with very little drinking and driving.

Coles' first job was an apprenticeship at Ford in Dunton, which was built near to where plotland dwellers once frolicked. The 20-year-old test drove Ford Escort Cosworths, a favourite of car-cruise enthusiasts doing burnouts down the seafront over the years, taking on high-banking corners at 120 miles or more, and recording the information for the

A modified Ford Focus on Southend seafront, 2021

engineers. He was always souping up his motors to impress onlookers: a new and bigger engine, a custom white paint job and perhaps the addition of nitrous oxide to boost power further. He joined an American car club, and when he wasn't cruising from Rayleigh Weir on the A127 to Southend he was street racing down the side of the oil refinery on Canvey Island. 'It's a dead straight road. There's fields on one side and the refinery on the other. It's probably about a mile and a half long but we only used a quarter of a mile at the very end. There'd be people up the top, they'd sit there and if any cops came, they'd radio down and say just park up, don't race, just park up.' These wild excursions into the night might seem different, even opposed to, the more collective instances of Essex's pioneering spirit and modernism, from the colonies to the new towns, but looked at another way they were perfect articulations for a place that had 'set its face to the future', as Kate O'Brien wrote of Southend. The ascent of the car was a thrillingly visual articulation of an individualism that, in truth, was always in existence; only now, technology had caught up with desire.

As teenagers, instead of driving, me and my mates used to walk down the Prittle Brook or beside the estuary itself on the way into Southend from Leigh. We'd buy all-day rovers and hop on buses or sometimes get the train into London. Perhaps we were wary of driving in Southend because there wasn't a lot to recommend it to a bunch of music-obsessed kids like us. I remember the news reports about the danger of the A127, and a particular bend between Southend and Rayleigh notorious for racing and accidents – a 17-year-old mechanic was killed 'when the Ford Escort he was driving skidded out of control and crashed three days before Christmas'. Digging further back, I realised the road had a bad reputation for years. The earliest instance I could find of the phenomenon of the A127 boy racer was in 1908 under the headline 'Essex Gentleman Fined', when Mr Frederick Wingford Leith of Mersea Island was found to have measured a speed of 29 miles per hour, according to the *East Anglia Daily Times*. A pattern emerged as Essex grew: 'A souped-up car swerved across the A127 reservation at East Horndon, took off and crashed into a car going the opposite way, a Brentwood coroner's jury heard on Thursday,' read a September 1970 *Brentwood Gazette* report. This particular accident, involving a modified Ford Anglia saloon, was one of an increasing amount that took place on the A127, with the same newspaper reporting in May 1970 that 100 people had died and nearly 3,000 been injured on Southend's 'death road' during the 1960s, leading local MP Eric Moonman to stand up in the House of Commons: 'I am absolutely shocked at these figures on such a modest stretch of road. It is incredible and tragic. We never thought they would be so high.'

The urge to get in the car and drive out into the darkness

of the rural Essex fringes is one that leaves a residue around the county. Sometimes, going for a burn might be taken too literally. Once, when we were walking on Radar Hill (so named after the huge Marconi antennas once tested there), which overlooks the sprawling town of South Woodham Ferrers and the wider Crouch Valley, we came across a burned-out Smart car on the edge of a ploughed field. Its squat dimensions made it appear as if it'd been compacted in a Thames Estuary wrecker's yard prior to being set alight. The carcinogenic hulk against a pastoral backdrop seemed a particularly Essexian sight, as was the detritus scattered around it: a chalky, transparent baggie and a discarded Durex packet – Es and sex. On another occasion, I drove through the darkness on the way back from the Dengie Peninsula one night, and passed an overturned car just left there as if that's the way the owner had meant it, the bent body of the vehicle an expression of pure abandonment against an uncanny, ask-no-questions countryside.

Boy racers are just the latest speed demons careering under Essex skies with the wind in their hair, owning tarmac just as the 'free-trade' smugglers who could outrun customs boats once did the water. In the eighteenth and nineteenth centuries fast vessels such as cutters, luggers and smacks were designed for maximum speed for legitimate purposes, such as delivering oysters to Billingsgate Market, and the men sailing them were well skilled in navigating the tricky rivers and creeks of Essex. This meant they were also well suited for more nefarious activities, such as unloading illicit cargoes from larger ships anchored off the Essex coast and passing it to waiting horsemen on land or sinking contraband to the bottom of creeks to be retrieved using devices known as 'grapnels'. They would race out to the estuary and rescue boats from the mud, but take a bounty for their trouble; if they were jailed for taking part in smuggling or other illegal activities, they were often freed by aristocrats to man their racing boats. The links to London, the waterways and ports have suited smuggling for centuries, and continue into the present day, with Essex's large open fields ideal for plane drop offs, while today's illegal goods are shifted quickly thanks to the ease of access to motorways.

A Southend car park was sparking into life on a cold November evening. Lighting rigs illuminated the growing crowd, most of whom were looking at a car parked in front of a row of nightclubs made dormant by the new lockdown. One of the clubs had been repainted to resemble Raquel's, the now-closed venue 14 miles away in Basildon made notorious in the mid-1990s as the place Leah Betts sourced the ecstasy that reports said led to her death during her 18th birthday party.

A group of about five or six teenagers asked me what was happening. They were making a film, I said. What about? I told them it's the latest about the Essex Boys' firm of wannabe gangsters.

Their eyes lit up. 'Essex boys! I've heard of them!'

How could they not? Pat Tate, Tony Tucker and Craig Rolfe were aspiring gangsters who helped flood south Essex with ecstasy pills during the 90s while working in a security firm on the doors of such nightclubs as Raquel's, a former dance-hall complete with a spring-loaded floor that had, even by then, seen better days. They might have disappeared without a trace, succumbing to the inevitably slowing passage of time or dying of a heart attack after one too many steroid-pumped days and cocaine nights, but their spectacular murder put paid to any notions of an inglorious retirement. They were killed, inevitably, in a car: gunned down by their killer or killers in a Range Rover, while waiting for an apparent drug pickup down a farm track in the village of Rettendon, as snow fell heavily on the night of 6 December 1995. The killing has fuelled decades of films, true crime books and tabloid intrigue ever since. The original film made out of the killings, *Essex Boys* (2000), took the title provided by the tabloids and starred Sean Bean as a seething fictional hardman hybrid of the characters involved in the gang. We were out here on a cold November night more than twenty-five years after the death of the three men to see the latest example, *Rise of The Footsoldier: Origins*, being shot in Southend. Starring Terry Stone, the One Nation nightclub impresario, as Tony Tucker, and the beefy former *EastEnders* actor Craig Fairbrass as Pat Tate, the franchise of films depicts a gleeful 90s lifestyle of violence and excessive consumption.

Since the original *Essex Boys* film, a growing amount of pop culture based on the initial bloody murder and the activities has been made. You could call it Essexploitation, a genre that takes advantage of the morbid curiosity behind a story that has lingered like a bad smell in these lowlands. Andy Loveday, the Canvey Island-born producer and co-founder of the Essex-based company that makes the *Rise of the Footsoldier* franchise, told me the film before this one broadened the appeal further than ageing boy racers and ravers in Essex. *Rise of the Footsoldier: Marbella*, a sun-kissed heist caper, featured a cameo from *The Only Way Is Essex* reality show star Jessica Wright, and was 'popular in North America, Germany, Australia, Benelux, Japan, Korea'. In the UK, it 'unlocked a whole brand new audience. A lot of women liked that film.'

Tony Tucker fell into the doorman racket after a chance meeting at Hollywood's club in Romford. He found his way to the Essex firm via Raquel's and capitalised on his position in club security during the heady days of acid house, starting a business to supply security to raves and wider events and recruiting doormen from bodybuilding gyms in Essex and east London. Ray Newman was a police inspector in Basildon at the time the Essex Boys were in town. He arrested Pat Tate after he robbed a Happy Eater restaurant, holding up the staff at knifepoint. 'He beat up a member of staff – he was just a drug-dealing thug,' said Newman. Tate's legend hangs on the fact he escaped from the ensuing court proceedings in Billericay, jumping on a motorbike waiting outside and fleeing to Spain. But even this caper shows Tate to come up short: he went to Gibraltar and was recognised by a British policeman there. 'They were thick, but they thought they were invincible,' Andy Loveday adds.

Those close to the group say to call it a firm or a gang was to oversell it. In a sense they were a legitimate security outfit that bit off more than they could chew. 'It's always the door security that basically runs the clubs,' said Loveday. 'They run the drugs. Slapping people left, right and centre – you never mess around with these people.' There was a lot of money in it, because if you controlled the door, you controlled the drug supply. 'I've worked at raves and I've seen people putting bin bags full of money in their car at the end of the night,' said Bernard O'Mahoney, a former doorman who ran security at Raquel's with Tucker and Tate. 'That's what created the violence.'

The Essex Boys phenomenon has its roots in the true crime series largely written by O'Mahoney, who has based an entire 'straight' career on publishing book after book promising the 'truth' about the Essex Boys, with each instalment peddling a truer truth than the last. *Essex Boys: The Final Word: No More Myths, No More Lies – The Definitive Story* was published in 2015. For all the talk of 'truth' in relation to the Essex Boys myth, there is precious little about it that feels definitive. O'Mahoney in particular, while on the face of it a detail-heavy and straight-talking narrator, is anything but reliable. The former bouncer was outed as the 'Judas of Fleet Street' by the *Guardian*'s Nick Davies in 1997,

We Play for Real

The Rettendon murders, as reported by
the *Daily Mirror*, December, 1995

a 'scoopmonger' whose stock in trade for some years had
been befriending people accused of crimes through writing
complimentary letters, often peddling mistruths and under

129

pseudonyms, before extracting sensitive information and details of their lives to sell to the tabloids.

Roads facilitated the fantasy life of the Essex Boys. O'Mahoney's books are full of driving-based incidents: the police following them onto the M25, the kids in the Ford Fiesta and the Commer van pulling up at the lights and screaming, 'You're gonna die, O'Mahoney.' It is ironic, then, that he actually helped build the south-eastern section of the M25 motorway, opened by Margaret Thatcher in 1986. Interviewed by Iain Sinclair for his psychogeographic treatise on the fallout of Thatcherite Britain, *London Orbital*, which itself took the form of a journey around the motorway ring road, O'Mahoney remembered the early days of the road's construction: 'There was a lot of car dealers and scrap dealers and the like. They got involved with drugs in Essex because they had a lot of money to wash.' The opening of the M25 did indeed lead to an increase in crime. According to the International Centre for the History of Crime, Policing and Justice, by 1987, crime in the Eastern Division was up 10.4 per cent partly due to the opening of the final sections of the M25 and the use of the new road by criminals from outside the area, 'some travelling substantial distances'.

On the night of the Range Rover murders, the story goes that Tucker, Tate and Rolfe had parked down a track next to a field to wait for a plane carrying cocaine, as arranged by drug smuggler Mickey Steele and his associate Jack Whomes. Whomes and Steele were jailed for life in 1998 for the murder of the three men on the evidence of supergrass Darren Nicholls. O'Mahoney once campaigned for their innocence, but said he is now convinced of their guilt due to the amount of evidence – including mobile phone location data – that proves they were at the scene. Whomes was released in March 2021 after serving twenty-two years, while Steele's release was blocked by the parole board.

Despite the convictions, other stories still do the rounds. In 2017, *The Times* reported that a crime boss was recorded telling a Met detective he could 'take out' the three dealers who supplied Leah Betts, just days after her death. This bombshell led Whomes and Steele to lodge an unsuccessful appeal against their conviction with the Criminal Cases Review Commission after a team of former Met investigators said this and other evidence supported the story of an East End criminal Billy Jasper, who told the police he drove the actual killer to the site on that cold December night.

Perhaps it is the murkiness of the narrative, the lack of a final word on who killed the three men, which has made the Essex Boys genre last so long. True crime YouTube channels posit outlandish theories (there is even a documentary about what has happened to the Range Rover since). Google-image search 'Essex boys' and you might see more than you wanted to, grotesquely deformed skulls and bloodied stone-wash jeans. When a collective fascination with the macabre enters this kind of fine-grained level of microscopic obsession, with 'fans' poring over pictures and facts on one of the many Facebook groups devoted to the burgeoning Essex Boys subculture, it has long stopped being about a search for truth, and becomes, as with the conspiracy theorists, a stab at control, about finding the answers that have been kept from 'us'.

What is certain in the fog of addled or unreliable memory is that, one way or another, the death of Leah Betts, after she took a clean ecstasy tablet purchased at Raquel's and drank seven litres of water, put the spotlight on the protagonists, on the club and on O'Mahoney, who said he felt under pressure to write about the drug deals, violence and eventual murders following the media scrutiny after Betts's death. The Essex Boys achieved notoriety, not in the way the Kray twins did in the East End, through an exercise in gentlemanly psychosis, but instead by being on the wrong side of a moral panic, maniacal no-marks elevated above their station by the accidental association with a suburban tragedy.

After an awakening at acid house raves in the late 1980s, the film producer Andy Loveday learned to DJ, sharing bills with Brandon Block, Colin Hudd and other names of the era, and from the early 90s to the mid-noughties, was resident DJ at the clubs he now used as film sets, before becoming a club promoter himself. These were the boom years of legitimate clubbing in the UK. Back then, between the raves and the nightclubs, Essex was filled with parties. Take your pick from Epping Country Club, Legends, or Joe Fridays. 'At that time the club was all about drugs, it was all about ecstasy,' said Loveday. 'People didn't even wanna drink. And you didn't wanna go home. It was euphoric. It was like the best thing in the world, you'd go back to people's houses and you'd sit there and have a joint, coming up . . . people only used to do a line of coke if you had enough money at the time to bring your E back up.'

Essex provided fields for raves and the roads to get you there, ports for drugs and the barns to hide them in, and towns for the nightclubs to sell them in. After new Essex towns and suburbs appeared from nothing, you might say it took a little while for a kind of shared, accepted culture to come to the fore. Good times filled the gaps and south Essex became synonymous with entertainment venues. The area prided itself on its nightclub culture, the site of one of the pre-rave tectonic shifts in youth culture: Essex soul boys and girls dressed up to the nines and shimmying towards euphoria. Mike Fordham grew up in Ilford and emigrated to the US. He had been living in New York and San Francisco for a couple of years but moved back to the UK in early 1989 just as acid house was exploding. 'I moved back into my nan's house on the Hainault Estate. It was like a light had switched on,' he said. 'Most of our raving was done either up the West End or in the big warehouses around the M25 – but it's always been my contention that the Essex soul scene of the late seventies and early eighties was rave before rave.' Working-class kids drove from miles around to cavernous spaces like Zero 6 next to Southend airport, Ilford Palais and the Goldmine on Canvey Island to dance to music produced by black American artists in the industrial hubs of Detroit, Memphis and New York. 'The thing about this scene was that it was fuelled by lager and Yves Saint Laurent rather than pills. It took a while before those same suburban kids took it to the centre of London and then back out to the orbital flatlands.'

After they finished the doors around midnight, Tucker, Tate and Rolfe sometimes went to Legends or Tommy Mack's Black & White dos in London. 'They'd see all the nightlife of London, all the glitz and the money,' said Loveday. 'They'd come down [to Southend] and play that role that they'd seen in London. Everyone's aspirations were that they wanted to be the type of guys who buy themselves a brand new BMW.' Yet the reality was quite different. 'They've got all the clothes on but they financed the BMW, they spent their wages on an eighth of coke and they're skint in the week,' he said. 'But they wanna portray that they are the big Charlie bananas.'

It is a scene that has since fallen away, like one of the unlucky beach huts on the front during a storm. 'They're gone,' said Loveday of the future of Southend's nightclubs, a strip of cavernous spaces that face a giant car park that is no longer filled up after dusk settles. 'They're like dinosaur relics of a bygone era that you're never gonna get back. These are gonna be flats, apartments overlooking the seafront. The only value in this now is real estate.'

The plight of the murdered trio tells a story about the excesses of late capitalism as much as it does the boom of the drug trade after the rise of rave. 'All this, "We control Essex." They couldn't control themselves,' said O'Mahoney. 'These "international drug dealers" drove to the meeting in a Range Rover which was on HP [hire purchase], the driver was uninsured, and it wasn't fucking taxed. That's how savvy they were. Pat Tate didn't have enough money to get buried. They had to borrow the money to bury him.' In trying to project some deranged and over-steroided version of Thatcher's upwardly mobile Essex man, they ended up, two bouncers in their late 30s and a 26-year-old stooge, immortalised as Boys.

Anton Johnson owned a pub near to where the Essex Boys' murders happened. 'The boys were all in there before they got killed,' he told me. 'I knew 'em all. I can see 'em now, they all had their coats on.' Johnson used to have a bit of a name for himself, too, not just in Essex, but all over the country. He was a regular in the British tabloid press at the time he was being investigated by the ITV current affairs series *World in Action*, before he was sacked as chairman of Southend United for stealing funds ('SOCCER BOSS "STOLE"' – *Daily Mirror*, January 1986), which Johnson has always denied, and still did when I brought it up. With Johnson, in fact, it didn't seem to damage him much. He was innocent, he said, but he still seemed to thrive off his image of an Essex entrepreneur gone rogue. Articles were often accompanied by a picture of him dressed up like Thurrock's answer to Pablo Escobar, all fur coat, aviators, moustache and a perpetually lit cigar.

I met Johnson, now in his late 70s, at a Starbucks off the A127. It felt apt: an illicit meeting in plain sight of a kind that happens between businessmen and gangsters on TV. Easy access and easy escape. Johnson's style was to bombard me with anecdotes, and God knows, he's lived a large life. He isn't the only man in south Essex to claim he was one of the last to talk to Reggie Kray before he died – he isn't even the only man I have interviewed for this book to have claimed it. Kray had asked Johnson to run a pub for him, but Johnson declined. Instead, he agreed to sell Kray-sponsored champagne in one of his own pubs, the Orsett Cock, in Thurrock. 'It was dealt through a guy from Essex who had a little vineyard in France,' Johnson told me. 'Can you imagine? Nobody said "No" to Reggie. We must have done over 1,000 cases of it. Barbara Windsor was having two cases a day.'

Johnson grew up at a butcher's shop in Grays, Thurrock, and he made a lot of money from meat. He told me one of his luckiest breaks came when he worked supplying pork to London Cooperative, which had 650 shops, and Portsmouth Cooperative, with its 450 shops; he had to shift so much pork he had out of work actors and reporters working for him. He told me he had always worked under the assumption that once he had cut the meat, the bones were of no consequence. 'Nobody wanted the bones; they only wanted the meat. So you used to get all these great big bins and chuck the bones in.' One day, he said, a guy from Whitechapel came in. 'He said there's a Chinese man here who wants to talk to you. You've got to remember, I'm taking 3,000 sides of pork off of Smithfield each day, which is a lot of pigs. He said, "What are you doing with the bones?" I said I've got these barrels. He said, "What do you do with those?" Spare ribs hadn't even started [in a big way] so I had been throwing them all away. So he said, "I'll buy all those off you." I ended up getting five grand every week off him in cash. So I bought my first Ferrari.'

It is the type of lucky break story that began to typify life in these parts as the post-war years drifted on. And Johnson found his figurehead. In 1975, after Margaret Thatcher had just beaten Ted Heath to replace him as the leader of the

Conservative Party, then the opposition party in the United Kingdom, Johnson, who was trying to make it as a singer, phoned up her press agent and made a proposition. Sensing an opportunity that chimed with his own political persuasions, he told the agent he wanted to break the record for the world's biggest Valentine's Day card, by sending it to Thatcher herself. 'They said Margaret would love to do it – you know, good publicity,' he said. The card, which read 'To Margaret, Love Anton', was reportedly carried on the back of a pink lorry on 13 February 1975. 'The press wanted it the day before Valentine's, so it came out on all the nationals on the front page [on the 14th].' Johnson arranged for six men in toppers and tails he called Anton's Messengers to arrive with red roses and this great big Valentine's card. 'They carried it right along the Embankment – red roses for a blue lady.' Thatcher gratefully received the card and the resulting publicity, before posing for press photographs and inviting Anton in for tea and sandwiches.

Johnson's meat money was a gateway to other pursuits, the most infamous being the purchase of football clubs. His first came in 1979, after watching *Match of the Day*, which had an item saying the South Yorkshire club Rotherham United was for sale. Johnson said he phoned up early Monday and spoke to the secretary. Not known for his understatement, Johnson rented a helicopter and took off from Southend Airport for the North. 'I landed and shook on the deal straight away; I mean it wouldn't matter what I signed. It was my dream come true.'

From meat into show business into football – there had always been so much opportunity for Johnson, so much to exploit. His stories pitch his life as a series of sliding doors moments. He has always dealt in bombastic, ephemeral gestures – tabloid explosions that weren't worth the chip paper they were printed on, ill-thought-out business ventures that ended in surreal implosions. He wanted to hit the big time and very nearly did until it slipped through his fingers. Sat here before me in this roadside coffee franchise, Johnson, grinning his way to the end of another exaggerated story, was the personification of Essex's lucky streak – its profligacy, its excess, its vulgarity, its tall tales, and its ultimate failure to capitalise.

But the money, however fast he would burn through it, would always open new doors for Johnson. He had told me when he went to college to study meat, he started putting concerts on at the huge Queen's Hotel in Grays, from Status Quo when they were a new band, to the Marvelettes, to Fleetwood Mac. My mates and I used to go out pretty much every Friday or Saturday night to the Pink Toothbrush in the former market town of Rayleigh, a club I later found out was started by Johnson. Over sticky drinks like snakebite-and-black people used to tell each other the story of when the venue was known as Croc's, named after a hair-brained idea of Johnson's to put a pond with real crocodiles in the middle of the space. Croc's was also infamous as the place where Depeche Mode first played. You can watch videos online and survey the awkward cuteness of Dave Gahan, Martin Fletcher, Martin Gore and Vince Clarke on stage all dressed in black and making twinkling and embryonic new synthpop sounds. Their name, Depeche Mode (at first pronounced 'Depeshay' by fans and journalists), was an off-the-cuff appropriation, which translated into French as 'fast fashion'.

Depeche Mode's debut record, 'Speak and Spell', was a clarion call of synth-pop optimism that started life in the experiments of Vince Clarke and the band in a Basildon garage. 'My family moved to Basildon from South Woodford when I was five,' Clarke told me. 'There was absolutely nothing to do [in Basildon]. When I was a kid there was just one Indian restaurant and one Chinese. Somebody asked me earlier why there were so many people from Basildon into music. I think that was the reason. If I hadn't joined the band, I'd still be working at the yoghurt factory.' Frontman Gahan reminisced about his Basildon bad boy past during a mid-80s interview. 'I was pretty wild. I loved the excitement of nicking a motor, screeching off and being chased by the police. Hiding behind a wall with your heart beating gives you a real kick – will they get you?'

Critics, particularly in the US, assumed Depeche Mode – with their leather trousers and caps, blouse-like shirts and pirate boots – were gay. They weren't, but it spoke to a truth about Essex synthpop, a subculture that included musicians, artists and members of the public seeking out queer alternatives to the machismo and fixed gender roles that dominated the culture around them. Gahan used to drink at Southend's long-running gay pub the Cliff, which became a key part of the New Wave scene in Essex, a place people could wear adventurous clothing without worrying about the threat from more conservative mindsets.

'Makeup, hairspray, dodgy looking clothes. Couple of bottles in the park where you'd talk about music and try to avoid getting punched in the face.' Douglas McCarthy of Nitzer Ebb was telling me of the inevitability of the beating he would receive for dressing as what was known as a 'positive punk', a kind of proto-goth, in Essex. 'We weren't exploring being gay or bisexuality but we weren't bothered if we were gay or straight,' McCarthy said. 'There was a typical homophobia based on a doubt of your own sexuality. There was no chance in their [majority of Essex men on nights out] minds with their set of friends that they could discuss if you want to kiss a bloke or even say another bloke looks good.'

Nitzer Ebb are a band that could only come from Essex. Almost the whole schtick is a pulsating dugger-dugger beat behind the flailing mock-machismo of Douglas McCarthy, who is perhaps the most Essex frontman who ever lived (and I mean this as a total compliment). During his 1980s on-stage pomp he was a lolloping bundle of constant movement and threat, careering around like an escaped clubber, accentuating the unhinged brutality of the band's weaponised brand of techno. Short back and sides but slick and long on top, T-shirt with the sleeves cut off, McCarthy had the demeanour of a *Grange Hill* bad kid at the weekend, flick knife in pocket. They had started out sounding like a junior partner to the sprightly Depeche Mode but even at the start seemed more bodily, more likely to break out into nervous, wanton violence, than their more famous peers. They riffed on the disco of Sylvester, the unrestrained and unhinged performances of the Birthday Party and the darkness of Bauhaus to create something I think hasn't really been surpassed in terms of what it set out to achieve: body music that satirised the lumpen immovability of the geezers who would call them 'poofs' and want to fight them on a Saturday night, creating music that willed people to move out of their cul de sacs of identity.

The band moved through the more obvious shock tactics to get a reaction – getting 'Krauted out' in cod-Nazi garb, Russian Soviet shirts with the Red Star, German jodhpurs, boots and braces and military buzzcuts – meant to antagonise and to make their name, to get out of Essex. And it worked (Douglas was talking to me on Skype from L.A.). As the band told Luke Turner for the *Guardian* in 2019, the producer Phil Harding, making a name for himself with Stock Aitken Waterman hits including Dead or Alive's 'You Spin Me Round (Like a Record)', came to a gig in Brentwood, Essex, during which the group stopped playing to fight with some stage-diving punks in the audience. 'We thought we'd blown it,' McCarthy told Turner, 'but he said: "Blokes dressed in leather, banging music, a fight, home by 10 – that's a great night out!"'

McCarthy's family had moved to Canvey from Barking. His dad was a lagger who had to get a 5 a.m. coach all the way to the Isle of Grain opposite Canvey on the Kent side of the Thames. Douglas linked the aggression to the displacement of the East End out to Essex, in a testimony that contrasts with the visions of Essex as an uncomplicated promised land. 'Everyone had come in the late 60s as transplants from east London and Barking. I remember talking to my mates, wishing we were in London, like we were in this second-rate place, so we didn't really care about it.'

Young Douglas played for Methane football club, which was associated with the methane gas terminal on the island, right by the Lobster Smack pub on the Thames, and when he wasn't doing that, he would go and smash up caravans with the son of the owner of the holiday park that housed them. 'Not to glamourise it but there was a touch of the underworld about everything,' he said. 'There were a lot of things that fell off the back of a lorry that were given to us as birthday or Christmas presents. That was just part and parcel of life down there. There was a slight hoodlumness about it, which was evident from where everyone's parents had come from.' The McCarthys moved out of Canvey when they feared Douglas had fallen in with the wrong crowd after they found him throwing stones at passing cars from the top of a bus stop when he was eight. When the family moved out to leafy Danbury, in mid Essex, from Canvey, Douglas was seen as an outsider for having a thick 'East End' accent.

Before the family left the island, McCarthy's dad used to drink with a more established crowd of musicians at the Canvey Club, centred around the island's prime musical legends, Dr Feelgood. The band have seeped into the lore of these parts. Lee Brilleaux and Wilko Johnson were also child emigres from London. They formed Dr Feelgood in 1971 with two local friends, bassist John B 'Sparko' Sparks and drummer

John 'The Big Figure' Martin. Brilleaux was a full blues obsessive, having 'nicked' his style from Howlin Wolf after seeing him perform wearing a tatty mohair suit in the function room of a Romford pub. Though Johnson was the Feelgoods' principle songwriter and is recognised as the band's true musical original for his choppy guitar technique, it was the fist-pumping, beer-sweating, groin-thrusting Brilleaux who forged Dr Feelgood's tough-guy character, the persona for whom Wilko Johnson's songs were written. The handful of records released in the band's original iteration inspired punk in the UK and New York new wave acts such as Patti Smith, Television and Blondie. The mid-70s, coiled-spring menace of Dr Feelgood's Essex came from its estrangement – and Canvey Island is estranged twice over, misunderstood or mistrusted by mainland Essex as much as Essex has been by the rest of the United Kingdom. The island was back then a heavily industrialised place – the birthplace of natural gas in Britain – and Dr Feelgood put its imagery in their songs, such as the 'towers burning at the break of day' at Coryton oil refinery. You can practically taste the acrid air of the height of Canvey Island's industrialisation listening to the growling, starchy recording of the band's debut album, *Down by the Jetty*. The cover of the record, too, seemed to stamp the band's credentials as unfussy, working-class outsiders: crumpled shirts and anguished, tired stares against the shoreline of the island at dawn.

Alison Moyet started off in a pub rock band on the same circuit as Dr Feelgood. Her howling vocal added a new depth to Essex synthpop. Vince Clarke left Depeche Mode mere months after their breakthrough appearance on *Top of The Pops*. He rang Moyet and formed Yazoo, a fascinating cultural proposition that welded his bubblegum synthpop with Moyet's butch blues. They too quickly made it onto the BBC's flagship music show. Alf, as Moyet was known to her many friends, was the talk of Basildon when she went on *Top of the Pops* in an outfit she had sourced at the market. 'My mum lent me twenty quid and I bought the cheapest fabric we could find and my mate who was on the dole whipped me up a dress on her sewing machine,' she told me. Watching that first appearance, it is striking how unprepared for fame Moyet seems, devoid of the cockiness of Depeche Mode's Dave Gahan. She was still living on pocket money at home. 'Dave was a market boy,' she told me, 'a cheeky chappy, so to see the band then so coiffed was quite a surprise – we were all boracic, just local people.' As Clarke shied away from the spotlight, Moyet became a household name, the biggest selling female singer in the UK when she was 22 and her first solo album, *Alf*, went quadruple platinum. She remains, as far as I know, the only musical artist to get into the UK charts with an album called 'Essex'.

Talk to Moyet about those days and, instead of stories of glitz and glamour, she is more likely to tell you about how her sudden fame distorted her social position within Basildon, leading to a profound sense of alienation. She cherished the community she grew up in, until stardom got in the way. 'I think it is really difficult to come from that kind of background and one of you has done so well, but then is slightly hung up about doing so well.' She didn't want to be the one that people were looking at, but it was too late. 'I felt ashamed to be deemed to be in a different social or class group now because I wasn't in my heart. I would still want to go to the same pubs with my mates but I was so recognisable that even in Basildon I would have crowds of people screaming and chasing me down the street.'

As her fame grew, a crippling agoraphobia took over her life and made it quite difficult for her to work. It stemmed, she said, from an Elvis Costello gig in Southend. 'There was an after-show party at Dr Feelgood's place on Canvey and I had gone there because Elvis Costello had been my childhood hero. I absolutely loved him. He did this two-hour show and he was brilliant, really brilliant.' Costello told her he had heard Yazoo, and really liked it. 'I wanted to say to him, "You were fantastic, you were brilliant, two hours, so much energy." But what came out of my mouth was, "You dragged that out a bit, didn't you?" I felt like a popped balloon and the room was a million miles away. The shame that I felt made me determined to never want to speak to another person I liked ever again. I didn't understand these beautiful people; these easy, social, articulate, erudite people. I didn't speak the same language as them.'

The more I tried to fit together these contrasting stories of twilight Essex subcultures, the more I saw the connecting lines between. Perhaps the destructive appetites of the Essex Boys and daring articulations of estrangement from musicians such as Moyet were two sides of the same coin. The building of twentieth-century Essex had provided new urban frameworks, suburban domiciles and the tarmacked arterial roads that connected them. The explosion of Essex music, the dominance of car culture, and the successes and tragedies of the nightclub scene in the 1970s, 80s and 90s suggested the Essex experiment in twentieth-century living had succeeded. Not that they left much trace. Today, Raquel's is closed along with most of the Southend nightclubs, while Moyet and the rest of the 1980s cohort moved away a long time ago. But then architects and planners can never truly account for what happens in all that new and supposedly logical space. You can't make people act in a certain way, no matter what your intentions for them might be – not totally. You can't stop someone from wanting out of the lives laid out before them, by whatever means afforded them.

Back in the roadside Starbucks, I sipped my second coffee. Johnson launched into another story, about the time he used to own a farm across the A127 from here, where he bred Irish Wolfhounds. The RSPCA used to call him when they had a dog they couldn't find a home for. 'One day they called and said, "We've got a lion, it's only six weeks old." I had to go to London and pick it up. I said to my wife Jan she could have it on her lap on the way back. They gave me a cardboard box on the platform. I opened it up and this thing roared like a full-grown lion. So we put it in the back of the estate car.'

They called the lion, somewhat inevitably, Tiny, and did what any self-respecting animal lover would do – put him in with the dogs. Tiny started purring, Johnson told me, and tried to suckle from one of the mother dog's nipples. He even used to come into the house sometimes. 'When he caught himself in the mirror, he would jump.' After a few years, however, Tiny started to escape fairly regularly. 'I went to London one day and I got back to a load of blue lights: Tiny had escaped into another farmer's field. He said what happened was, there was a bitch in season over there and the mongrel had gone over, followed by the wolfhound, followed by the lion. A guy from the council said he'd never seen a wolfhound before, so that made him jump, and then the lion came along. So he's gone up the tree and no one could get him down.' After a petition to have Tiny removed from the farm, Johnson donated the lion to Chipperfield circus, driving it to London to make the donation, to the shock of a taxi driver who pulled up next to them at the lights.

Opportunity, quick bucks, image, having a laugh. Just don't take things too seriously, whatever you do. After all, if the lion doesn't work out, there's always the circus. As I left Johnson, we shook hands, and made our way to our respective cars. Before getting in his vehicle, Johnson stopped to wave. He looked like he wanted to say something, as if he was not quite ready to leave behind the opportunity to tell one more story, even if this one would need to be bellowed across the car park against the traffic noise. I got in the Fiesta and slowly approached the A127. As I tried to edge into the outside lane, waiting to find a gap in the whooshing traffic, I thought to myself in that anxious moment that this place, with its incessant speed and its sly roads off to the country lanes of Thurrock and beyond, was Essex's dominant energy. Keep moving, it hisses, keep talking. Don't stop 'til you're dead.

7

Doing Very Well

'There are three things of such a sort
that they produce merciless destruction
when they get the upper hand:
One is a flood of water,
another is a raging fire
and the third is the lesser people,
the common multitude;
for they will not be stopped
by either reason or by discipline.'
John Gower, extract from *Mirour de l'Omme*, 1376–1378

Fobbing, Thurrock, is one of those places that could only
exist in Essex. The village, credited with being the birthplace
of the Great Revolt of 1381, better known as the 'Peasants'
Revolt', sits at the threshold of a landscape that holds the
past, present and future tightly in its grasp. The broad lorry-
friendly sweep of the road by the Harvester chain restaurant
seamlessly segues into the ancient logic of the old High Road.
On one side of this road, rows of desirable detached homes
stand proudly, boasting lit-up driveways, bespoke gates and a
fast route to the M25 via the A13. Some of the bigger examples sell for the best part of a million quid. On the other
side of the High Road a discreetly complicated countryside

landscape unfolds. The Thurrock historian Randal Bingley wrote that Fobbing was 'devised as a long strip of territory', part of a 'jumble of boundaries, which few folk entirely understood', a border among many other borders, contested territories that overlapped from here to Brentwood, such as Warley, Dunton, Corringham and Shellhaven. At six miles long and a mile and a half wide, it was a wisp in the landscape.

On one of those mornings when Hayley and I would be puzzled as to what to fill Greta and Ernest's day with, I suggested making a picnic and heading for Fobbing. We drove west along the estuary from Southend, and parked outside a surviving timber-framed thatched cottage, which still went by the name of Fishers, 'a flimsily framed . . . minor yeoman's house of c. 1470', according to Bingley. It was a beautiful late July day, with plump cumulus clouds unable to make a dent in a dominant blue sky. We found a lane that the map said would take us away from the roar of the High Road. In Essex, some old lanes can take you back in time; Bingley called these types of tree-lined lanes the 'oldest man-made landscape structures'. We walked down it, to the edge of a farmer's field, and found a spot to eat our sandwiches. After lunch, Greta and Ernest took no small amount of joy in climbing a rusty old gate that looked like it was slowly bending back into the earth. We could hear the faint popping of a farmer's gun in the distance.

The field towards the Thames to our south looked scorched and dry and on the horizon I could see the great cranes of the huge container port run by DP World, a multinational logistics company based in Dubai, which the fishermen and the cocklers down Leigh-on-Sea say is harming their catch.

Thomas Baker wouldn't have stood for that. Baker was from Fobbing, and was widely reported through centuries of historical research to have been the no-nonsense mouthpiece for the south Essex peasantry during the revolt. Villagers from Fobbing, Corringham and Stanford Le Hope marched on the King's Judiciary at Brentwood against what they saw as an unfair demand of a tax already paid. Local landowner John Guildesborough, the knight of the shire of Essex (what we'd think of as an MP today), was chased out of the county.

The Great Revolt ripped through Essex and wider East Anglia. Of the 145 rebels named as the ringleaders of the Essex rising, 28 of them came from Fobbing, a huge number for a tiny village near the mouth of the Thames. The revolt kicked off in Essex and spread into Kent, which was also a relatively densely populated area of rural England at the time. The men of Essex and Kent were used to being drafted into the never-ending fight against France and so were trained in combat. South Essex was a drowned, yet fertile landscape and its waterlogged nature ensured it was an economically active place in the Middle Ages, the Thames being a main artery for goods going into London and trading occurring with Kent on the other side. It was this kind of organised self-determination that drove the revolt. Peasants were mobile and it was one of the most sophisticated areas in England in terms of communications, with messages relayed at speed on horseback. This animated scene contrasted with the conditions of their own serfdom: they were villeins, bondsmen, serfs, tied to the land of their lord, to whom they were expected to pay taxes, and unable to leave it for longer than a day without permission being granted. Demand for their labour was turned on and off like a tap. Punishments and fines were dished out for perceived wrongdoing, with no possibility of appeal.

The shock of an estimated third to half the population of England dying during the fourteenth century Black Death, and the subsequent labour shortages experienced after, meant the peasants began to wake up to both their value as individuals and their power as a collective. 'Let's just say every second person around you dies and you survive – in the end then you probably have a different outlook of society,' Herbert Eiden, a historian based in north Essex researching the revolt, told me. 'After the Black Death there were fewer labourers or fewer workers who could till, or plough, or sow, or harvest the land.' Some peasants' tenements became bigger as landlords were dying and leaving no heirs. 'People were getting better off but on the other hand their social status was still as it was before,' said Eiden. 'So they are increasingly at odds with the world around them.' In the areas the peasants' revolt was most potent, many had free tenure status, meaning their servitude was predetermined and of a higher status – ploughing the fields for a set time, chivalric duties – rather than the beck-and-call villeinage of the unfree.

The government introduced rules in England that you had to be employed by someone for one year before leaving the position. If you left early, because your neighbour offered you money, say, you were fined and if you did it again, you were outlawed – branded on the forehead for all to see and fear. I wasn't all that surprised when Eiden told me that England was one of the only examples in Europe where the government tried hard to save the business interests of the landed classes.

After the leader of the revolt, Wat Tyler, was killed in front of the crowds at Smithfield in London, local rebellions around East Anglia and the south-east of England were crushed, although accounts depict particular resistance in Essex, with bands of men holding out for their dream of liberty, and a much sought-after pardon from the boy king, Richard II, who apparently was having none of it. 'Rustics you were and rustics you are still,' said Richard, according to the admittedly heavily one-sided accounts of the chronicler Thomas Walsingham. '[Y]ou will remain in bondage, not as before but incomparably harsher.' The king's uncle, Thomas Woodstock, and Lord Thomas Percy were sent into Essex to lead the king's forces into battle in woodland near Billericay to put paid to the Essex resistance. There is a quietly sad line among many poignant details in Rodney Hilton's history of the peasant risings in medieval Britain and Europe, *Bond Men Made Free*: 'Such was the demand for freedom from serfdom, it was the one most persistently presented when the rebels were directly negotiating with the king and his advisers.'

The geography of the rising can be partly explained by the preponderance of wealthy landowning Christian institutions attracted to these low-lying, bounteous pastures. The land at Fobbing, for example, was owned by Barking Abbey, while Canterbury was the ecclesiastical landlord of Southchurch, where our family now lives. There was an attack at Southchurch Hall, a fourteenth-century building surrounded by moat and earthworks, now public park where I take my kids to look at the terrapins. The peasants who attacked the hall burned rolls of records about themselves, hoping that erasing the proof of their bondage would free them. Many may have thought they had destiny behind them, riding a wave to escape the indignity and unfairness of their positions in society, which ultimately ended in failure. Perhaps worse than the anguish of the peasants' perpetual servitude was the hope that any crumb of relative freedom brought with it.

Writing in the *London Review of Books* about the myth of Robin Hood, James Meek explained that for a myth to succeed, it had to be easy to understand. 'Myth is a story that can be retold by anyone, with infinite variation, and still be recognisable as itself,' he wrote. 'The entry level for national myth is high. It's not that the mythical hero must have some basis in historical fact; that might actually be an obstacle. It's that any individual must be able to interrogate their own memory to assemble their own version of the myth.'

While it is easy to conjure Robin Hood in one's mind's eye, even historians of the Peasants' Revolt can't close their eyes and conjure up who exactly Wat Tyler was. Hamstrung by having actually existed but there being no surviving evidence of his importance to the revolt itself, such details as his imagined physique were not as immediately obvious as Robin Hood's. Experts are not even certain which side of the river he called home, Essex or Kent (although Essex has claimed him through Wat Tyler Country Park, built on the former site of Pitsea Explosives Factory). Historian of the period Juliet Barker wrote that despite Tyler being described as 'a captain, leader and chief . . . of the county of Kent', the jurors in Kent said he was 'of Essex', specifically 'of Colchester'.

The peasants' myth lay in a state of dormant confusion for centuries. The post-war years that saw the NHS launched and the new towns ratified could be said to have marked an answer to the desires of the Peasants' Revolt – a lasting rejection of the kind of servitude that feudalism represented. But it is also interesting that the collective endeavour of the peasants was for years implicitly rejected. The problem of the Peasants' Revolt is the problem of any kind of discourse around 'the people' in a country as stratified by class as England and by extension the wider United Kingdom. The Norfolk-born emigrant to revolutionary America (and even-more-revolutionary France) Thomas Paine voiced his dismay that there was no commemorative statue for the Peasants' Revolt at the end of the eighteenth century. 'If the Barons merited a monument to be erected at Runnymede, Tyler merited one in Smithfield,' he wrote in 1791. Paine's quote is now etched at the site of Tyler's death in Smithfield.

There have been fragments of possibility that the heroism of the revolt might be better remembered. Partly by dint of sheer luck (more of his letters survived than other protagonists in the Peasants' Revolt), the name of John Ball has survived the centuries well enough to achieve a kudos among left-wingers and libertarians. He was claimed as a proto-socialist by William Morris in his novel *A Dream of John Ball*, where the protagonist is a time traveller gone back to tell Ball that the feudal conditions he had railed against had become replicated in the industrial nineteenth century. 'I come not from heaven, but from Essex,' is the immortal line Morris gives to Ball, who was thought to have been born in Colchester in the late 1330s. It would not be the last time a polemical writer has put words into the mouth of a semi-imagined Essex person to make a point.

While the Peasants' Revolt myth survived and grew into the twentieth century, the way it manifested in public life said a lot about the way things work in British discourse. Instead of a myth encapsulating a useful message for society, it became a shorthand for the sudden jostling of an unwashed, unworthy, un(public)schooled mass into view. In 1985, the *London Review of Books* twice referred to the rise of Margaret Thatcher and her supporters as a peasants' revolt. First in June by Peter Pulzer in a review of the Tory MP and journalist Julian Critchley's *Westminster Blues* ('In that respect the peasants' revolt which elevated her to power is irreversible'), the second by Critchley himself, taking the credit when reviewing a biography of Lord Carrington by Patrick Cosgrave: 'The author is a partisan in the civil war which has been quietly raging within the Conservative Party since it elected Mrs Thatcher as its leader in what I have called the "Peasants' Revolt" of 1975.'

Thatcher was the daughter of a Wesleyan Methodist shopkeeper in Grantham, Lincolnshire. Her biographers variously and often fondly describe her as a zealous conviction politician who had no truck with the gently deferential Toryism that dominated the politics of Westminster for years. The

Peasants' Revolt was therefore a perfect metaphor for her entry into British politics. Howell Raines in the *New York Times* in 1987 used the same metaphor, and wrote that 'Her election as party leader marked an end to the dominance of "the older-type, traditional Tory, mainly coming from public school, the landed gentry," recalled Labour's Denis Healey. It became more oriented toward small businessmen, middle-class professionals and strivers who, like Margaret Thatcher, had worked their way up from humble origins.'

Thatcher's Edmonton-born Rottweiler Norman Tebbit took upward mobility so seriously he ended up in Suffolk. After he greeted me at the door of his home in Bury St Edmunds, he immediately escorted me down some tricky steps to his cellar despite the fact he was almost pushing 90. I surveyed wooden beams made from trees that stood 1,000 years ago as the Tory grandee told me how locals built a battering ram to attack the monks during the Peasants' Revolt, as he grinned from ear to ear. Tebbit had never thought much of the landed gentry: 'I'm not against them but I'm not particularly in favour of them,' he said in 1990. 'Why should I be? I don't hold any brief for someone whose only contribution is to have been born in the right bed.'

The very land contested during the Great Revolt would eventually become a byword for self-determination via home ownership. After Margaret Thatcher became its leader in 1975, the Conservative Party ramped up its efforts to win over voters who had moved to the new towns. Their pitch was based on the promise of prosperity and home ownership, rather than the Labour Party's old appeals to class solidarity. Britain might have at times during the 1970s felt as if it was living through perpetual economic turmoil, yet the economy of the south-east flourished relative to other regions, particularly in comparison to the industrial north. People who had grown up in pokey London flats were saving for first homes outside London, looking for a bit more space, a garden and somewhere to park the car. The Conservatives were tapping into a desire that had come to shape the modern history of Essex – people moving north and east in search of more space and a home of their own. In 1980, when Thatcher's new Conservative government gave council tenants the right to buy their homes, the policy was launched with a photo opportunity in the kitchen of a terraced house at 39 Amersham Road in Harold Hill, the large estate in Romford. Built in the 50s by London County Council, the house had been sold to its council tenants, the Patterson family, for just over £8,000. The new policy sparked a grand sell-off along the Thames corridor, stretching from east London to the Essex coast, and across the country at large. Barking and Dagenham lost 48,500 council units to the policy, while in Basildon, home ownership shot up from 53 per cent in 1981 to 71 per cent in 1996.

It is assumed that Right to Buy was a purely Conservative idea, but to a degree the Tories were following the prevailing societal trends. Home ownership passed 50 per cent in 1970 – not under the Conservatives, but under Labour, the party that built the welfare state. In 1961 Britain's Central Office for Information released a pamphlet entitled 'Social Changes in Britain', essentially a marketing tool for advertisers to learn more about television audiences. The findings it recounted painted a picture of a new consumer Britain. Hire-purchase debt had doubled in a little over five years, from £461 million to £927 million. Almost 40 per cent of new houses and flats were privately built, and when they moved in, new homeowners would buy their new sofas and fridges on credit. Reporting on the pamphlet in January 1963, the *Television Mail* wrote how the 'London ITV area' – an area of transmission that took in Henley-on-Thames to the west of London, to Southend and, across the Thames, the Isle of

Margaret Thatcher hands over the deeds of 39 Amersham
Road, Harold Hill, to the Patterson family.

Sheppey to the east, and from Bedfordshire to the north of
the capital all the way down to the south coast – had experienced a population increase of 6.4 per cent. At the same time,
the population of Greater London had declined by 2.1 per
cent. 'Thus "Greater London" – with its wealth and prestige

– now reaches out beyond the Green Belt, beyond even the new towns, to a circle with a radius of 50 miles from Hyde Park Corner.'

The relative affluence of the Londoners moving out to Essex and other parts of the south-east piqued the interest of advertisers. 'With personal incomes 5 per cent above the national average, these figures indicate a uniquely prosperous and concentrated consumer market.' A table at the end of the *Television Mail* article displayed the stark difference between this newly minted patch of south-east England and the rest. For example, the percentage of houses built privately in the London ITV area between 1945 and 1961 was 41.1, compared with 34.1 across Britain. There were 127.2 cars per thousand in this area as opposed to 107.8 in the rest of the country. Thirty per cent of homes in the sweet spot had refrigerators, compared to 19.7 per cent everywhere else.

The existence of this new London ITV Area would suggest that the metropolis had broken out of its borders years before the fact was recognised by more official channels. Greater London was born on April Fool's Day 1965, after which the Essex boroughs of Barking, Chingford, Dagenham, East Ham, Hornchurch, Ilford, Leyton, Romford, Walthamstow, Wanstead, West Ham and Woodford were dissolved into five new Greater London boroughs: Barking and Dagenham, Havering, Newham, Redbridge and Waltham Forest. The electrification of trains meant that the new suburbs and towns in Essex were now viable options as bases for commuting workers. A piece in *The Sphere* magazine in 1956 fretted over the news that the railway line from Liverpool Street in the City of London was being electrified all the way to Chelmsford, Essex's county town. 'London was growing ever nearer. Would the electrification result in suburbia engulfing the ancient county town of Essex?' Chelmsford feared the invasion, reported the

Essex Chronicle three years earlier, of not only 'the bowler hat brigade with their brief cases and their umbrellas', but also of the less well-mannered 'barrow boys and spivs'. 'The Invasion Is On!' reported the *Essex Chronicle* after being told that Chelmsford's estate agents reported hundreds of interested enquiries from London once the news of electrification was out.

The rise of the commuter created a countryside backlash. 'People who live in the real country, that is Lincolnshire or Norfolk, believe that London begins at Chelmsford, and most very good country addresses can be assessed by their varying degrees of incommutability,' wrote the chronicler of village life, Ronald Blythe, in *Tatler and Bystander*, 1962. 'East Anglia at its worst is only three hours from London but its gateway is Liverpool Street station, a place of Doré-like horror which has kept all but the very brave and the quite insensitive out of the region for a century . . .'

The concept of classlessness has long been trumpeted by a type of pundit we might now call neoliberal. However, the idea of classlessness as a goal to strive towards did not begin as a Thatcherite or Reaganist idea that typified the transatlantic aspiration of the time, but one originally touted by the left only to be later appropriated by the right. Alfred Salter, the Bermondsey MP from 1922 until 1945, in laying out his plans for his south London constituency, said: 'We do not merely want to ensure a rather more tolerable existence for the "working classes". We are out to abolish the working classes as such and create a classless society. That is what we mean by socialism.'

Classless, by the 1960s, was beginning to mean something different entirely. In her 1966 piece for *New Society*, Anne Lapping painted a picture of a new kind of commuter future, with bowler hats and umbrellas becoming a thing of the past. 'Commuting is no longer an upper-class activity.' Lapping described how rising house prices were driving young Londoners 'from the swinging city' to new builds in Essex and Kent.

The consumer instinct was starting to pervade the previously pragmatic approach to housing city wantaways typified by Becontree and the new towns. Under the heading 'Sub American Dream', Lapping reported elements of cutting corners for quick sale, eschewing experimental or communal architectural practices for profiteering, and she wrote witheringly about the way the new estates seemed to work against the fight for gender equality. 'Well-paid secretarial work in London was swapped for local work – from £13 a week as a typist in London to £8 as a telephonist in Ashford.' Women found it hard to adjust, and the sudden divorce from the wider family networks in London was also hard to take. Lapping told the story of a woman who was 'bitterly upset at not being able to travel into town from Chelmsford to see her sick father, and who missed all her old friends'. The sweetener for some of the women came in the form of a pay rise for their commuting husbands and the opportunity of a bigger house, a state of affairs that seemed to circumvent the nascent feminism of the times.

As many working-class voters simultaneously migrated both out of the city and towards the Conservatives, London's increasingly Labour-voting middle classes were plugging the gaps they left. A wave of gentrification crept eastwards from Islington as bedraggled Georgian terraces were snapped up. 'The burrowing out of new postal districts inside the city is like a drive into a new frontier,' wrote Jonathan Raban in his 1974 book, *Soft City*. 'Like a frontier, it produces edgy and painful encounters with the indigenous population (the sitting tenants, some of whom are immigrants, some cockneys), who are alternatively harassed with eviction notices and raised rents, and romanticised, like Fenimore Cooper

Alison Steadman and Tim Stern in *Abigail's Party*, 1977

Indians, as "real" people.' And like any idealised protagonist, they aren't supposed to leave their rightful, authentic place.

In 1977, Mike Leigh wrote a play that would come to be seen as emblematic of the moment, a satire of the new individualism taking shape within and without the capital – and a seminal document in the invention of Essex. *Abigail's Party*, which played to packed houses over 104 nights in Hampstead and was later adapted for TV for the BBC's *Play for Today* series to popular acclaim, told the story of a suburban soirée that descended into a tragic farce. It was set in Romford, the old market town turned commuter town that was subsumed by London's boundary changes in 1965, but which many still regard as 'culturally Essex'.

The play's most enduring creation was Beverly, a monstrous, power-dressing proponent of bettering oneself through consumer choice. In developing the character, the Liverpudlian actor Alison Steadman, who was married to

Leigh at the time of the play, drew upon her experiences at East 15 Acting School in Loughton, Essex in the late 60s. 'There wasn't that thing of Essex girls, yet,' Steadman told me on the phone. 'But I knew of a girl who would say: "Oh, me and my sister went out at the weekend." They would pick pubs that had posh cars in the car park. You look for a pub where there is an Aston Martin parked outside and say: there is money in there.'

These women were the early adopters of the consumer lifestyle that became so tightly linked to Essex. 'The life I'd come from was so different to that,' said Steadman. 'It was Liverpool, the start of the Beatles and all that, but there was no sense of being "upwardly mobile".' Whereas Liverpool and other northern towns and cities had their own industries, traditions and rituals that set them apart from London, much of Essex had become a place to escape family memories of poverty in the city. 'People weren't satisfied at what had been going on for years and years with their parents and grandparents,' Steadman said. 'This was a new time when they weren't just going to sit in some little house somewhere and put up with it.'

In 1979, two years after *Abigail's Party* made its debut, the working-class Essex enclave of Basildon, along with many Labour-voting constituencies in south-east England, switched to the Tories as Thatcher swept to power. For many observers, *Abigail's Party* had become a warning about where this new assertive individualism would lead. In a 2002 article marking the play's 25th anniversary, the writer Simon Fanshawe expressed what had, by then, become a familiar view of the new Essex voters who had helped sweep Thatcher to power. 'These were the people who turned their backs on Labour and thought that by buying their own houses in a new neighbourhood, hanging net curtains to shut themselves off from a world they didn't have to look at and thus care about, they could take over the country for themselves.' Then, in words that seem like they could have been lifted from a more recent jeremiad against people who voted for Brexit or Boris Johnson, Fanshawe continued: 'Not that they knew that was what they were doing, or understood the effect it might have on the rest of us. They were far too self-centred for that.'

One day in 1990, the journalist Simon Heffer was travelling from Essex to London to attend the funeral of Claudie Baynham, the wife of Peregrine Worsthorne, his editor at the *Sunday Telegraph*. On the train, Heffer encountered a fellow commuter, a City trader who was travelling in from Essex and talking on a brick-sized phone. But instead of making an important multimillion-pound deal or explaining to his boss he was held up on the train and was going to be late, he was on the phone to his bookies. 'He was putting money on a horse,' said Heffer incredulously.

At the wake in Kensington, to cheer everyone up, Heffer told the story about the bloke on the train. One of the attendees, the *Sunday Telegraph*'s deputy editor Frank Johnson, who had himself grown up in the East End, told Heffer that he had identified a fascinating social phenomenon. 'I said: "Yes, he's Essex man!"' recalled Heffer, 'and Frank said: "It's brilliant! Do it, do it!"' So I went away and wrote the piece and it appeared the following Sunday.'

Essex man, in Heffer's portrait, was in thrall to excess without necessarily being able to handle it. 'When one walks through the City most evenings, the pools of vomit into which one may step have usually been put there by Essex man, whose greatly enhanced wealth has exceeded his breeding in terms of alcoholic capacity,' he wrote. The phrase, Heffer told me, was a deliberate echo of 'Neanderthal man' – implying that Essex man was the missing link between

'He expects to win, whether he is the best man or not'

Edward Collet's Essex Man illustration
for the *Sunday Telegraph*, 1990

the lumpen proles of the new town estates and the bright new citizens emerging under the stewardship of Margaret Thatcher's party. The editorial was published in the *Sunday Telegraph* and accompanied by an illustration by Edward Collet depicting a small-foreheaded individual in a shiny suit standing in front of his brand new Ford motor and (presumably former council) house replete with satellite dish. It appeared just before the prime minister's final Conservative Party conference and seemed to rubber-stamp her legacy.

In all his boorishness and bigotry, Essex man was offered by Heffer as England's saviour: 'He is as Boswell said of Johnson, a stern, true-born Englishman, and fully prejudiced against all other nations.' Recreation was 'drinking with his mates, watching sports on Sky' . . . Milton Friedman and Ayn Rand were his heroes (which was probably a fit of projection for Heffer) and self-improvement was the central tenet of his existence. 'He is unencumbered by any "may the best man win" philosophy,' Heffer wrote. 'He expects to win whether he's the best or not.'

The editorial might be described as a form of revenge. On his first day of term in 1966, six-year-old Simon Heffer had gasped at the shocking sight laid out before him. Before the summer break, his school, in the lower reaches of an Essex village called Woodham Ferrers, had backed onto fields. Now, it was surrounded by hundreds of houses. 'It was awesome to see that transformation,' he told me on a warm late-summer afternoon in his vast back garden in Great Leighs, an Essex village not far from where he grew up. 'That was the moment I realised that nothing is for ever.' Yet Heffer said he saw something in these incomers that seemed new in the scruffy agricultural environs of his home, something he admired. 'They had a serious work ethic,' he said. 'They did anything they could to better themselves.'

In Heffer's editorial, Essex man was depicted as escaping

life in one of the new towns, described in the editorial as 'nasty workers barracks' that were 'among the closest representations in Britain to the crushing townscapes of Stalinist Eastern Europe'. But it wasn't just the architecture that put Heffer off the new towns; it was also the fact that this was a state-run initiative and therefore counter to his high Tory ideology. In Heffer's editorialising, Essex man had risen to prominence in reaction to the contempt shown 'by his patronising masters' – so he 'chose to fight back by economic means'.

Essex man was not a complete fiction; he described something rooted in the reality of south-east England. In making the caricature so cut and dried, so against the implicitly socialist principles of the new towns and so pro new-build homes, fast cars and credit, Heffer was describing the conscious realignment of what social mobility in Britain now looked like after more than a decade of Thatcherism. What Essex man was, however, was an exaggeration, and one that was useful for the Tories as it claimed working-class social mobility exclusively for Thatcherism, rather than it being part of a longer process you could trace back to the rise of Keir Hardie and Labour in metropolitan Essex in the late nineteenth century. The editorial freely admitted, too, that Essex was more an ideal than a location bound by geography: 'For spiritual purposes, Essex is to be found all over the newly affluent parts of the outer London suburbs.'

For the rump of Essex who identified with Essex man, here was a prime minister turned godhead who, if not actually omnipresent, managed to achieve the closest thing to it as she was transmitted into the living rooms of the voters in newly bought council houses ready to lap up rhetoric on low taxation and self-determination. When we spoke at his house in Bury St Edmunds, Norman Tebbit didn't recall having discussed Essex with Thatcher after she became leader of the Conservative Party and eventually prime minister of the country, putting him in a prominent cabinet position as minister for trade and then employment. But he was clear, he said, that it 'fitted with what I wanted to do and what she wanted to do'.

There was, and still is, a genuine affection for Thatcher in the part of Essex I grew up. Bill Sharp, a 'self-confessed "Essex man"' who had a picture of the former prime minister in his bedroom, was interviewed after the death of Thatcher, for the BBC. Indeed, Sharp even has a good shout at the title of the world's first example of Essex man, though he might claim his manners were better than Heffer's portrait suggested.

Sharp grew up in Manor Park near Romford. His father was a foreman stevedore, a manual labourer who helped unload the great ships at the Royal Albert Docks. It was precarious work, where each morning the foreman picked gangs from the gathered labourers. In the early 1960s, Sharp's dad took him there at 15, to see if he wanted to follow in his father's footsteps. 'I asked where the toilets were, went into the toilet, and there was just a plank of wood with six holes in and people sitting there. No doors anywhere. I thought, that's disgusting, I can't handle that, I'm not gonna do that.'

When Sharp was a teenager during the 1960s, a career adviser at his school in Forest Gate, which was then still in Essex, suggested becoming a stockbroker in the City. So eager was he to join the besuited commuter ranks that he told his mum he wasn't feeling very well and bunked off school to seek his fortune as a messenger in the City at five pounds a week. He worked his way through the system, eventually going down to the floor as a trainee, then a dealer, and then, on his 21st birthday he became the youngest member of the stock exchange. Sharp recalled that it 'became a bit of a thing' in the City to hire East End boys, who were regarded as 'barrow boys'. 'That was a logic that I used when I employed people. I thought about their ability to buy and sell and be streetwise . . . We needed to change the system and these guys were young, eager, keen and hungry.' Sharp said he remembered he hired one guy after encountering him cleaning his car at a petrol station in Kent. 'He's now a major name in the City running a huge concern of his own.'

In the same year, 1968, Sharp got married and bought a house on Canvey Island, which had only just started to issue mortgages fifteen years after the flood. Sharp suggested his move to Canvey Island was part of a wider rejection of the politics of his old stamping ground. 'I looked around in Manor Park and East Ham, which had been socialist automatically all my life. People automatically voted Labour, and I didn't understand that when I saw the state of the place.' The slow decline of the industries that once supported East Ham was showing in the streets. 'You looked at East Ham Town Hall and that was splendour personified but you looked at people's homes that people were living in and the state of the streets, it was quite dreadful.' As Sharp made his way in the City, he noticed the ascent of Thatcher in frontline politics. 'Let people decide what they want to do with their lives. Magnificent. From then, I was hooked.' Sharp told me he saw the unionised country as not a collective entity, but a place where people were controlled. He was, he said, a 'big supporter of looking after your own wallet'.

The arrival of 'Essex man' dovetailed with a general upturn in the fortunes of a City of London that had for years existed under the threat of obsolescence. There had already been hints of a more vibrant future for the Square Mile, such as the rise of eurodollar loans and the eurobond markets in the 1950s and 60s, but controls still applied to the stock exchange during the 1970s, the Labour government stopping capital investment abroad unless it had permission from the

Treasury. When Geoffrey Howe abolished foreign exchange controls in 1979, just months after Margaret Thatcher was elected, the Conservative government signalled an end to such caution.

If the foundations for the modern idea of Essex were laid during Thatcher's first term with Right to Buy, it was the deregulation of the City of London in 1986, during her second term, which gave rise to Essex man. The arrival of the London International Financial Futures Exchange (LIFFE) in 1982 had constituted a brave new world, a 7,000 square-foot trading pit built over the cobbles of the Royal Exchange courtyard to resemble the raucous American-style arenas. It filled the old building with a cacophony of the new city, the roar of commuters after long boozy lunches.

The Big Bang reforms brought in by the Thatcher government were helped by huge advancements in information technology. The City of London's position grew in relation to its rivals New York and Tokyo, globalisation favouring London's time zone between Wall Street and the Asian markets. Thatcher launched the new Broadgate development next to Liverpool Street in 1985, observing that it was the largest single development to take place in the City of London since the Great Fire of London in 1666. Essex man's rise was also a story of modernisation, dissolving the centuries-old rules of rank and file. Suddenly it didn't matter as much if you had been to the right school. 'City firms could no longer afford just to take people from Oxbridge or old Etonians to work,' Heffer told me. 'People who came from council estates who had that instinct for making money – this was their opportunity.'

In his editorial, Heffer wrote how Essex man had 'transformed the social mix in the Square Mile' and 'the Big Bang', as it became known, scaled up the City to become more outward facing and less beholden to the clique of wealthy financiers that had long held sway, making it easier for those outside of the fraternity to join the London Stock Exchange. Foreign financial operations moved in, often as a reaction to restrictions in their own countries, resulting in huge influxes of capital. The reforms meant an end to the cosy cartel of British financial firms and the volume of dealing ballooned.

Essex man's brashness became a shorthand for a reanimated City. Heffer achieved what every political journalist surely wants to – to invent a phrase that passes into not just common parlance but into the chamber of the House of Commons. Essex man became such a gargantuan figure in the landscape of UK discourse, public figures and politicians felt the need to proclaim whether they were for or against this imaginary (but very real) figure, and what he represented. There was an Essex man cartoon strip in the tabloid, *Today*. The *Guardian* reported that Ford were to launch an 'Essex man' Fiesta in 1992 (although it never seemed to materialise from the production line). It entered the Oxford English dictionary: 'British derogatory, a term used to denote a supposed new type of Conservative voter, to be found esp. in London and the south-east of England in the late 1980s, typically (esp. contemptuously) characterised as a brash, self-made young businessman who benefitted from the entrepreneurial wealth created by Thatcherite policies.'

And yet, although Essex man became representative of the salt-of-the-earth common man, its success was powered in no small part by the wishes of the politicians and journalists behind it. It told a story that was both extremely general (Essex man was a heterosexual male who desired improved material circumstances) and extremely specific (Essex man loved the Conservative Party because they promised to improve his material circumstances through low taxation and a raid on welfare spending, under the guise of promoting meritocracy).

Doing Very Well

When Andy Coulson was hired by the then Conservative leader of the opposition, David Cameron, as his director of communications in 2007, it was described in the right-wing press as the return of Essex man to the Conservative Party after they had been scared off by John Major and the fallout of Thatcher's poll tax debacle. Coulson brought with him no small amount of baggage – he had resigned as editor of the *News of the World* due to a reporter and a private investigator being jailed for phone hacking under his watch – but the Tory leader obviously thought his supposed common touch was worth the risk. Here was access to an electoral soothsayer, a direct link to swing-voting Essex man. Coulson resigned in 2011 when it was clear phone hacking at the *News of the World* had reached industrial levels. He was arrested and charged with conspiracy to intercept voicemails, sentenced to eighteen months and taken to Belmarsh prison in south-east London in 2014.

The boom of Essex and the power of a British journalism pumped full of advertisement money were interlinked. Coulson's first job was at the *Basildon Echo* as a trainee at 16 and it was there he did his journalism indentures. After the reporters had filed, they could go down a staircase to the print hall and see it come off the press for the evening edition. 'The building would rattle,' Coulson told me. 'That bit was romantic, to see a freshly minted paper come off a press and you open it up and even if your name is on a piece about a cheque presentation, which I think my first piece was, it was unbelievable.'

Coulson has long traded off the fact he was born in Basildon, describing his family as 'classic London overspill', his grandfather a 'pioneer ... a proper trade union, flat-cap-wearing, travelling the country kind of blue-collar worker'. He told me he remembered Depeche Mode's Dave Gahan coming round for dinner (he was friends with Coulson's brother). 'He can't have been more than 14, 15. I just remember him being stunned by the fact that we were eating spaghetti Bolognese, which was a new experience for him – it was a relatively new experience for us too – and my mother was teaching him how to use his fork and spoon.'

New towns encouraged people to swap the solidarity of London streets for new car-dominated environs, and to expect more than the familial tales of impoverishment downriver. At the same time, decades of improvement in workers' rights and the growing strength of the unions paradoxically created the perfect opportunity for the forthright Thatcherite politics that followed. Essex man did not grow in a vacuum. Britain was already becoming an individualistic place in the 1970s. That decade is remembered in Britain for being a volatile period for industrial action in part (in addition to the effects of inflation) because the growing individualism of the age had brought about a fragile and combustible collectivity. How the unions bargained – free, collective bargaining, negotiating aggressively for their own members – had been verging on the individualistic for years. Trade unionism was changing: in the 1940s and 50s members were deferential to their headquarters but by the late 60s there had been an explosion in unofficial strikes, part of an anarchic, febrile culture that often held union bosses based in London in contempt. Although this brand of bombastic and chaotic union action grabbed the headlines, what it in fact reflected was how collective effort was fragmenting as society became more materialistic.

Unions became, like the country, assertive about the individual rights of individual members of particular unions against everybody else. To a degree, trade unionism itself was becoming less ideological, and the perception became that people going on strike, such as at Ford Dagenham in the 70s, were maybe doing it for slightly selfish reasons: prioritising protecting their holiday in Spain rather than thinking about how, if they bring down Callaghan's Labour government, Thatcher's Tories will be waiting to form a government.

The fabled 'Winter of Discontent' wave of industrial action from November 1978 to March 1979, which contributed to Thatcher's successful election bid, began when Ford workers, including those in Dagenham, rejected a 5 per cent pay offer. Dagenham had long been at the centre of the struggle between ideologies within trade unionism. The shop steward combine committee (essentially a group of elected union representatives) in Dagenham was attacked for being 'a union within a union', controlling funds and enjoying huge support, and even publishing its own newspaper. *New Society* reported on 13 May 1965 that the management at Ford Motor Company in Dagenham had successfully broken up the Communist organisations that were once thriving there. The notorious Dagenham women machinists' strike in 1968 triggered Barbara Castle's white paper, 'In Place of Strife', which set out how to curtail industrial action, signalling the beginning of the end of national tolerance of industrial action and was built upon with glee by the Conservatives. In came a more punitive and employer-centric work culture that is actively hostile to unions, one which we are still living in the reverberation of: in 2022, in the context of a much more stagnant wage economy, MPs approved plans drawn up by the Conservative government to allow agency workers to replace those going on strike, potentially leaving strikers without any real power and ripping up workers' rights in the process.

The decline of the unions, through consensus, coercion and the political warfare of the Thatcher government, created the conditions for Essex man. Although men tended to dominate the discourse of unionism, this disguised the fact that the unions had become extremely mixed, with many of the newer members being women and minorities. Indeed, *Race Today* reported in 1976 that 60 per cent of workers at Ford Dagenham were black or Asian. A lot of the people who went on strike during the 'Winter of Discontent' were 'very badly paid women', the political historian Andy Beckett told me. 'You can almost say trade unionism that stayed in London rather than going out to Essex and other places, was GLC [Greater London Council] trade unionism, which was very politically ambitious, and evolved into Corbynism.' Unions split between those committed to a kind of internationalist solidarity that is still recognisable today and those with more parochial, materialistic concerns. Unionised workers started to represent a strange and historically novel class position: the skilled elite of the working class.

The rise of a new white-collar working class was singled out for a 1968 Cambridge study, *The Affluent Worker*, which suggested that the embourgeoisement of the new working class had led to a transactional rather than emotional attitude to employment. It could therefore no longer be assumed that workers would vote Labour in their own collective interests (although the study stopped short of suggesting the seismic shift from Labour that was to come). The migration of industry to the new towns fragmented the cause further, with unionised incomers from the East End such as Basildon's Joe Morgan coming up against an already entrenched, and unsympathetic, Tory coalition of local politicians and gentry types. Morgan reminisced about how he was told to 'get back to London' by Conservative MP for Billericay Bernard Braine when standing up for the plight of his fellow new arrivals, and was repeatedly sacked from building jobs for organising workforces into unions, which the Development Corporation, the ultimate employer of all builders in the town, was not too keen on. The BDC apparently threatened to evict anyone who went on strike.

Paul Harrison's book *Inside the Inner City* painted a bleak picture of the collapse of manufacturing in London in the 60s and 70s. He visited Lea Bridge industrial estate on the marshes of the River Lea on the old Essex / east London border, near to where the industrialised miracle of West Ham occurred to the south. '[T]he place, like so much British manufacturing, was coming to resemble the aftermath of a neutron-bomb,' he wrote, describing a sea of To Let signs and abandoned warehouses where there were once vibrant workplaces. GLC manufacturing jobs were disappearing and opportunity was displaced to the new towns, where many of the factories and the offices were moving, while Islington was becoming a byword for unemployment, something that sounds ludicrous when considering the much higher than average house prices and median incomes to be found in the north London borough today.

The Long Good Friday, a 1979 film which centres around a corrupt deal between criminals and local politicians to develop the London docklands, starring a peerless Bob Hoskins, in hindsight betrays a sense of knowing where the country was going better than most observers did. The movie's East Ham-born writer, Barrie Keeffe, utilised his years as a journalist on the *Stratford Express*. 'My impression is a lot of money changed hands in town halls,' he told the *Guardian* in 2015. 'It was secretive. You could sense something enormous was about to happen.' The upshot is London Docklands Development Corporation cleared out the rusting docks, resulting in the departure of any lingering cockneys. 'They went to Harlow, to Essex. Some of them were happy,' Keefe said. 'But it wasn't London. It was a purge, really.'

The tectonic shifts in class expectations in the decades after the Second World War, the establishment of commuter trains directly into the City and Thatcher's reforms meant that Essex man was in the right place at the right time to return to the old stomping ground and exploit the new opportunities on offer. When the new business district Canary Wharf was built over the derelict docklands, the city's financial industry expanded eastwards, its suited employees ending up in the same place their parents once lived and worked, ensuring the legend of the barrow boy done good in the City grew even greater. Former East Enders who had swapped London flats for a house on the other side of the green belt were now commuting back and forth, and doing very well for themselves.

The lives of those who had left London were becoming a popular cultural trope in themselves. Mike Leigh returned to the London–Essex aspirational borderlands for his 1983 made-for-TV film *Meantime*, which signified the sudden estrangement between escapees and their supposedly less well-off extended families they had left behind, through an awkward opening scene in which the forthright uncle John welcomes his Bethnal Green-based nephews and brother-in-law into the new-build family home in Chigwell, fussily commanding that they take their shoes off before coming in. *Birds of a Feather* was also set in Chigwell, and the BBC sitcom about two sisters who end up living a life of luxury after their husbands are sent to jail for bank robbery put the Conservative-voting south-west Essex town on the map. The show's creators Laurence Marks and Maurice Gran came up with Chigwell in the late 1980s after a policeman told them it had more houses paid for in cash than anywhere else in Britain. More broadly, Chigwell 'represented new money, unabashed,' said Gran. 'There is a lot of snobbery involved, and it can be liberal metropolitan snobbery as much as Home Counties conservative snobbery. I don't think people have to apologise for striving and achieving.'

While *Birds of a Feather* was a warmer and more subtle commentary on class than many remember, the sitcom helped give the world the female counterpart to Essex man:

Essex girl. Over time, the names of its lead characters, Sharon and Tracey, came to represent a type of sexually promiscuous and somewhat dim woman said to come from the county. By the mid 90s, the threat of Essex girl was everywhere. 'Is Diana now an Essex Girl?' the *Daily Mail* fretted in 1994 while reporting on an editorial in the society magazine *Tatler*, which begged: 'Will the real Diana please sit down, turn off *Birds of a Feather*, forget the Queen Vic [the pub from the soap *EastEnders*] and dress like a princess.' In the *Mail* the following day, the writer Anne de Courcy recoiled at the 'Sharonisation of Diana'.

The Sharonisation panic peaked when it was reported later that year that Volkswagen had dropped the name for the British version of its new people carrier, Sharan, because it sounded too much like the *Birds of a Feather* character. 'Some years ago we could probably have stuck with Sharan for the UK, but this Essex girl thing has arrived and we don't want to risk it,' a Volkswagen UK spokesman told the Press Association. (Volkswagen's head office in Germany eventually overruled the decision.)

In typical tabloid fashion, alongside all the stories poking fun at Essex types, there came the occasional article that relied on the opposite premise: that people from Essex were good-hearted strivers cruelly judged by the old establishment elites. In 1998, an 18-year-old student from Harlow called Tracy made the front pages after she was ridiculed by a Cambridge don during her interview for a place at Trinity College. 'There was a poem by TS Eliot which included a line of Greek,' Tracy Playle told the *Daily Mail*. 'Dr Griffiths said: "Being from Essex you won't know what these funny squiggles are."' Playle left the interview in tears.

When I spoke to her, Playle remembered the incident well. 'Everyone loves a good Essex girl story, don't they? And I'm Tracy from Essex as well,' she said. In the end, Playle secured a place at Warwick University, while it came out in the press that Griffiths, who died recently, was the son of a Liverpool docker. 'He should have had a level of empathy he clearly didn't,' said Playle. 'The fact that we even call it "upward mobility" is questionable – it's not very upwards in my perspective.'

In 1992, the *Essex Chronicle* commissioned an Anglia University academic to write a report about the way people from Essex were portrayed in the press. 'In exploring the stereotype,' David Crouch concluded, 'we discover more about the media than those it sought to depict.' While Essex man was valourised by politicians for challenging class boundaries, Crouch suggested that the persistence of the Essex caricature actually proved the opposite – that snobbery was still alive and well. 'Is the myth, then, a search for the New Classless Britain,' he wrote, 'or an extraordinary example, by its own action in erecting the stereotype, of exactly the reverse?'

Where the Peasants' Revolt failed, the contemporary Thatcherite reboot, speeding forth and vanquishing everything in its wake, succeeded in becoming an archetype recognised by the country at large. By the 90s, Essex was no longer just a county in south-east England. It was a shorthand for the way the whole country seemed to be changing, for the emergence of a brash, crass new individualism – and soon, it would become a shorthand for the discomfort with those changes, for a fear about what Essex man and Essex girl threatened to reveal about the true nature of Englishness.

The easy (going on cheesy) smile of David Amess, my MP growing up in Southend West, seemed to sum up the confidence felt by Essex in the 90s. When he was murdered during a violent attack by a knife-wielding terrorist sympathetic to the causes of Islamic State in his constituency surgery on an October Friday in 2021, it felt like Essex man himself had been killed. In a way he was a Thatcher creation: 'the working-class boy made good'. He grew up in an old, terraced house in Forest Gate, Newham. His father was an electrician for the London Electricity Board, his mother was a seamstress, a cook and, later, a tea lady in the City of London. Amess proudly told of how, when growing up, his family didn't have a car, telephone, or fridge. He walked two and a half miles to school every day. He was in awe of the House of Commons after he became an MP, and was confronted by so many colleagues who were more eloquent. He didn't have any connections, so did not push to be a minister. He instead decided to spread the gospel of the Essex constituencies that he represented: first Basildon (1983–1997) and then Southend West (1997–2021). He became a publicist for his community, forcing his 'I Love Basildon' and Southend City campaigns onto any parliamentarian who would listen, often bringing the matter up at prime minister's questions.

I grew up a few roads away from Belfairs Methodist Church, where Amess was killed. My parents still live in the area, an edge-of-nondescript working- to lower-middle-class suburb that is slightly estranged from the better-off side of Leigh-on-Sea nearer the estuary. The church squats at the end of a banal, just-so drag of shops: chip shop. Off-licence. Co-op. Bakery. Beauty salon. Hairdresser. Chinese. Balloon shop ('Balloonacy'). A vigil was held for Amess at the old Woodcutters playing field, where I used to play football. By the time I arrived, most mourners had left, but the circle of candles they had lit illuminated the patchy turf around them. By the church, outside broadcast vans were pitched for the night. A woman wiped away a tear and comforted her teenage daughter as they laid a bouquet on the floor outside the church, where a pile of flowers had been left by residents. Amess was remembered fondly after his killing, although my parents – an art graduate-into-trainee-into-teacher father and hospital-cleaner-into-trainee-into-teacher mother – weren't his target audience. But he fitted the area like a glove, a champion of property ownership and leaving the EU, even if some found his grinning and constant PR drive for Southend hollow and hammy and believed that it did the cause of the town some harm. He dressed up in armour on horseback to celebrate receiving his knighthood from the Queen. When Southend was awash with drugs in the 1990s, he tackled the issue with misguided gusto, standing up in the House of Commons and arguing against 'Cake, the made-up drug' after being sucked into an infamous stunt by the comedian Chris Morris for the satirical show *Brass Eye*. But then attention-grabbing interventions were Amess's stock-in-trade. He won his first seat in 1983, but by 1992, it looked like the writing was on the wall for the Tories in Basildon. He was teased by Labour activists confident of a Kinnock government that he was on his way out. But he won again after fighting a campaign that saw him utilising his own motorhome, decorated with blue balloons, as an election surgery.

Basildon, once a beacon of Labour's post-war consensus politics, voted for Thatcher's party in every election she fought – until the name of the town itself came to somehow represent the societal shift that had taken place from socialist-influenced policymaking to a more cut-throat neoliberalism. '[The] organised working class is disappearing as people have more individualistic aims, more privatised aims,' Amess, told *Channel 4 News* with an air of triumph in 1992, despite his slim majority in that election. 'They buy their houses, they purchase their shares.' For Basildon, and by extension Essex, and maybe even the country itself, there seemed to be no coming back.

After Amess's famous 1992 victory, a new subspecies was born: Basildon man, who was really just Essex man under a new, more pointedly localised name. The new town might have been built in an era of post-war welfarism, but by the 90s it was treated by the political press as a window into the voting intention of the sought-after 'C2s' – advertising speak for the skilled working class, who were seen as able to swing British general elections. But Basildon is where the Essex myth collided with reality. While the new town was painted as the centre of the Essex phenomenon, it didn't fit into the picture of Essex as a place for the newly wealthy to make hay. In the 90s, the centre-left thinktank Demos conducted a survey of skilled workers in Basildon: in 1992, 64 per cent earned less than £15,000 (just under £30,000 in today's money), not exactly loadsamoney by the standards of the south-east; by 1997, 32 per cent earned less than £10,000.

The Conservative Party may have succeeded in identifying the desires of these children of London, but it didn't offer much to satisfy them. What it offered instead was an illusory promise. 'There was this false understanding that Margaret Thatcher was a strong woman who could provide economic opportunities, she understood you wanting to get on,' Basildon's former MP Angela Smith, who won a majority as Labour returned in 1997, told me. 'But the policies were so damaging if you look at unemployment, you look at the industry. Look how Basildon has changed.'

Data gleaned from a 2018 council study showed Basildon to be the sixth most unequal town in the country: a place that contained a quarter of the most deprived areas of Essex, despite housing an eighth of its total population. Pitched against such evidence, the myth of Essex as the great Thatcherite success story says more about the will of the Conservative commentariat than anything else. Right to Buy drained the fabric of society as the money received was never invested back into building more housing, and created inequality street by street between those who had bought and those who hadn't. In the mid-1980s, my parents bought the council house my sister and I grew up in, but we didn't feel like triumphant beneficiaries of some economic miracle. A microclimate of inequality existed on our street, separating homeowners from council tenants. I remember my mum and dad refusing to sign one London-born home-owner's petition to have a renter (his sister) evicted for being the mother of a 'problem family'. No one seemed any richer, just further apart.

Amess's successful capture of Basildon in 1992 was organised by the now-MP for Rayleigh and Wickford, Mark Francois, then a burgeoning Basildon councillor. 'I have no doubt that his ability to find prospective Conservative voters and get them out to vote on polling day was instrumental to my election success,' Amess said. Francois, the anti-EU MP for Rayleigh and Wickford, who grew up in Basildon and worked in the City before entering politics, was lovingly described as 'every bit an Essex man' by Quentin Letts in the *Daily Mail* in 2009. In the same year, after Francois had become an MP, David Cameron promoted him to the shadow cabinet as a sop to the Eurosceptic wing of the Conservative Party. His star rose in line with an increasing demand for polaris-ing soundbites after the Brexit vote; infamous moments include Francois angrily quoting Tennyson beside a portrait of Margaret Thatcher, angrily ripping up a letter from the German CEO of Airbus about Brexit on live TV and angrily making a throat-slitting gesture as Theresa May spoke in the Commons. 'Essex man' is still a template for the barbaric, tell-it-like-it-is tone of the right-wing press – and, increasingly, the hard-man posturing of today's insurgent reactionaries.

The genius of 'Essex man' was the licence it gave politi-cians and the tabloid press to mobilise the figure's apparent authenticity to push policies further rightwards, advancing an agenda of cuts to public services and lower taxes for the rich. Essex man benefitted New Labour as much as the Tories.

'Essex man and Essex woman are coming over to today's Labour Party,' Tony Blair told the press in 1996 during a visit to Basildon. Essex man's rejection of John Major in the 1997 election dramatised a national shift from blue to red after market turmoil and repossessions put an end to the Tories' economic miracle. Yet, instead of discrediting Thatcherism, some commentators read Essex man's defection as vindication that the Blair government was right to stay close to the iron lady's economic policy.

There have been signs that the thread linking the idea of Essex to a distinctively Thatcherite model of 'every Essex man for himself' has been wearing thin, as Essex grows tired of cuts to public services after perpetual austerity and a permanently combusting Conservative Party. Perhaps one reason the Essex myth persists is the allure of an 'authentic', salt-of-the-earth England – whose views coincidentally always align with the politician currently invoking them. Right-wing ideologues, to whom Brexit was only the start of a bonfire of regulations, make confident pronouncements about 'what the working class wants' (a rhetorical style that the writer Joe Kennedy calls 'authentocracy'), fixating on flags and foreigners rather than a living wage and local services.

'We're an entrepreneurial county, we don't like being interfered with, we don't like bureaucracy,' the MP for Harwich, Bernard Jenkin, told me when I asked him why Essex voted Brexit. 'If you go to Surrey or Sussex or Buckinghamshire and the university cities like Oxford and Cambridge, you really are still in the M25 bubble. Essex is not part of the metropolitan bubble . . . People have got their feet on the ground.'

This, finally, is the magic power of 'Essex'. For it allows Jenkin – the Cambridge-educated son of a lord – to confidently proclaim that he knows the desires of the 'common man', merely by the mention of this most misunderstood of counties. If Essex did not exist, they would need to invent it.

8

Reality Bites

The A12 to Dedham Vale is a time-travelling road, a route back to the cobbled old seafaring town of Harwich, Roman Colchester and Suffolk, a county that, unlike Essex, is still celebrated for its dishevelled country squirisms. Up here in Essex's further reaches is the land of the old antiques drama, *Lovejoy*, which followed the roguish antiques dealer played by Ian McShane who never ventured south of Ingatestone but somehow reflected a more agreeable version of the swash-buckling, corner-cutting and off-the-books moonlighting of the Thatcher years.

This part of the county north of Maldon, I am often told, is the real Essex. It is an attractive narrative – that there is a sacred part of the county that has never changed, ever threat-ened by the fake Essex of the tanning salons, 'well reem' haircuts and souped-up cars creeping up from the south like a pernicious alien.

Nowhere in Essex is realer than Dedham, the old village at the heart of 'Constable Country' that is characterised by the tufty banks of the River Stour and cottages with thatched roofs that were a treat to our south Essex eyes as we got out of the car (in Southend you have to go out of your way to find a genuinely old timber-framed house, of which there only a smattering). Dedham Vale is an undoubtedly picturesque, classically English landscape – a place often considered *only* as a landscape. We walked into this flattish valley that tapers out from the Stour, a river of rambunctious English-ness, frayed grass rather than the concrete protection of the Thames sea wall. John Constable was born in 1776 in East Bergholt on the Suffolk side of the Stour, but was educated in Essex at the local grammar school at Dedham. (Both Essex and Suffolk claim Dedham Vale.) He was the son of a busi-nessman who ran the corn mill at Flatford memorialised in one of his most famous oil paintings, and so he must have felt a sense of ownership over the landscape, which was part of his family and part of him. Constable did not idealise the plight of the labourer, nor accentuate the grotesqueries of the lower orders to make a moralistic point, as William Hogarth sometimes did. His paintings instead were an attempt to convey a kind of reality, albeit a reality perceived from a place of comfort. 'His landscapes were real and familiar, not wild and remote,' wrote John Hunter in *The Essex Landscape*, 'and when figures appear they are the workers who contributed to the agricultural prosperity from which the Constable family benefitted.' While of higher status than the majority of those living around the Stour, Constable was by no means lord of the manor; as an artist he was at the mercy of patronage, and would have been painfully aware that his own class was something elusive, outside of the establishment pulling the strings.

We all stopped to eat our sandwiches. Hayley and I looked at the river as Greta and Ernest played out their injection of carbohydrates in a procession of wonky limbs and giggles. Hail came down lightly as we ate but was punctuated by bright flashes of sun, then hail again. It was a changeable day, one you felt Constable, with his obsession with clouds, would have approved of. For him, nature was always in con-stant motion, the English weather, even on the Essex-Suffolk border in summertime, liable to change. Constable's biog-rapher CR Leslie wrote that the artist painted 'atmospheric truth'. Constable himself wrote in a letter of his sensory passions for his landscape. '[T]he sound of water escaping from mill dams etc, willows, old rotten banks, slimy posts and brickwork. I love such things. As long as I do paint I shall never cease to paint such places. They have always been my delight ... I associate my "careless boyhood" to all that lies on the banks of the Stour. They made me a painter (& I am grateful), that is I had often thought of pictures of them before I had touched a pencil.'

Constable's favourite spot was Gun Hill, Langham, a vantage point from which he produced sketches in sharp pencils, soft pencils and oils that captured the swooping folds of the hills, the clusters of trees, and cloud after cloud after cloud. The critic Conal Shields suggested the fact Constable grew up under the threat of French expansionism created the conditions for a rarely unified Englishness of 'ardent patriotism and togetherness'. The wheels of the industrial revolution, of which his family business were a small cog in rural Essex, were fraying the fabric of society. In the context of the threats of a revolutionary enemy abroad and what EP Thompson called the 'erosion of traditional patterns of life' at home, Constable became 'a chief protagonist of, the myth of paradisal English past ... where winter arrived infrequently and mildly, where rich woods and ceaselessly fecund fields supported a benevolent patriarchy and a decent crew of labouring mutes'.

EH Gombrich wrote *Art and Illusion* in part to unpick how representation in art had become increasingly mixed up in the 'psychology of perception'. Constable features heavily to aid Gombrich's inquiry into whether painters are 'successful in the imitation of reality because they "see more", or do they see more because they have acquired the skill of imitation?' Either way, a painter such as Constable is, like all artists, playing a trick: they are not a clear pane of glass

The Hay Wain, painted by John Constable in 1821,
depicts the River Stour between Essex and Suffolk

through which one can see the truth but a reflection of the
artist's *perception* of reality. His paintings, wrote Gombrich,
were no more a simple representation of the 'real' than a more
abstract artist's might be. It is better to think of his work as
an inquiry, a series of experiments in recording the truth of
the movement of the landscape. 'Not the dry but the humid,
not the linear but the atmospheric, not the lasting but the
transient,' as Gombrich put it. Or in Constable's words, to
give 'one brief moment caught from fleeting time a lasting
and sober existence.'

During the nineteenth century, Constable's cherished
yeoman plenitude was threatened by what we now know to
be the story of Essex. Farmers started losing out to foreign
imports as the nineteenth century progressed, selling land
off to the railways and then to wannabe homeowners by the
plot. London's seepage, beginning in earnest when West Ham

industrialised in the nineteenth century, had created a split between the materialists and industrialists who were interested in Essex as a site for accumulation and the romantics wanting to rescue the county's sacred heritage. Dedham Vale remains an outpost for the latter. It was designated an Area of Outstanding Natural Beauty in the late 1960s after years of threatened development reached boiling point. The proposed new estates would have included 260 houses at Dedham in Essex, 220 houses at Stratford St Mary, Suffolk, and the expansion of East Bergholt, Constable's birthplace, from 2,000 to 4,000 people. The development threatened to almost double the population of the three villages, while it was feared the ever-expanding towns of Colchester and Ipswich would drip, drip into this unspoiled patch. The Dedham Vale Society, active in protecting these parts since the 1930s, stepped in, and the development was halted. The society helped turn the area into a static curiosity, using Constable's work to guard against the horrors of modern development. A fussily romantic intervention that told people what to regard as outstandingly beautiful: what could be more English than that?

There is of course something stultifyingly limiting about the terms on which we engage with Constable because of this fact. Constable paintings act as a pleasing simulacra, a shorthand destined for a cosy sitting room, a required reference for a visit to a picturesque spot in the south-east of England. If the 'unspoiled' north of the county, a shambling pastoral scene assiduously cultivated since the days of Constable, constituted the real Essex, then so must raw sewage, rheumatic infections and the high infant mortality rates that accompanied the plight of the agricultural workers who maintained the picturesque landscape. 'The Housing of the Agricultural Labourer in Essex', an 1891 report in the first ever issue of the *Essex Review* by medical officer for health for Chelmsford and Maldon Sanitary Districts Dr Thresh, was a devastating account of the sanitary conditions of rural Essex communities still reeling from agricultural depression. Dr Thresh depicted cottages bundled together on waste land – damp, rotting structures that were freezing in winter. Rheumatic and chest infections were a result. 'The air space in the sleeping rooms is found to average very little over that which is found in the worst slums of Manchester.'

With Constable Country, then, one has to fight against seeing it through the eyes of what we have been told to see. But then, has Essex ever been any other way? The Essex of the rural idyll stubbornly persists in part as a commuter ideal, divorced, as we are, from the days of Essex when the county was a shorthand for agricultural toil and bucolic muteness. 'Restaged and reappropriated as the past, history is often also appreciated for its "timelessness",' wrote Patrick Wright in *On Living in an Old Country.* 'This paradoxical sense of time-lessness existing where one could be forgiven for expecting to find a stress on historicity and change is in part a measure of endurance – the object or traditional practice which has "come through" the trials of centuries.' Dedham, then, is a historical English landscape made immoveable and stately, something 'worn self-consciously as finery over the merely ageing body of society'.

It's ironic that one of the most lasting achievements of Constable, an artist celebrated for capturing the movement and changeability of nature, is that he helped to make a land-scape stay still. Some weeks after we travelled to Dedham Vale, I returned to meet Justin Hopper, a writer based in Dedham who explores the British landscape for uncanny coincidences and poetic connections. 'It didn't *stay* the same,' he said of Constable Country. 'What they have created is an uncanny Victorian theme park. It never looked like this when Constable was here.' In Constable's time it was agro-industrial, 'absolutely loaded with people. It was a busy waterway. It was the way that every one of those villages got all of its coal and sent stuff back. He was painting it in a nostalgic way for his childhood the way he remembered it as opposed to the way it really was when he looked at it.' He told me he thought the Dedham Vale AONB should be considered the greatest conceptual artwork ever made.

Hopper, who moved here with his family from Hackney, east London, likened what has happened in Dedham to a craze during the height of the nineteenth-century pictur-esque landscape movement. Tourists would visit a landscape such as Dedham Vale and refrain from looking directly at the beautiful countryside they had come to visit. Instead, they would turn around so their back was to it and look at it through a little mirror, called a 'claude glass', so you could curate the landscape into exactly what you wanted, and to see it as a painting. 'So it's a way of essentially transforming a lived-in and worked-in landscape into a painting in person before you had a phone.'

The BBC screened what was perhaps the first Essex reality show in 1957, by sending an outside broadcast team to Harlow to document the new town. The team followed a competi-tion to find the 'ideal family' – first prize was a brand new home offered by the developer, Wimpey. The strange, new kind of dullness the show offered was commented upon in the *Architects' Journal* notes and topics section: 'Those are the shops,' said the commentator, as the camera swept by a row of plate-glass windows, staring bleakly into the premature dusk. 'And . . . funnily enough . . . a lot of them seem to sell . . . tele-vision sets . . . oh, and prams.' The *Journal*'s reaction to this television production company seemed to anticipate cri-tiques of reality TV half a century before the fact: 'The BBC still gets overawed by "actuality" programmes. Most of us are so used to the thrill of knowing that "it's really happening" that we are forgivably bored when what does happen is rather dull, and even more bored when we have to wait about in darkened streets for that dull happening *to* happen.'

Following the Essex Shock of the 1980s and 90s, the county's image softened into a more cuddly, approachable form at the turn of the millennium. The BBC sitcom *Gavin and Stacey*, first broadcast in 2007 and revolving around the love story of a boy from Billericay and a girl from Barry in South Wales, helped launch the career of James Corden, while Alison Steadman turned her previously beastly Essex observations into something altogether warmer in her role as the oh so recognisable Essex mum, Pamela. Unlike Beverly in *Abigail's Party*, Pamela isn't obsessed with drinking the right drink or buying the right furniture. 'She's moved on from there,' Steadman told me. 'They're comfortable with where they've come from and who they are. And they've got a bit of money as well. [Pam's husband] Mick's got a good job, he earns decent money, so they're not always worried about how they are going to pay the bills.' The Billericay home of Gavin's family in particular, led by the goodtime charms of Steadman and Larry Lamb, who played Mick, felt like it represented a country finally at ease with itself in the last years of New Labour as a place of gentle banter and simple – often alcohol-based – pleasures. Essex now seemed a perfect backdrop for the days of early millennial drift, when it was assumed that the majority of the country was now comfortably middle class and would carry on being so in perpetuity, before the financial crash in 2008 revealed a trap door in the end of history.

The year before *Gavin and Stacey* appeared on screen, Chantelle Houghton became a reality TV overnight sensation, as the blonde Essex girl who won *Celebrity Big Brother* despite not being a celebrity. The *Daily Mail* called her the

'Eliza Doolittle of our age'. For once rags to riches wasn't far off the mark. When I asked Houghton what class she identified as when growing up, she asked me what the definitions were. After I told her the three traditional ones were working class, middle class and upper class, she replied: 'I'll put it this way: I grew up with bailiffs, and also my dad, when the neighbours went on holiday, would get the hose pipe from their house and then put it through the window of our bathroom and fill up our bath so we could wash. I don't know what class that is.' The Wickford-born former barmaid, who was reported to be earning a living as a lookalike of the multi-millionaire heiress Paris Hilton before fame came calling, earned her first million within six months of winning *Big Brother*, £250,000 of which came from a single interview with *OK Magazine*. When she married her television housemate, Samuel Preston, who fronted the indie band the Ordinary Boys, they were paid £1 million for the exclusive rights to coverage.

Houghton's family came to Essex from Bethnal Green, her grandparents buying a place on Canvey Island – for the weekend at first, before being enticed to live there full time. She told me she used her 'Essex' identity to achieve a more stable life financially than her parents, turning a negative connotation into a way of earning decent money. Before *Big Brother*, she used to play up to her blonde bimbo persona when working in pubs in Essex. In 2010, she was dressed as a Christmas fairy and lifted by crane to the top of an enormous, 54 foot, Christmas tree outside Lakeside shopping centre in Thurrock, despite the fact she had a huge fear of heights. 'I was so frightened, my legs just went limp.'

Houghton invested the money she earned in property. She moved to east London and then to an apartment in a converted psychiatric hospital in Brentwood in 2008. (It has become a draw for celebrities: Gemma Collins, Ferne

Chantelle Houghton at Lakeside shopping centre, 2010

McCann and Russell Brand have all lived there at one point or another.) Although when Chantelle was appearing on *Big Brother* it was on its way to becoming a comfortably bougie Essex commuter town, Brentwood would soon be transformed by the rise of a new breed of reality show – one that riffed on the stereotype that had helped to make Houghton rich. By the mid 2010s, devotees of *The Only Way Is Essex*, or *Towie* as it became known to a generation of reality fans, were making pilgrimages to Brentwood and the town morphed into the home of opulent chain bars where chandeliers hung above boozing City boys and glamorous twenty-somethings sat on crushed-velvet chairs. The tourists initially came from the UK and Ireland, but then locals started to notice visitors from further afield: the US, Canada, even Australia. Enterprising Essex duly went into overdrive, turning the town into an unironic celebration of retail England. The queue for the Sugar Hut, the bar most associated with *Towie* (which in a former life was the fifteenth-century-built White Hart Inn noted by Pevsner for its 'remarkably good coaching yard'), would spill halfway down the high street at weekends. The Premier Inn did a roaring trade, as did Murphy's, the bar next door, which invented a shot in honour of *Towie*. Two-for-one cocktail deals abounded.

Ryan Fleming, a taxi-driver and security guard turned filmmaker, took a sip of his pint in yet another pub where chandeliers, pastels and pinks had replaced the more traditional timber and oak. We were talking about how his hometown had become a dream destination for young people to visit from all over the country, in particular the north and even as far as Ireland. 'The tourists like it until they get the bill! Everything's more expensive down here,' he said. 'Often you'll go into a pub like this on a Sunday and you'll have a table of about eight girls with all their hair in curlers, beautiful clothes on. Nine times out of ten they're from somewhere in Ireland, probably the first time they've been out of the country. They've all spent about 400 quid each to come to sit in a pub in Brentwood.'

The change could be described as an accentuation, not a reinvention. Brentwood's main drag looked like any prosperous high street in the all-right-Jack south-east – only more so. Tourists ignored the history of the town in favour of salons and shops; Essex girl archetype Amy Childs opened a boutique opposite a monument commemorating the protestant martyr William Hunter, who was burned at the stake there in 1555. The remnants of a ruined chapel built by the monks of St Osyth in honour of Thomas Beckett is a reminder of the tumultuous fourteenth century and Brentwood's role as the place where it all kicked off in 1381. But while Essex had (eventually) earned freedom from serfdom, it had not been so lucky with voyeurism. To watch the rise of *Towie* from afar was bemusing to me and other Essex natives. We'd grown up with Essex-girl jokes and white-van stereotypes but now Essex had gone global, morphing into an adjective that described a permatanned and cosmetically enhanced pursuit of beauty, wealth and celebrity. '*The Only Way Is Essex*'s popularity is mystifying,' quipped comedian Gráinne Maguire at the 2012 Edinburgh Festival. 'Nothing happens in it. It's like a never-ending hen night mixed with Samuel Beckett's *Waiting for Godot*.'

Implicit within the series is the void of consumer life: relationships, clothes and cars are acquired without effort; the countryside became a backdrop for group getaways to lather up the tension. Only nothing is particularly tense. Events seemed to be set up in a way that made certain you knew they were staged, producing a distancing effect that does feel somehow akin to Beckett, with the viewer stuck out on the periphery of the narrative, estranged from the proceedings: 'Nothing to be done.' *Towie* was fascinating in its flatness. A reel of viewer tweets preceded each advert break. *Towie*-centric 'news' lined the *Daily Mail* website: bikini selfies, who-shagged-who stories and liposuction disasters provoking reader responses in the comments section.

The strutting competition and petite dramas acting themselves out on Brentwood high street every weekend mirrored *Towie* itself. The company behind the show, Lime Pictures, had the aim to make it reality TV's version of *EastEnders*. The show's executive producer Daniella Berendsen described *Towie* as a 'living soap': the show's 'story team' talked to the cast before every series to plot it out based on what was going on in their personal lives, creating a strange, designer version of reality, with each episode turned around in three or four days. 'People think we're just mucking about being silly but it's not easy putting your life on camera at times – especially when things aren't going well,' one of the show's main stars, James 'Arg' Argent, told me. 'Everyone knows your business. If I break up with [his on-off love interest] Lydia, everyone will know about it. Everywhere I go it will be, what's going on with you and Lydia? I'll see pictures of her in the paper. You can't ever get away from it.'

One reason *Towie*, and programmes like it, became part of the televisual furniture was that they reflected a way of life in which people had become performers of their own situations through social media. *Towie*'s success chimed with the triumph of commerciality in the lives of young people in the guise of makeup tutorials, vlogging, working on your personal brand. 'Structured reality' fed this, filtering out through social media, adhering to fans' desire for fame – a fame that never felt too far from reach – through the digital mirrors of social media.

The stars of the show cashed in on this connection. Fans could pamper themselves with Amy Childs 'sleep-in rollers' or Joey Essex 'D'Reem hair styling wax' (named after his catchphrase, 'Reem', which sort of just meant 'really cool') while kicking back and reading *Basically*, the autobiography of Gemma Collins, *Towie*'s deadpan queen of meme-worthy moments, or covering themselves in *Towie*'s own 'Love Addict' perfume before a night out. *The Only Way Is Essex* phenomenon was, like Essex man and Essex girl before them, reported on in the tabloids as a kind of moral panic that in truth was more about a general rise in easily accessible celebrity style. The *Daily Mail* reported that the show had made stilettos 33 per cent more popular, false eyelashes 249 per cent more popular, while vajazzles had gone up by 400 per cent and fake nails rose by 567 per cent, according to research company Mintel. The show was attacked in passing by the Essex MP and hardline Tory minister Priti Patel in 2015 when she announced a new plan for youth employment was being implemented 'so that no young person thinks that *Towie*-style fame is the only way to get ahead'.

Essex turned its five minutes of fame into an industry. *Towie* was popular in part because it was about the winners of the working classes, the glamorous residents of the south-west of the county, Buckhurst Hill, Epping, Loughton, Chigwell all the way out to Brentwood. Through years of representation in Mike Leigh films, *Birds of a Feather*, newspaper editorials and the rest, the idea of Essex had manifested into a kind of performance. The vulgar Essex person was in part invented by the media, but in lampooning self-made men and women for luxuriating in their sudden wealth, it created an adoptable persona, gifting the children of the original Essex men and women a lucrative commodity for an age of communications: themselves.

Southend-based part-time actor Louise Stanton smelled opportunity and set up a bus tour of Brentwood, starting with irregular one-off trips before business boomed to three four-hour tours every Saturday, with thirty people per coach. 'It's usually women: hen parties, makeup packages to look like a *Towie* star,' said Stanton. It was a shopping tour by default, which took in Joey Essex's shop Fusey, Sam and Billie Faiers' shop Minnies, and Lucy Mecklenburgh's and Amy Childs' boutiques, before travelling to Loughton to stop at Lydia Bright's shop. Often the cast were waiting to greet the lucky tourists.

'Ten years ago, if you went abroad or out of town, people would ask you where you were from and you say London, because they wouldn't have heard of Essex,' said Ryan Fleming. 'Now, you say Essex it's like: "Oh, *Towie*! Reem!"' His friend Aaron added: 'Our mate went to LA and thought it was a dump. He said Brentwood is more LA than LA; it doesn't make sense.'

And you didn't have to be from Essex to be 'Essex'. Yasmin Bettis, a hairdresser from Hemel Hempstead, a new town just over the border in Hertfordshire that welcomed its first residents the same year that Basildon did in 1949, was 22 when the show started. She moved to Brentwood when her boyfriend got a job as a senior planner in the town. 'I was excited when I first moved here. I would see them all walking about: oh my God, I've just seen Mario, I've just seen Lucy.'

I met Bettis during *Towie*'s heyday in the mid 2010s. She told me how she played up her apparent 'Essexness', putting on an accent. 'When you go to Spain you want to see people speaking Spanish,' she told me. When the girls came into the salon, often from a town or city in northern England, she and her colleagues really hammed it up, so they felt like they were getting 'the full Essex experience'. 'There are a lot of Geordies and northern girls, who come to get their hair done. They say, "I want to look like an Essex girl", and in my head I know what they want,' said Bettis.

The way Bettis described her job suggested that those

denigrating the experience of these tourists visiting the realms of English caricature have missed the point. There was always a humility, a knowingness and an irony to the excess. 'When people have had their hair blow-dried really big, everyone knows it looks really ridiculous,' she said. 'People take the Mickey out of themselves for wanting to be orange and have big hair. It's gone beyond wanting perfection. It's almost like the peacock look. Wanting to be a character. The biggest, brightest, the most stand-out in the place.' But, as a Disney employee might say after a few full days in a Mickey Mouse suit, the gig was starting to grate. 'After a ten-hour day, where you've done the same thing the last few times, it does wear thin,' she said. 'It's like acting basically.'

Bettis said she understood the appeal for people not as well off as the cast of *Towie* as she grew up on a council estate. 'If you wore your slippers to school in Hemel Hempstead, no one cared – if someone brushed their teeth before they went out, they did well.'

The main difference, she noted, between Essex and where she grew up in Hemel Hempstead was the locals she met coming into the salon were of a higher wealth bracket. 'Brentwood is an affluent area and a lot of people who come into our shop are quite well off. It's not as diverse as where I used to live. There are lots of rich housewives and people like that.' I asked her if it made her feel jealous. 'No, it just makes me want to work harder to achieve what they have. It is nice to see people who have done good, managed to brand themselves. It gives you a boost, that morale – they've got a nice car, they've got this, they've got that, and so maybe I should really work hard to get that. It's a good thing really, it makes you want more.'

Like what?

'It does make you look up to these girls. I always want to look immaculate as well. I try my hardest. They've got nice clothes, nice house, nice car, they're self-sufficient. I wasn't very academic at school, that's why I went into hairdressing. Some of the people on *Towie* are not very academic but they've still managed to open up salons, shops. People like myself can relate to them: if they've done it, I can do it.'

But Yasmin also seemed frustrated at something about the *Towie* phenomenon that put paid to the myth of meritocracy, that if you just strived and worked for it your reward would come. The thing with *Towie*, she said, was that you had to be quite well off in the first place to be considered for the show. 'I never got given a brand new Jeep that everyone else seems to be getting,' she said. 'I had to work hard to get where I am now. Most of them come from well-off backgrounds anyway, you're not going to get a leg-up onto that show unless you live a lavish lifestyle.' When I met her, Bettis was aspiring to be a model and celebrity, and had recently been named Face of Essex in a beauty competition. She yearned to be a *Towie* celebrity and had auditioned for the part of a main character at a bar in Romford but wasn't selected. 'I knew my lifestyle wasn't going to be that interesting. Me working ten hours a day and going home and watching TV; I knew that wasn't going to sell any stories.'

Of course, it is not just in Essex that young people from modest backgrounds talk plainly about their aspiration to make money and own nicer things. Perhaps it shouldn't have been surprising, so signposted had this side of Essex been throughout my childhood, and particularly not now it was back in vogue with *Towie*. Yet I realised that this contrasted deeply with the hopeful, radical Essex I had been reading about. The Essex dream might have always been about materialism, but it was a tangible, reachable materialism, about moving out into space and improving living conditions for you and your family.

What struck me about Yasmin's dream to be a *Towie* star

is not how impossible it sounded, but how lightly exploitative the process was. Yasmin had been an extra in *Towie* a few times, which meant 12-hour days, sometimes until one in the morning, for nothing in return aside from the experience itself. She had met some really nice people doing it, she said. Girls from Scotland who travelled hundreds of miles simply to stand in the background for a scene or two of the hit show. The extras were from far more economically diverse backgrounds than *Towie*'s big names, she said. 'Some people are single mums or on benefits and some people are really well off, it's a mixture of everybody.' The main difference between haves and have nots, I suppose, is haves get to make, and buy, and do, whereas the have nots peer on voyeuristically and wish.

As the 2010s progressed, *Towie*, with its oversized hair and heavily tanned complexion, felt like the capitalist-surrealist end point of a journey that began when the first cockneys were attracted to Essex in the nineteenth century. Go back a generation or two and these Essex answers to Beverly Hills families were emigres from Shoreditch, Walthamstow and Leyton. The grandmother of one of the show's initial protagonists, Mark Wright, who also starred as the much-loved Nanny Pat, used to run a pub with her husband Charlie in Bromley-by-Bow before moving to Essex. There is an area of housing in Brentwood known as the East Ham estate after Londoners were decanted to the development following the war, and Newham Council still runs the properties.

The origin story of escaping the East End was important to the cast of *Towie*. One of the stars, Ferne McCann, lived a few minutes away from Brentwood's main drag when I visited in 2015. She said she believed Essex people have been hard done by. 'There's such a misconception of people around here,' she said. 'The work ethic in Essex is just second to none.' McCann's nan came from a family of fifteen in Stepney and moved to Essex after she married. Her dad went straight from school to the City. 'The majority have all come straight out of the East End – working-class families that are humble and genuine, who have still got that neighbourhood vibe about them. It's flash, but why shouldn't people celebrate because they've worked so bloody hard.' McCann seemed to sum up the appeal of *Towie* to those who hadn't made it but wanted to. Her wealthy friends grew up rich, she said, because 'their granddad or their dad or their great granddad set up a plumbing business: working-class families who have cracked it'.

But while this self-made tradition is admirable, it ignores the geographical luck of these tales of working-class derring-do, that London's endless flow of capital explained why affluent Essex successfully turned its five minutes of fame into an industry whereas other reality shows set in Liverpool, Newcastle or Wales didn't so much (while hyper-affluent west London's version, *Made in Chelsea*, was never going to fill Sloane Square with boutiques run by stars of the show). In addition to financial services jobs in the City of London and Canary Wharf, there was the volume of work in London and the densely built pockets of south-east Essex for people in the building trades, and other subsidiary jobs that feed off London's ability to create and sustain wealthy people.

Essexness once again represented something greater, yet also something more limited and less nuanced, than the county boundaries allowed. It represented the industrial-to-post-industrial trajectory of south-east England, how suburbia and new money had won, and how their representations on flat screen televisions around the country had become the thing that young people were aspiring to countrywide. And yet, scratch the surface and Essex has never felt like a non-stop party, of youth revelling in its demographic primacy. (At least, not to me.) Essex was loud – but never proud, at least not without complication. I met Hayley in the upstairs room of a sticky bar in Southend when I was 18, she 19. I thought she seemed quite posh, posher than me anyway, as she was from a place I had never heard of called South Woodham Ferrers. This turned out to be a new-ish and respectable commuter town surrounded by Essex countryside and marshland, and not the sprawling, scruffy seaside town of knob-gag postcards and easy access to class A drugs that I was from. She even pronounced her Ts and everything. By the time Hayley and I arrived at university in 2003 (Falmouth in Cornwall), some housemates in our halls of residence laughed away my suggestion that Hayley didn't much sound like she was from Essex, and to prove it they did an impression that sounded not far from the televised caricature of an Essex girl straight out of *Birds of a Feather*.

When I first arrived in London in the mid-noughties, to take a junior job on a national newspaper, my glottal stops and too-fast speech confused colleagues, so I straightened it out and slowed it down the same way many people with regional accents do when they move to London. But at parties after a few drinks I'd lapse back into a glottalled Sarfend flow until I was questioned by a forthright editor at the broadsheet magazine I used to work at why I was suddenly talking in a sort of Mockney accent. 'You never used to speak like that in the office.' Conversely, back in Essex, I probably came across a bit middle class and softened around the edges. Coming back home to visit I would usually feel like a hybrid, a half man, an imposter, although since I have moved back, I can feel my carefully constructed pronounced Ts starting to erode.

Ferne McCann said the perception that the protagonists of *Towie* were brainless Essex girls was eventually crushed by the sheer success of this new breed of reality star. 'I feel like the whole Essex girl bimbo thing has died a little bit of a death because there's so many young girls and young men who have been so successful, so it's not really like the whole thick bimbo thing any more because they're all sitting there in their one-million-pound houses.'

But what if they feel trapped in those houses? Celebrity woes are the ultimate first world problems, but being a reality TV star has always struck me as a potentially more stressful and isolating existence than is ever accounted for: a world of sniping, hating and empty beef as you desperately try to stay relevant. Chantelle Houghton told me some of the *Towie* stars had been sucked into the dark side of the reality TV-social media-tabloid press continuum, entering an endlessly narcissistic spiral about how they look, how they are perceived. 'It's very worrying because I think people are so absorbed with it that when it does one day disappear – and it will, of course it will – I think it will be really hard.'

Brentwood is now part of the new Crossrail railway development, bringing London closer, and perhaps diluting the town's distinctively 'Essex' vibe. Louise's bus tours ceased years ago. Most of the stars' boutiques have closed, at least one – that of Gemma Collins – due to financial difficulties. Meanwhile, the Essex stereotype is being eroded by the passage of time. The term Essex girl was taken out of the Oxford Dictionary in 2020 after a lengthy campaign backed by the likes of novelist Syd Moore, and which memorably included an appearance by Collins, on Sky News to say she was 'a massive fan of the dictionary' but thought that it should still pay 'everyone in Essex some compensation' for the years of the derogatory name being printed in its pages.

And yet, the surface preoccupations of *The Only Way Is Essex* and these PR-driven attempts at promoting a more genteel county than is usually reported feel two sides of the same coin, an attempt at putting on your best face to the exclusion of much of the actual lived experience of a place. Constable Country is no more indicative of Essex's peculiarity than the translucent mud and the sky. One should not negate the other. It feels like a mistake to try and create a fixed idea of what Essex is, as if it is against the county's eroding, sinking, but always somehow reanimating nature. There is no 'real Essex' to be unearthed if we can just crack through the veneer of the mediated, overdone, 'fake' Essex of TV lore. (Can I just shock you – I have seen Botox and fillers in Constable Country, too.) And this is perhaps what is so strange about the idea of 'Constable Country': a place that has grown out of the artist's obsession with *catching* his fleeting perception, the way his sketching out the pencil lines of the landscape before he blotted and stroked the canvas has led to all the car parks and the restaurants, ice creams and gift shops. In a sense this is the key to Essex, from the plotland dreamers to *Towie*'s Brentwood, new realities have been forged only to disappear again under the weight of time.

I gave the Stour, Constable's curvaceous muse, a last look before we headed for the car. It was teeming despite the changeable April weather. There were people wedged into kayaks or gingerly balancing on paddle boards. A swimmer in a wetsuit trailed by waterproof bags was followed by her still-dry partner and daughter who sauntered along the bank. She powered on ahead as they followed her, until she reached the part of the bank she had decided to use to make her exit, and lifted herself out, dripped off and dried to greet her family. An Essex landscape upstaged, as ever, by so much human activity.

9

Unstoppable, Immovable

Under a blazing midday sky, my friend Luke and I snaked around the tidal tributaries of the River Roach, passing the islands of Rushley, Potton and Havengore, which shyly presented themselves as mere suggestions on the landscape. It is at points like this on walks in marshland Essex – we had come to walk the coastal path from Shoeburyness to the village of Barling – where it feels like you have broken through into an unreality of your own imagination. In 30-degree heat the terrain turned into a looping miasma of stunning white light and scorched flattened marsh. At one point we found ourselves walking nonsensically around a promontory that brought us back almost to where we started. We encountered a herd of cows casually grazing up the steep, sloping banks of the sea wall, unfussed by our interruption into their daily routine. The water glistened so intensely it took a while until we noticed it was teeming with shoals of mullet that had swum in on the incoming tide. But we didn't see anybody fishing all day. In fact, we hardly saw anybody else, aside from a group of teenagers whooping and cheering as they splashed into the creek, and the boat-owners in the marina at Wakering, who tetchily enquired what we were doing near their patch.

Essex is characterised by barriers and buffers, roads and rivers, fences, gates and sea walls. Some of its islands, especially, can feel as if they have hermetically sealed themselves from the chaos of the world. The predominance of the sea forces decisions, accentuates obsessions, drives characters towards unthinkable actions lest they succumb to oblivion, and action must be taken to resist it. When I met Flavian Capes, the marshman of the Blackwater Estuary, he told me the story of the Tollesbury cannibals. In 1884 Captain Thomas Dudley sailed a boat, the *Mignonette*, which was built at Brightlingsea and had been moored at the spot we were looking out to. After it was repaired at Southampton he picked up a crew of two adult men and a 17-year-old cabin boy. North-west of the Cape of Good Hope, the *Mignonette* was smashed to bits by a storm. The men and the cabin boy were cast adrift with little food and no water, surviving for days on a tin of turnips they had brought with them and a turtle they'd managed to catch. When the cabin boy fell into a coma after drinking too much seawater, Thomas Dudley followed the 'custom of the sea', and, with fellow crew member Edwin Stephens, cut his jugular vein. The story goes that they feasted on the meat of the dead boy to survive out at sea until they were rescued after twenty-five days adrift. The resulting case, 'Regina v. Dudley and Stephens', is still studied by law students to this day, while locally the tale has grown taller over time, with stories that the Tollesbury fishermen used to eat the Mersea fishermen from the other side of the estuary being shared down the generations.

The sea forces other extremities on individuals; those involved in trying to navigate it, but also those trying to protect their land, like John Harriott, the man on Rushley Island who spent his life trying to stop the tide and failing. Canvey islanders still rely on the sea wall for their survival. After the 1953 flood, millions of pounds were spent on protecting the land and the people from future inundations. It didn't happen without a fight: there was talk from the authorities about leaving Canvey to the fate of the tides, but local pressure ensured a suitable defence was built.

I first visited Foulness Island as a teenager, when Mum and Dad had the idea of Sunday lunch at the George and Dragon pub on the island. Dad phoned ahead to the pub's landlord, Fred, who passed on his number plates to a multinational defence technology company – as the Ministry of Defence is the landlord of the 6,000-acre island, which is operated by the private firm QinetiQ, you have to have a good reason to visit; you can't just walk onto Foulness. After a cursory check of Dad's car boot, the barrier lifted and we were in. It was a good meal served with frothy pints of real ale but, Fred and his wife told us, the effort involved in running a pub with the MoD as a landlord had long been a thankless one. Who comes for a pint if you have to get past the army before you can reach the bar? The pub finally closed after Fred lost his twenty-seven-year battle to attract punters into a danger zone against the backdrop of ever-rising MoD rent.

While researching this book, I was invited onto Foulness again, this time by Mary Reeve, who lived there, in the rectory in the village of Church End. As well as the pub closing, the village shop had too, and Mary said it was a shame that the island had lost a lot of its community spirit. When her family had first moved there, they had found produce on the doorstep – a variety of vegetables and even a goose. Friday nights at the pub turned into a veritable vegetable swap shop. 'We'd take fresh eggs and come out with a courgette and a cucumber,' said Mary, 'it was like the old bartering system.' Born in Rochford on the mainland, Mary grew up by the sea in Southend before moving to the island with her husband, daughter and son more than twenty years ago. The appeal, for Mary, was partially nostalgic. 'You'd drive through the village and there'd be an old boy leaning against his gate talking about the size of his chrysanthemums. It was as though you had passed through a time warp to 100 years ago.'

You could call Foulness Essex's biggest gated community,

and Mary said she appreciated the peace of mind the military's barrier fence gave her: the fact that nobody could get in or out had lent the island a pleasant feeling of stasis. After signing in at the gate, I crossed the bridge over Havengore Creek and continued in a straight line towards the village of Churchend, the car gliding along a landscape of serene flatness alongside fenced off fields of rape that blazed bright in the sunshine. Mary described her feeling coming home over the bridge as though she was leaving the world behind her. 'QinetiQ always knows who is here, which gives you a great sense of security. At night, they patrol, so I can be walking the dog and if one of their vehicles passes, it's comforting. It must be how it used to feel with the local bobby.' The image struck me as simultaneously idyllic and horrific: a dreamlike vision of England in aspic that relied on this heavily guarded militarised zone to keep it that way.

The Olde Essex feel of Foulness, with its villages of weatherboarded cottages and bushes of plump sloe berries, contrasts somewhat with the fact it was for years a secret site, where Britain's first atomic bomb was assembled in 1952. Put together in Explosive Preparation Lab X6, a drab looking flat-roofed building within the Atomic Weapons Research Establishment on Foulness, it was transported to Shoeburyness by lorry before being loaded onto a barge and shipped to the remote Australian island where it was detonated. (This was the first of many similar journeys from Foulness to north-west Australia, and the effect on the aboriginal Australians living closest to the blast zone, including reports of higher cancer rates and early deaths, is still being reckoned with.) Following 9/11, assessments of the military capabilities of organisations such as al-Qaeda were made on Foulness, including the testing of explosives that resulted in the death of MoD scientist Terry Jupp after a 10kg mix of chemicals exploded during an experiment. Do residents notice this side of island life? 'There's the odd occasion when it will rattle the windows but it's just like having trains at the bottom of your garden. You get used to it,' said Mary.

The more I read about Foulness, the more I started to think it had been shrouded in mystery for as long as it has been known, a place where anything can happen. Samuel Purchas, in the fourteenth chapter of the ninth book of his popular and surrealistic travelogue, *Purchas, His Pilgrimage* (1613), recalled seeing clouds of flying ants on 'the island of Foulenesse on our Essex shore . . . that filled our clothes . . . the floores of some houses where they fell, were in manner covered with a blacke carpet of creeping ants; which they say drowne themselves about that time of the yere in the sea'. Purchas was the Vicar of St Laurence's, in Eastwood. He earned a significant reputation in the early seventeenth century with his exotic tales of far-flung fantasy – King James read his first book *Purchas, His Pilgrimage* seven times. He was an inspiration to Milton, Defoe and, most famously, Coleridge. The latter based his most famous poem 'Kubla Khan' on a passage from the seventeenth-century Essex villager's tome: 'In Xamdu did Cublai Can build a stately Palace, encompassing sixteene miles of plaine ground with a wall, wherein are fertile Meddowes, pleasant Springs, delightfull Streames, and all sorts of beasts of chase and game, and in the midst thereof a sumptuous house of pleasure.'

Coleridge's version, 'Kubla Khan', was unfinished after he was interrupted while writing in an apparently opium-induced reverie in Somerset, halting work at, 'For he on honey dew hath fed, And drunk the milk of paradise,' and never again being able to recapture the imagery. As James Canton points out in his book *Out of Essex*, the poem doesn't just feed off Purchas's passage on 'Cublai Can' but also from the Essex author's account of the Old Man of the Mountain that appears forty pages earlier in *Pilgrimages*: 'Aloadin', who

A plane taking off at Southend airport, seen
from the graveyard at St Laurence's Church

'inclosed a goodly valley, situate between two hills, and fur-
nished it with all variete, which Nature and Art could yield,
as fruits, pictures, rills of smoke, wine, honey, water, pallaces
and beautiful damosells richly attired, and called it Paradise.'

Purchas, His Pilgrimage and the 1623-published *Purchas,
His Pilgrimes* documented Essex as a place that received exotic
voyagers from such far-off places as India, Japan, China,
Africa and the West Indies during the age of discovery, before
such adventure became so heavily weighed down by the bru-
talising forces of empire. Sailors straight from their boats
told Purchas fantastical tales in the pubs of Leigh-on-Sea.
But he had no desire to escape to the unknown, in a physical
sense; his purpose, he felt, was to document those who had
lived lives of such rare incident that they must be written
down and communicated. Purchas still haunts St Laurence's
Church in the form of a stained-glass window depiction,

with his Shakespearean ruff, book and quill, but these days has to contend with the modernity of London Southend Airport. At one point, the church was threatened by a project to enlarge the airport due to its inconvenient position on the site of the planned runway extension. The airport's owner, Eddie Stobart, planned to move it, brick by brick, stone by stone, so he could extend the runway. In the end the church remained, but not without a fight that dragged on for more than a decade. That Purchas's legacy might have been moved aside for the expansion of an airport specialising in low-cost flights to Tenerife, Majorca, Amsterdam – the Southend day trips of our age – seemed perverse but somehow fitting. In the end, only the Victorian wall was destroyed. The church and graveyard remained, with orange and white jets trundling to and fro beside them before take-off.

Foulness Island, too, almost became an enormous airport in the 1970s. (The plan was shelved once a Labour-led minority government replaced the Conservative government of Edward Heath, whose pet project it was.) To fight the development, a consortium of local, national and international ornithological organisations – from the International Council for Bird Preservation to Foulness Wildfowl Counting and Birdwatching group – was set up to gather and proffer evidence of the unsuitability of Foulness as a site for a major airport. The Defenders of Essex formed to fight for the protection of the county's rural character that could be lost to the devastation caused by yet more suburbs and transport links, not to mention the threat to the Brent geese who flocked there in great numbers. A petition was sent to Parliament listing the Defenders' concerns that the ministers backing the scheme were overseeing the destruction of a unique area for wildfowl.

'Essex has suffered so much: the new towns, the vast growth and overspill of London, the lancing through of motorways,' wrote the Chelmsford-based naturalist and author of *The Peregrine* (1967), JA Baker. *The Peregrine* is a tautly vivid document of a place, the Essex of the rivers Chelmer and Blackwater and the Dengie marshes and fields, where his favoured fowl would stalk their prey or take rest; he allowed the specific Essex place names to erode until they become 'south Wood', 'north Wood', 'the estuary'. Baker articulated a disgust at the despoliation of the countryside that would later become common. The writer despised the militarisation of Foulness and he dreaded the destruction a proposed airport would unleash on the wild hinterlands, home to his beloved raptors. In a 1971 diary entry, tracing a walk along the River Crouch, he described the disquieting scene from afar: '[F]ive miles removed, is the faint blur of Foulness Island and the uplifted thorn of its church spire. Foulness. Already the name has a cold and final sound. There is barbed wire in it and emptiness. It is the future.' And yet the barbed wire and emptiness may have contributed in part to saving these salt marshes from development. While the island's isolation has worked against the human population, it has proved immeasurably better for conserving the island as a wildfowl sanctuary.

Implicit in Essex's hostility towards development was the fate of that other London-bordering Saxon county, Middlesex, which after years of massive growth of the city's northern fringe ceased to exist when the London Government Act came into force in 1965. By contrast Essex, wrote historian Gillian Darley, was 'bubble-wrapped by the Green Belt against accidental breakage or spillage'. The idea of a sacrosanct ring of greenery to hem in the rapacious capital city was hundreds of years in the making, but by the early twentieth century, with the advancement of London an ever more political problem, it became a question of not if, but when, and in 1938 the Green Belt Act was drawn up in reaction to

Bernard Braine MP speaks against the creation
of the airport at Foulness, 1971

the type of endless sprawl that befell Middlesex. A small item
in the *Architects' Journal* in October 1936 detailed how 1,000
acres near Purfleet had been secured for the Green Belt and
how belts in Buckinghamshire, Middlesex and Essex were to
be considered. In 1940, the journal reported that, despite the
war effort, the Green Belt scheme was still going ahead – and
Essex County Council were doing their bit. 'A contribution is
being made towards the cost of the acquisition, by the Essex
County Council, of more than 2,000 acres of land which are
to be added to the Green Belt in Essex.' I don't know if it is
due to the fact that I grew up in Essex but I always found the
concept of the Green Belt confusing. After all, green was just
what you saw on journeys to your aunt's out in Hockley or on

coach trips with the cub scouts. I'd look at green fields out the window and wonder to myself, 'Is this, this bit – is this the Green Belt?'

Questions surrounding the Green Belt were not always directed at the land in question, but at the people who might frequent it. In 1935, *The Sphere* claimed in an item entitled 'The Green Belt of the mind' that although the Green Belt was finally coming to fruition, the march of the London suburbs had created a mass of people unskilled at appreciating the countryside that would suddenly be protected for them. 'It is largely due to the lack of taste and understanding in local authorities, and in part to the absurd veneration which we accord to scientific inventions, that today the citizen is not worthy to enjoy green spaces when he possesses them.' The article claimed local and national politicians had failed urban and suburban citizens, cruelly divorcing them from the cleansing disorder of nature. 'Bureaucracy has driven man from the Garden of Eden, with railings, gravel paths, notices and litter boxes, and today the best use which cockneys can make of their green spaces is to turn them into a setting for their mechanical sound boxes and their public house recreations.' In a fit of Maoism for the conservative English middle classes, *The Sphere* argued that any money spent on the Green Belt must be accompanied by re-educating the public. 'Before the government and local authorities spend the ratepayers' money on new open spaces, they should set aside a large sum to be spent educationally in reclaiming green spaces in the public mind and making the citizens of great towns better fitted to enjoy, and more worthy to own, green spaces in their midst.'

There would have been no Essex as we know it without the Green Belt. 'I think you probably can't think about the character of southern Essex without thinking about the fact that it is [the] old East End having moved out, and the Green

Belt is a key part of that story,' said Jonn Elledge, who writes about London urbanism and transport for the *New Statesman*, and grew up near Romford on the edge of the Green Belt. 'On the most basic level if you look at a map of the Green Belt the bits of Essex it covers are almost exactly a map of that London-flavoured southern Essex [which] sort of arcs from Harlow round to just south of Chelmsford and then across to Southend. It's all the bits that sort of fit into the Essex stereotype. The bits of Essex that are more rural, which don't fit into that, are all outside the Green Belt. Just on that sort of level the fact that the Essex of the popular imagination that people make jokes about is basically surrounded by Green Belt, but the nice Essex of the well-to-do cream tea antiquity bit is outside it.'

Without the Green Belt, Elledge points out, people would have still moved to Essex but the decision to leave the city or not wouldn't have been so totalising. 'To an extent the Green Belt hasn't stopped London's growth, it's just dispersed it. One frequent argument in favour of retaining a tight Green Belt policy is that it directs people and resources back into the cities. On the contrary, it has forced people to leapfrog it and actually to move further away from the inner city.' Development that could have happened closer to the city is instead 'pushed out to Chelmsford and Southend and Harlow and so on,' said Elledge. 'These places just beyond the Green Belt, where it is still possible to build stuff. It is still the same sorts of people doing the same sorts of jobs and getting trains into town – they are just having to skip over the Green Belt to do it.'

The existence of Green Belt land has led to protests across Essex. In Rochford and Great Wakering, near Barling, it takes the form of a coalition of your usual concerned residents and Green Belt evangelists, but with a new collaborator, Extinction Rebellion environmentalists. I talked to Johanne Deverrick, one of the organisers who got involved with campaigning against a Green Belt plan drawn up in response to government housing targets in Castle Point in December 2019, which she said would 'destroy the borough'. A figure of 5,300 houses might not seem like that big a percentage of a 90,070 strong population, but Castle Point, an early recipient of the plotland bungalow boom, has some of the most densely populated neighbourhoods in Essex. In Daws Heath, where she lived, she told me there were three big Green Belt plots earmarked for development. Daws Heath felt like one of those areas in Essex that is folded away by the happenstance of infrastructure, protected from the relentlessness of the A127 by the ancient woodland of Pound Wood with an old church, St Michael's, and a 'villagey feel' – at least compared to the rest of the borough. The plan would lead to 700 houses being added to the three plots. Excess traffic would spill onto Daws Heath Road, little more than an old country lane widened over the years, turning it into 'a car park', she said. Deverrick lived in Chadwell Heath near Romford before she and her partner decided they wanted to live somewhere with a bit more open space and so made the leap over the Green Belt. Pleasantly surprised with how bucolic the area was, they couldn't believe their luck. 'And then we find out they are going to build everywhere!'

Essex has form when it comes to protesting developments. I found some grainy news agency footage on YouTube; filmed in the late 1980s, it looked like a clip from the height of the Troubles. Breezeblocks and timber sit in a frozen cascade where a house should be. The whole frontage of someone's dream home has spilled out like innards as firemen tread carefully over a carpet of bricks. But the aggressor here wasn't fighting a revolutionary battle for a united Ireland. They were fighting a cul-de-sac. The Essex dream of a brand new detached house in the country required an obliging countryside, and this time it found no such thing.

On Sunday, 21 August 1988, an explosion woke the villagers of Barling at 3.30 a.m. Local resident and former RAF pilot Peter Smith said the bomb 'sounded like one of the smaller ones we used to drop – a 200-pounder'. The target was a brand new five-bedroom house that was being built on Green Belt land by a firm of developers in Upminster, that had been the subject of much ultimately unsuccessful objection from the villagers in Barling, a marshland village tucked away in an estuarial fold north-east of Southend.

It was reported that the Barling Bomber, as the culprit was

EXPLOSION LEAVES VILLAGE IN FEAR

Police hunt for bomber

By HELEN MORGAN-WYNNE

A CRACKPOT bomber's war against developers could have ended in death, a senior detective said today.

Forensic experts are now examining parts of a home-made bomb taken from a £300,000 luxury Barling home, which was destroyed in a 3am blast on Sunday.

Police revealed they are investigating the possibility that someone has a grudge against the development, which provoked protests from villagers.

Gas

Det Chief Insp Ivan Dibley, head of Southend CID, said: "We are taking this very seriously. If it had happened at any other time than the middle of the night we would have had a death on our hands or a very serious injury.

"The site hut was completely destroyed in the blast and somebody working on the site could have been caught in the explosion."

Experts are now examining wires and tubing found in the rubble and believe the device was gas or petrol-powered.

Police are still making extensive door-to-door inquiries in the area and searching fields.

An article on the Barling Bomber, in the
Evening Echo, 25 August, 1988

soon to be known, made the incendiary device from instructions contained in *The Anarchist's Cookbook*. Police believed the suspect was a resident who had previously written to the council to object to the development. 'An incident room has been set up by the local constabulary,' wrote Tim Walker in *The Observer*. 'Council files containing the names of twenty-five people who objected to the development have been turned over to detectives. Forensic scientists have visited the site.'

The event was the talk of the village, although some, such as the vicar at the local All Saints Church, wished to play down the possibility that the blast was intentional. Yet it was soon apparent from newspaper reports that many in Barling saw themselves living under siege from development. 'It's been taken over by the nouveau riche,' a local stonemason told *The Observer*. 'Perfectly respectable Tudor homes have been turned into horrible pseudo-Regency monstrosities.'

Was the Barling Bomber – who was never formally identified – a paramilitary manoeuvre against the tide of uber-capitalism sweeping into south Essex and threatening to take over these ancient villages, or a disgruntled nimby with too much time on their hands? Either way, they didn't stop at a cul de sac. They bombed a barn that was in the process of being converted into a luxury residential property, a listed building that was being renovated, and a yacht club based on a barge that was moored down Barling Creek. They also targeted a landfill tip where every day dozens if not hundreds of lorries were coming to dump their rubbish, with twelve incendiary devices placed in the cabs of the lorries, bulldozers and diggers that were going to be used to build a new stretch of road to carry 360 dustcarts a day. 'It caused about a million pounds' worth of damage, I think,' said DCI Ray Newman, who had worked in Basildon and run into the Essex Boys before he was appointed the head of Rayleigh and

Castle Point CID in the mid 1990s, and was given the case to try and finally solve.

Although this local whodunnit went national, it remained a mystery deep into the 1990s. 'The Sunday papers ran it a bit like Agatha Christie writing about a sleepy little village,' said Newman. He tried extracting information from villagers but came up against the same omerta as his predecessors had, so he looked into deploying some leftfield tactics. It had been reported that someone had signed the visitors' book of the All Saints Church in Barling, 'Guy Fawkes of London', and the police later were shown threatening letters they thought could have been sent by the bomber. 'We published pictures of the letters, just like the Yorkshire Ripper,' Newman said.

Newman enlisted a graphologist who described the suspect's handwriting as that of an older person with a formal education. The stunt and continued media drive helped pick up interest and detectives launched a fresh appeal on the back of the new line of enquiry. Two thousand copies of the suspected bomber's letters were delivered to homes in Barling and the nearby villages of Little Wakering and Great Wakering in the hope someone who recognised the handwriting would come forward. 'Eventually someone did come forward and they gave us the name of a local family who [they said] were involved,' said Newman. 'One morning we did the proverbial dawn swoop and rounded them all up and interviewed them.' Two men aged 58 and 64 were arrested. The detectives found materials at their property that matched the makeshift bomb materials they had recovered after the explosions. The improvised explosive devices used to blow up the houses and other locations were made from 'a combination of wires, plastic and all sorts,' said Newman, but he wasn't sure if there was a timer on the bomb as had been rumoured in the press. 'I seem to remember it involved filling up some bin bags with gas and sealing them and placing them around the house so when the fire did take there were a series of explosions.' In the end the police didn't have enough evidence that the materials found at the house were an exact match and the case fell apart. 'So we were never able to charge them but it was a matter of record that there were no other attacks [after the police attention] so I drew my own conclusions.'

Despite the frustration of never catching the elusive Barling Bomber, Newman could afford a little empathy towards his old nemesis. He said that he understood the resistance to change if you had lived in the village all your life. 'Even if I escaped to the country and moved somewhere, it would probably take me about twenty years to be accepted, and can you imagine if I had gone down there and done some damage or some unwanted development as well,' he said. 'They just took the law into their own hands, I think. They obviously didn't get anywhere with any planning enquiries.'

It was a crisp and blue January day when Paul met me from the train as I arrived in his home town of Grays in Thurrock, where Essex bleeds into Greater London. Mates when we were teenagers –Paul would stay round after a night spent wandering the estuary, staring out at Coryton refinery, which transformed into an emerald city after spliffs and tabs – we grew apart when we went to different universities, but he tracked me down when I started writing about our shared home county and we decided to meet up. We sized each other up a bit, each of us a little worn out by parenting and the day job. He said we should go for a walk, which lasted only until we were standing outside a pub, waiting for it to open. We gulped down our first pints of Guinness. During our second, Paul told me that he voted Brexit. Separated by the years, as much as the M25, we had moved further apart than the 20-odd miles between our flats. Paul described himself as a pragmatic libertarian. I thought I was a left-wing urban liberal, a lifelong Labour voter. Paul worked in house clearance, a gig that took him to some of the grottiest residences in Thurrock. I was a fully paid-up member of the metropolitan elite, sitting at the desk of a national newspaper office each day, supposedly insulated from reality by a mediated veneer.

Paul described his family as being about as 'typically Thurrock' as possible: large in number, still quite tight-knit, half Irish/half white British. His aunts and uncles were a collection of entrepreneurs, ex-dockers and plant workers, most with strong socialist and Labour backgrounds, with the occasional vocal outlier supporting an English or British nationalist movement. His local paper shop used to sell more copies of the left-wing *Morning Star* than *The Times* and the *Telegraph* put together, but not any more. 'Obviously, I live in a slight bubble here,' he told me of his experience of the Brexit vote. 'Everyone was out, out, out. But I still didn't take the decision lightly.' Nor did Paul think it would happen. 'On the day of Brexit I sat there, bruv, I sat there in the fucking morning with about 150 quid in my Sky Bet account. I was, like, shall I do it? Seven to fucking one, mate.'

Paul said he voted for Brexit as he didn't think this country was a natural fit for continental Europe. His libertarian politics about shaping our own destiny as a nation often echoed the anarchic elements of Essex's growth; Paul also said the decision came from his sense of fairness and unfairness linked to the post-war settlement that built much of the county. He wasn't interested in the bombardment of statistics from each side in the run-up to the referendum. Instead, he relied on his own eyes. 'My nan and granddad, my mum and dad and me have paid into a system all our lives. The idea that someone could jump on an easyJet flight from Riga tomorrow and get exactly the same level of services when me and my family have contributed for years – these services are not built overnight, it takes decades and decades of investment.'

Four pints in and Paul and I were still not convincing each other, so we headed to the pie-and-mash shop for some stodge. 'Rarely do good things happen when people have been drinking, but what's worse?' said Paul. 'People have a drink, or all the pubs go.' Such considerations are part of the reason identity is such an important political subject today. The pub's identity as a working-class space might be under threat, but it has survived all manner of change, often change for the worse. In Grays, the local theatre was set to close. The ground of Grays Athletic football club, which stood for over 100 years and was a point of local pride, was bulldozed to make way for flats. It's sights like this that help explain the fatalistic, fuck-it mentality of much of south Essex today.

In a bid to help stave off further closures, we headed for another pub. On the corner of the high street, Paul pointed out the office where he had one of his first jobs at the UK's longest-running sex chat-line company. 'I was general manager for seven months. They started in 2001. Phone sex happened before that, of course, but the rest have chopped and changed since. They're invariably run by cocaine addicts. The geezer who ran that one died of a cocaine overdose. He was pulling ten grand a month out of it, snorting all of it.' By the time we're walking to The Traitor's Gate, our third pub, I'm well pissed. As the street curved psychedelically round by the old Co-operative Society dairy, a gap in the terraced housing revealed the sun going down behind the factories on the industrial riverside. It was a glimpse of a workers' town built for a purpose it will never again fulfil. Thurrock has become a well-worn backdrop for anyone who wants a sense of decay in their film or TV show. Around the time I met Paul in Grays, I read of an arson attack on the East Tilbury library. Someone reversed a car into the entrance and set it on fire, completely destroying the entrance and lobby, along with artefacts belonging to the Bata heritage centre, a local initiative run by volunteers to keep alive the story of the company town.

But there is still work in Thurrock, quite a lot of it. I noticed a bus route in Southend that advertised a new worker colony in Thurrock: AMAZON TILBURY: AMAZON WORKERS ONLY. Although the Bata factory at East Tilbury closed in 2006, after years of scaling back once the company had shifted business overseas, a few miles away is a very modern version, which sucks in workers from all around the Thames Estuary. Amazon's 'fulfilment centre' was built in the years after the opening of the London Gateway port. I met a worker at Amazon who didn't wish to be named for fear of being sacked for speaking to me; they told me of how they saw the fact their Tilbury workplace was named a ful- filment centre in two ways. In one sense it was a description (although a slightly dystopian one) of what the workers do: they fulfil the wishes of that ever-important figure in the Amazon mythos, the customer. But they said they also saw it in an 'Arbeit Macht Frei' way, in the sense of fulfilling your destiny as a worker. The canteen was full of slogans, he said. 'Like "Always challenge authority", things that were quite contradictory, doublespeak and things like that.' (Christmas, at Amazon, is simply known as 'Peak'.)

The Worker had been there three years in a low-level management role in a department that dealt with deliver- ies, but they said they never felt like it was a permanent job, precisely, as it always felt as if you were one step away from doing something wrong. If workers are 'on task', they wear readers that can calculate their speed and their accuracy, and a superior would go round with a Kindle showing people their figures, and where they had made mistakes. 'One day the manager said, "Good news, everyone, last night we did

300,000 units. We've never done that before, that's really great. Tonight we're gonna go for 320,000 units." So we'd broken a record and they were still pushing us and pushing us, and they were like this needy friend you've got: whatever you give 'em, they want more. That's just the Amazon way.' He had seen ambulances outside the facility. 'I don't think it's to do with any kind of industrial accident. I think it's more to do with people just collapsing. A lot of the time it's old women.'

Tilbury is a small port town with a big name. It's most often talked about in terms of its illustrious past – from Elizabeth I's speech before the Spanish Armada and Daniel Defoe's business dealings to the docking of the *Windrush* as shorthand for Britain's post-war immigration policy. Its Empire-facing past is reflected by the road names – Calcutta Road, Adelaide Road, Malta Road – and the weight of history can often lead one to believe that whatever happens now doesn't matter. Joseph Conrad lived at Stanford-le-Hope – and *Heart of Darkness* begins with a journey downriver towards the sea. In opening pages seen by many as the Thames Estuary's greatest depiction in literature, Marlow and his vessel the *Nellie* depart London via the 'interminable waterway', leaving for colonial Europe's African 'horror' in the Congo.

Global trade built the Empire, and Tilbury was the entry and exit point. Conrad's dark tale based on his life on the swell reflected a wider curse for humanity, exposing London as the dark heart of an ever-exploitative capitalism, a generator of wickedness in warmer outposts all over the Empire that simultaneously fed the modernisation of home. 'A great future lies before Tilbury Docks,' wrote Conrad in the nonfiction work *The Mirror of the Sea* (1907), bewitched by the striking modernity of the hydraulic cranes. That future is now gone, along with the dockers clocking in, clocking out. Labour is no longer so visible but hidden beyond fences and gates and behind desks. Unions fought to bring workers into the realm of time-mastery, standardising conditions to give dockers such luxuries as working hours and fixed shifts. These days, Tilbury floats sedately on the edge of a void, its illustrious past haunting it in flashes of memory. The mud by the cruise terminal glitters grey-brown under bright September skies, as the oil and water collected in pools separates into a murky yet twinkling rainbow. Stacks of containers and gleaming new cars reflect the systematisation of globalised capital set against the prematurely old and cracked nature of Tilbury's town centre.

By the 2010s, the decline of Tilbury had fed into something that was gaining more traction in the British media: the idea of the 'white working class'. The charity-shop-kebab-shop scruffiness of the industrialised dockside town became typical of a neglected town in Brexit Britain, a cradle of the 'left behind'. Port towns reflect decline more starkly than most places; it feels that more than anywhere, Thurrock is at the sharp end of the south-east. Despite the stumbling blocks of Brexit and Covid, almost all British trade, 95 per cent, still comes through ports. Yet, there isn't a great deal of work to be found in the ports themselves. Port traffic increased by 35 per cent between the early 1980s and the turn of the millennium, but over the same period, the workforce was decimated.

Tilbury still holds on to working-class traditions of solidarity. The Tilbury Band, the town's brass band founded by the National Union of Railwaymen in 1919, symbolises this, a stoic anomaly with a lightly worn communal spirit that alleviates the prevailing cynicism of England. Members meet to practise in an unassuming building near the docks, in which cardboard egg boxes line the ceiling of the hall to stop the noise from annoying the neighbours. They are fiercely proud of Tilbury, while acknowledging its reputation might have some truth to it. Horn player Paul Carver was mugged on his way to practice, but he says that could have happened when the town was still thriving. The band no longer paraded around Tilbury before Christmas. 'The local kids worked out if they were at the other end of the street to us, they'd knock on the door and get the money that was meant for charity,' said Carver, whose granddad joined in 1933, and who followed his father when he picked up the French horn with the band in 1978. 'When I was a kid there were six or seven working men's clubs in Tilbury and the majority of the band worked on Tilbury Docks,' says Paul. 'You'd be lucky if there are two operating now.'

When I visited the band in 2015, Thurrock was included on the xenophobic, Europsceptic party Ukip's 12-strong hit list for potential seats in the forthcoming general election. 'The whole thing about immigration being peddled by Ukip is that, if you actually live in an area, it's different,' said Brian Martin, the chairman and tuba player in the Tilbury Band. 'The people who stir up that kind of thing are always from outside. In one of the local schools I'm governor of, 57 per cent of kids have English as their second language. Last year, they got 'good to outstanding' in an Ofsted inspection. You hear all sorts of languages at the school gate. But once you get inside, no one thinks, "Well, he's an Albanian, he's a Sri Lankan" – there is still a good community in the area.'

Essex has long been painted as a hotbed of bigotry, the place where white people moved to escape parts of London that were no longer white enough for them. In 1994, Lord Inglewood, a pro-European Conservative MEP, told a newspaper that the 'Essex view of conservatism' was threatening the 'more generous, less xenophobic historic tradition'. This is of course not the whole story: much as in the country at large, electoral support of the far right has always been a minority pursuit in Essex. Essex has been a welcoming place over the years to the migratory flows of people, from Jewish groups to Westcliff or, later, Canvey Island, or the Irish, who helped to build much of Essex, or the Ugandan Asians coming to Basildon as refugees fleeing Idi Amin's regime, or the people of colour now choosing Essex after they have been priced out of London.

That is not to say that there have not been racist flash points, often in places where migration is high and wages are low. Tayo Yusuff, a producer and director, moved from Wood Green in north London to Tilbury in Essex in the 2000s, when he was 13. 'It was obvious I wasn't from there. One, I was black. I remember being at school on the first day and being, like, something is really weird about this school.' His mum was a poor single parent who moved to Tilbury so she could buy her very first house, one of the first people on the street to do so. At first, Yusuff was surprised by the bouncing violence and glottal stops of his new classmates' accent. But that wasn't exactly what felt so different. 'It took me 'til lunchtime to clock that I was one of two black people there,' he said. 'In my old school, I guess if you were white British you were in the minority, and then there were people who were close to that skin type, the Turks and the Kurds. Other than that, it was Somali, Jamaican, African from all different parts. It was a bit mad – I'd never seen so many white folk.'

At first he wanted to be accepted as a Tilbury boy, 'wearing tracksuits because that's what they wore, being rude to your parents, teachers, being unruly, naughty, not listening in class.' Some Saturdays they would head to Lakeside shopping centre. They tried to terrorise security guards, create a big rumpus that might get attention and, speculated Yusuff, help them forget about their daily lives. He was offered alcohol for the first time in his life. 'It was Saturday daytime; we got four cans of Fosters and went to this ditch. We got drunk and passed out. That was my first time experiencing the world of Tilbury.'

Yusuff described how a violent atmosphere began to take hold. 'There were loads of attacks,' he said. 'It was more racially aggravated. At the time that I was moving in, we were one of the first few branches of black people to move here. But when more and more came, the more racist tendencies began to appear. I remember the first time someone called me a black cunt, I said, "What?" When I was in London, I'd never ever had anything racist said to me before.'

Yusuff said racism towards him knew no age limit. The comments came from girls, young kids, 'super young kids', adults, old people. Not everyone was racist, he stressed, it just felt like it. 'There was a lot of resentment there for people of colour, because things weren't going well in their lives: there were generations of families that were on the dole, they couldn't get jobs, and the reasons they thought they couldn't was these foreigners taking their jobs.' Physical violence was part of his daily life, such as the time Yusuff managed to make a lucky escape when five cars pulled over on his road, and out of each one jumped a man carrying a different weapon, including a pole, a bat and a Stanley knife. Or the time he spent hours scraping off a painted message, 'Niggers live here', from the front of his mum's house. When I spoke to him in 2018, Yusuff said that integration had improved but incomers were still being targeted. 'When I first moved here it was the blacks, now it's the Poles.'

Tilbury is also remembered for the dockworkers' support of Enoch Powell in the 1960s. But by rights, Tilbury should represent a very different story for people of colour. In 1948, Essex became the destination for the *Windrush*, the ship that carried about 500 immigrants from the Caribbean and docked in Tilbury, with thousands more people arriving in the ensuing years. Lord Kitchener performed for Pathé News:

'London is the place for me. London this lovely city.' Essex didn't get a mention.

'With the *Windrush*, Essex actually symbolises the rise of multicultural Britain,' said Southend-based artist Elsa James. But the symbolism sits uneasily with the lived experience. 'There is still a conversation, even today, black folk in London saying to me, seriously: "What are you doing in Essex?"' James grew up in Acton, west London, moving to Chafford Hundred in Thurrock with her husband before choosing Southend in order to bring up her family by the sea. I met her when she burst onto the Essex cultural scene with her *Forgotten Black Essex* project in 2018. One of the stories she unearthed with the help of historian Steve Martin was that of Princess Dinubolu of Senegal, whose entry into a beauty contest held at the Kursaal in Southend was held up as an early example of black resistance in Essex. James doesn't

Jamaican immigrants are met by RAF officials after the HMT *Empire Windrush* landed at Tilbury, 1948

know if she really was a princess or from Senegal; Martin thinks Princess Dinubolu was a local mixed-race girl who had agreed to take part in a media stunt. 'What would a princess be doing in Southend?' In that sense, however, her story is still at home in Essex, a place of canny self-mythologising as a tool of defiance.

The overwhelming sense I have had talking to James about living and working in Essex is a feeling of tiredness at the constant micro-battles and sweepings under the carpet that is still everyday life for minority cultures. She told me that since the Brexit vote her family had avoided certain pubs in Southend, while her husband, Leroy, had found that people would stare at him in the gym because he was black. (He went to a gym run by the same company, in London, and 'there was nothing, no drama'.) Elsa and Leroy wondered about moving back to London but couldn't afford it, and equally James wanted to stay and fight and conquer Essex. She told me there are reasons to hold out hope for the black experience in Essex. At the brutalist buildings of the University of Essex on the banks of the Colne in Colchester, for example, there has been an increase in the number of black British students.

Sunder Katwala, a writer, activist and director of think-tank British Future, also sees the potential for optimism. Katwala, whose mother was born in Ireland and father born in India, grew up partly in Southend, and believes Essex has been on its own journey into multiculturalism, albeit not such a heralded and visible one as somewhere like Walthamstow or Hackney, which once had similar problems with the far right to those Thurrock has today. Katwala first encountered this multicultural Essex on the terraces of Southend United. He told me about how a chant about the racial makeup of Southend's strike partnership Brett Angell and Andy Ansah – 'Ansah's black, Angell's white, we are effing dynamite' – felt to him like the formation of a kind of meritocratic anti-racist folk art. 'I remember once at Southend, somebody did make a racist chant about a Wolves player, and a guy on the North Bank says, "Oi, mate, what's Andy Ansah going to think of that?"'

In Essex, I couldn't shake off the feeling that the gritted-teeth harmony of all these houses, Green Belt fields and roads had created the kind of fervent, sometimes violent, energy we were seeing play out in pockets of the county. After all, the infamous stand-off at the Dale Farm Travellers' site in Crays Hill near Basildon in 2011, which exploded into pitched battle when activists defending the eighty Traveller families' right to remain clashed with police, had its roots in a single neighbour's complaint that the Travellers' presence was devaluing the price of his parents' property. Travellers have been part of the Essex scene for centuries. 'The Essex working class may be caricatured, but Gypsy residents are tolerated only if frozen on canvas in the nineteenth century, rarely as living persons,' wrote Professor Judith Okely in a letter in reply to a *Guardian* article I had written about Essex in 2019. 'The MP for Harwich and North Essex, Bernard Jenkin, said in his 2010 election leaflet: "This is a precious corner of England. Our countryside is precious . . . wind farms, traffic, phone masts, gypsy sites: local people should be able to decide these issues." No matter that this precious landscape depicted by Constable in *The Vale of Dedham* has a tent-dwelling Gypsy woman and baby in the foreground.' Despite Essex's Traveller heritage, Basildon District Council took the Dale Farm families to the High Court for expanding the site onto Green Belt land. Once the Travellers had been cleared, the homeowner in question, Len Gridley, had expected it to be turned back into Green Belt land. 'Ten years later nothing has been done,' he told the *Guardian* in 2021. 'They [the council] don't want to clean up the mess.'

A retired chartered structural engineer who lived in Castle Point told me he voted for Britain to leave the EU due to immigration, yet when I pressed him further, it seemed immigration was just a different way of saying housing development. 'The government have asked Castle Point Borough Council to make provision for 8,000 new homes,' he said. 'Of course, that's all based on population projections, and that's just because we've got 300,000 new people a year coming into the country. It's not that the population of Castle Point will naturally expand to require 8,000 more homes. It's people coming in from outside, and we can't cope. What they are looking for is to make a lot of the Green Belt land into housing'.

He told me about a section of land on the edge of Castle Point, a bit of Green Belt between Benfleet and Basildon. 'They've been wanting for twenty-five years to build on that, and I've been on several committees to try and stop it. We stop it every time. You would get this urban sprawl all the way from Basildon right through to Southend, with no green. They want to put 200 houses on there, and Castle Point can't cope with that. Infrastructure is a problem. Right through the country it is a problem. There are not enough hospitals, not enough police – I mean, with all these things, there is a huge pressure on the country. So, yeah, immigration was a big problem for everybody, I think.'

There is always a convenient scapegoat in the person from the other side of the wall, and so immigrants are blamed for the failures of economic planning, failures in infrastructure, becoming victims of a political short-termism that is typified by the Conservatives' proposed extension of Right to Buy, which – if it were to be pushed through – would let a small number of people gain a very valuable asset at the expense of future generations, leading to further societal decay in the not-too-distant future. At the time of the Brexit vote, Castle Point, which had one of the highest votes in the country to leave the EU, was also one of the whitest places in the UK, which in the years preceding the referendum, 2014/15, saw net migration of just 81 people. (When I pointed this out to the Castle Point resident, he sounded a little put out. 'No, there aren't *at the moment*,' he said. 'There's no room for them to come. Castle Point is full!') After the country voted to leave the EU, I was still living in London and so took it upon myself to try to get the measure of why different parts of Essex voted the way they did. I talked to Beryl Allen, 79, who lived in Benfleet in Castle Point and had taught in one of the local secondary schools before she retired. 'The whole time there I could have counted the immigrants on one hand,' she said. 'I don't understand why they should vote in so many numbers to leave.' One reason, she posited, was the changing face of London's East End. 'Is it seeing what's happened to those areas where they've come from? My brother-in-law came from Ilford and he said it's "totally Asian" now. Do they look back there and think, "Oh no"?'

Essex after the boom years of growth came to represent the idea of 'white flight' in the UK, due to migration from London contributing to the relative whiteness of the county when compared to the capital's racial mix. 'White flight', the process of people moving away from an area deemed too diverse, has been debunked as too simple an explanation for the complex range of desires that explain why people move out of London. The BBC's controversial *Last Whites of the East End* documentary riffed on the idea of a 'white working class' that was 'forced' out of the East End, but ignored any notion of ethnic mingling and the fact that many ancestors of this supposedly 'indigenous' category would have come to the East End as migrants themselves.

Racism has historically clustered to the edge of the growing metropolis. The BNP and Ukip have made political hay in London-border edgelands such as Barking and Dagenham. When the 'historically Essex' London borough's housing stock fell into the hands of buy-to-let landlords, when job losses at Ford meant a cloud of resentment fell over the area, and when the ethnic mix reflected migratory patterns out of London, its politics changed. Eleven BNP councillors were elected in 2006. As Daniel Trilling noted in his book on the English far right, *Bloody Nasty People*, this was a story as much about Labour voter apathy in the face of New Labour's post-Thatcherite policies as anything else. And, as Trilling has noted, the people who campaign and eventually take on and neutralise far-right threats are from areas such as Barking and Dagenham. The recent presence of Britain First in Southend was met with antifascist protest, with one campaigner throwing a pint of cockles over one of the fascist visitors.

Myths are powerful, and the myth of the unshakeable, white East Ender is one that has endured more successfully on screen than it has in London's eastern boroughs, which are invariably more ethnically mixed than they were fifty years ago. For some British residents, their antipathy to change is articulated through practicalities. I talked to a man whose father, originally from Bethnal Green, had moved the family out to Upminster when he was 8; as an adult, he himself continued into leafier Essex, to Navestock and Kelvedon after that. A few years ago, out of the blue, his dad had the romantic idea of moving back to Silvertown, down the Camel Road and back to the East End he knew as a boy. But he moved back to Essex after he realised the East End he'd got cloudy eyes over wasn't there.

This is the flip side of the trailblazing Essex dream. In

zooming ahead into a classless future, some of the East Enders who left to buy a house in Essex expected their old haunts to remain exactly how they had left them. Now, Essex wasn't so much about the future. It was about what to do about the fact that the past they had left behind was no longer there. The gushing of London emigres into all these new towns and suburbs and suddenly swollen villages created two warring islands. London's former wantaways and London itself have ended up at opposite ends of the political spectrum in the UK.

Castle Point has the highest level of homeownership in the country, with 82 per cent of its dwellings owner-occupied, according to Office for National Statistics figures, while Hackney has the highest proportion of social rented property in the country, at 43 per cent. Coincidentally or not, Castle Point had the third highest Leave vote, 72.7 per cent, while Hackney had the third highest Remain vote, at 78.5 per cent. Add to the mix the glut of high-value homeowners in a liberal enclave such as Hackney, who were happy with the status quo, and the precarious, almost invisible class of people struggling to afford the rent in an Essex suburb in Castle Point, who *weren't* happy with the status quo, and you have a vision of a nation divided by invisible but dramatic lines of property, class and aspiration.

'White flight' is perhaps too easy a term because it supposes that a fear of the other was the main impetus for people leaving London. But what if people's views on immigration, as well as a grim outcome of living in the heart of a once powerful Empire, are tied up in the years of living in the same property in a place away from the tumult and flux of your old neighbourhood? Watching as civic life drains away in privatised England might do funny things to your expectations, making memories of the old city harden with a sepia crust and narrowing your view until all you see is the field over the other side of the road, and sense danger.

Unstoppable, Immovable

*

Luke and I eventually reached Barling as we started to feel the limits of our perambulatory endurance test and having just run out of water. On the way into the village there are some newer looking buildings, perhaps built after the Barling Bomber, or bombers, received their dawn raid warning from Ray. But as we approached the end point of our walk, the All Saints Church in Barling proper, we began to sympathise somewhat with the context of the local terrorist's ire. Ducks flung spray at us from the village pond as we caught sight of some ancient cottages: we had entered old, unchanged, rural Essex by the back door, as if our meandering marsh walk had opened a portal into the past. A village with a name rooted in ancient English, Barling still felt apart from the sprawl of Southend. The bomber's worst fears had never quite happened – at least not yet. We walked on and noticed that the inscribed year on the wall of each dwelling we passed got older and older as we got closer to the church, from 1738, to 1670, to 1480.

Viewed on an OS map, it can seem as if Barling has been pushed out as far as it can go against the encroachment of Southend. A village edging into a muddy fringe; any further and it would be swept out with the tidal River Roach. Perhaps the violent transgressions of the bomber were simply a refusal to accept a surge of yellow-grey Barratt Home blandness. As we marvelled at the shambling and incongruous magnificence of one of the oldest properties still standing in this area of south Essex, I noticed three old boys had their eyes fixed upon us from across the road. I asked this contingent of neighbours if they had any theories about who the Barling Bomber was. The older of the three cried out, exaggerating as if trying to deflect the inquiry of this visitor. 'Oooh, you be going back a fair bit now,' he said in his rounded-yet-clipped old Essex tones. But the one in the hat to his right looked more pensive. 'We all have our theories.'

Perhaps it was a little expectant to think the old boy might fess up to any knowledge of what truly happened. After all, the Essex villager's reputation as hostile to 'furriners' is well documented and centuries old. Despite my living a few miles away from here, we were outsiders from the big town of Southend. I couldn't work out if these men seemed indomitable examples of the grand tradition of suspicious and fatalistic rural life, or the end of all that. Villages have a cherished reputation as representing the true England of the green, the cricket team and even the undercover fox hunt. But the places I have encountered in recent years are often unsure of where exactly they fit in the world. South-east English villages are often dominated by a facade of wealth. The only new housing that arrives is expensive. Sometimes the local pub has become a boutique hotel or an Italian restaurant, so that locals don't go there any more, but tourists do, while the car park for the train station a few miles away expands massively to cater for the arrival of commuters who drive from new neighbourhoods that the Barling Bomber could not stop.

10

Mucking In

For my father-in-law, Cliff Hatton, the gravel pits, clay pits and sand pits of South Ockendon became, in his own excited words, 'a nirvana' after his family moved there from the LCC-built Harold Hill Estate in 1964. 'Being mad keen fishermen, we were more than keen to find out where we could put a line, and it wasn't very long before we discovered we had hit El Dorado, because in just about every direction there was a glorious pit.' Cliff and his brother Barry enrolled in the Moor Hall and Belhus Angling Society, which had waters in South Ockendon: the Hamble Lane pit, the Ripples, the main pool, and Arisdale Avenue, which was opposite Ford's Advanced Vehicle Operations plant at Aveley, which turned out prestige cars such as the Escort RS2000 and the Mexico. Cliff would often proudly tell of how he fished the pits during his teenage years. He visited after school and every weekend and spent spare time looking after the pits, picking up litter, which seemed like a futile exercise considering they were being dumped in on an industrial scale.

When Cliff and Barry arrived at the waters in South Ockendon, they had already been dumped in for many years, in particular their favourite pit at Hamble Lane. 'It could be quite an alarming experience,' he said. Things came to a head one Sunday morning when Cliff's mate Michael was visiting the pits without him. 'We'd grown accustomed over the months and the years to hearing muffled explosions and seeing plumes of smoke rising up from the ground, but God knows what it was that exploded on this particular morning, because Michael told me that there was an explosion so loud that it deafened them. It could have been something from World War Two, a huge explosion erupted in the middle of the Hamble Lane dumping site. What it was, heaven only knows.'

This juxtaposition of Edenic youthful dreaming and toxic effluvia speaks to Thurrock and, more widely, south Essex, home to landscapes that have become key scenes in the horrific sublime of anthropocenic south-east England. But back then the future of this luckless landscape was still up for grabs. Cliff and his fellow fishing club members knew the rules, knew the dumpers should respect the quality of the swims, and knew that the anglers were entitled to let them know they shouldn't be polluting the waters. 'Sometimes the dumpers would get perilously close to the waters. We were precocious kids of 13 or 14 years old, and such was our dedication to preserving the pits, we would quite boldly go up to these burly lorry drivers and order them back, tell them to back away from the water, lest their loads pollute it,' Cliff said. The drivers would do as the kids asked. 'They probably realised we were in the right and they had probably been instructed to keep away anyway so they did as they were told and backed off.'

Cliff was a big fan of local heroes the Small Faces and the music of the burgeoning 1960s mod scene that was filling Mecca ballrooms with R&B and soul from Forest Gate to Clacton – but it wasn't music that was keeping him up all night. As peers might be trying their luck with a potential squeeze in the dark corner of a parquet-floored hall, he was sitting under the moonlight with a rod, eager to catch a handsome carp, perch or bream. It wasn't long before the Hatton brothers became accustomed to the rumble of lorries and the reflection of headlights on the water of the pits. 'There was more activity in the site, which was hundreds of acres, during the hours of darkness than there was during the hours of light, even though everybody should by law have been gone,' he said. Lorries would be coming through the gates 'literally nose-to-tail' with sometimes up to fourteen in a convoy all through the night until sunrise. 'I hate to think of the nature of the chemicals that were being dumped there,' he said.

An elderly neighbour had asked Cliff to bring back some sticks from the dump that would be useful for his rose gardening. Remembering on the way back from fishing, after the sun had gone down, he climbed on top of the pile of wood to search for sticks, but changed his mind to carry out the search at the base of the pile. 'I just leapt into the darkness thinking I was going to land on solid ground,' said Cliff. Instead, he found himself up to his waist in what he believes was a caustic substance that was 'almost certainly dumped by May & Baker', the pharmaceutical company based in Dagenham. 'That led to me spending a week or so in hospital and many, many weeks after that invalided indoors with great burns to my legs and on my face.' Burning pools of solution had formed in cavities of bare earth, thick, black, glutinous, sweet-smelling stuff that burned into his legs, hands and face but spared his more delicate regions. 'I thank the Lord for good quality Lyle and Scott underpants,' he said.

Cliff's parents, knowing their place, never sought compensation. 'I am sure nowadays the parents would have taken the dumping company to court; they probably would have received many thousands in damages, but it was deemed at the time that there is nothing you can do and it was forgotten about and they just carried on as normal.'

Once recovered enough to return to the pits, Cliff found two half-empty drums of granulated cyanide floating in one of them. Another time, he and Barry came across a mountain of glass vials and realised that barbiturates and the like had been dumped a few yards from the school fence, again, according to Cliff, almost certainly by May & Baker. 'We took some samples to the local police station, and showed them these dangerous drugs and mentioned they were within yards of the school playing field, and the only question we were asked was: "What were you doing over there?" They were more worried about the fact that we were trespassing.'

Cliff quickly became a thorn in the side of the local authorities he was dismayed had allowed this to happen. As an outraged 15-year-old, he regularly wrote to the *Thurrock Gazette* about the issue. His letters were published but remained unanswered by the council. He escalated his campaign, dumping a sackful of poisoned fish on the steps of Thurrock Council's area office along with a letter containing his address – but again received no response.

As Cliff reached his late teens, some of the pits were being drained as they switched from huge fishing spots to desolate dumping grounds for good. 'When the water got low enough, each weekend club members would get together in working parties and rescue as many fish as we could,' said Cliff. Despite the efforts of up to thirty club members who plunged into the murky water in chest waders each weekend, Cliff said that they were unable to rescue the vast majority of the fish. He still winced at the thought of the fish floundering about in the couple of feet of muddy water; those that had not already perished were buried alive under tonnes of industrial waste. 'And of course with them went all the voles and the birdlife, including kingfishers and bitterns. It was dubbed the Ripples because when the wind blew on it and the sun shone on it, it was such a beautiful looking place. It sparkled. It was a paradise and it just went under a sea of filth.'

By 1971, the game was up. The *Angling Times* sent reporter Dave Nash to document the disaster that happened at the

Ripples. His resulting report was nothing less than the anatomy of a localised extinction. 'In less than a decade, what was one of the best fisheries in Essex has been savagely raped and despoiled. Seven hundred tons of household garbage is deposited into the pits every day, along with a similar undisclosed amount of industrial refuse.' Cliff sent me the page in the post, the top picture, taken by Nash, a shocking image of two men attempting to catch a pike between the scrap cars that lined the bank of the Arisdale lake. 'If it's not the water level dropping,' Jerry Hulbert, the vice president of the Moor Hall and Belhus AS told the *Angling Times*, 'then it's the rubbish encroaching a few feet every day.'

The lack of response from the authorities to the scandalous pollution that burned him as a teenager and destroyed the habitat he so cherished shaped Cliff. 'I don't know if it affected other people as profoundly as it affected me but I can honestly say that the whole experience of seeing my El Dorado disappear under a billion tonnes of chemicals and industrial waste, the effect that had on me, was to foment a lifelong grudge against authority. To this day, the very word or the very term leaves me with a bad taste in the mouth and I naturally assume that anything Thurrock Council have ever or will be responsible for will be second rate and unworthy. It really did have that marked an effect on the way I thought about things.'

South Ockendon today is a patchwork of suburbia on the edge of the Green Belt, a luckless residential zone impinged upon by the M25 motorway and the A13 road. Hovering above it is the endless industry of the Thames Estuary, all thick, acrid treacle air, and the fallout from the Lakeside shopping centre. Is this way of life going to last in perpetuity? What do we do if it does? What do we do if it doesn't?

*

The waste-filled shoreline seemed to carry on forever, sheets of asbestos lying over bottle caps and shards of glass that had been softened by the attention of the tides. Cascades of ragged polythene in off-whites, blacks and greys had been spewed out of the bank of earth and landfill, a layer cake of soil, rubbish, soil, rubbish, with plastic mingling with the thickets of brambles and green vegetation to become almost indistinguishable from it. Almost. But look for more than a second and its uncanniness hits you, as if you realise the landscape you were enjoying walking through was as artificial as a film set, but quite a lot less pleasant.

I walked out to this historic landfill beyond the old Coalhouse Fort from East Tilbury station with Professor Kate Spencer, an environmental geochemist at Queen Mary University of London (QMUL), who has dedicated more than a decade to studying the threat of historical coastal landfill, concentrating much of her research in south Essex. On the way we passed Bata's old shoemaking town, where his statue stood next to the long-closed factory in a state of ironic pride, like Ozymandias if he was an icon of benevolent capitalism. We were walking south to the river to look at two landfill sites that are eroding. There are around fifty historic coastal sites in the Thames Estuary area (out of 1,215 in England), but out of the Essex sites it was only Thurrock that was eroding.

We arrived at the first landfill site. Spencer and QMUL have analysed materials at this site and others in Essex and the Thames Estuary and around the country. 'It's definitely contaminated. If you were building a house here, you'd remediate or remove it, because the levels of contamination would breach human health guidelines and it breaches safe guidelines for ecology – there are invertebrates in here, but [the toxicity] is at levels that could cause them harm.'

The common way to deal with historic landfill has been capping the sites to try to stop contaminants and waste from coming to the surface. Spencer likened the act of dumping and capping to her grandmother who, when she got dementia, started to hide things that upset her, like old clothes or dirty dishes, putting cushions over them or placing them in cupboards. She said it would have been a really easy decision to send rubbish to the Thurrock tip. 'Put it on a barge, ship it down here.' It was actually the local authorities, or vestries, who first sent rubbish to Essex. East London vestries such as Mile End bought up land in Essex with the intention of using barges and steam tugs to shift the rubbish they didn't have space for. In 1889, Kensington began sending its rubbish to Purfleet, in what is now the unitary borough of Thurrock. The unpopulated wasteland of south Essex provided an extremely convenient place for London's political class to shift the stuff the powerful did not want in their backyard. As Lee Jackson recounts in his history of the filthy capital, *Dirty Old London*, an LCC official cut to the chase when describing the reason for using Essex as a place to dump waste: 'The natural solution is to shoot it in some sparsely inhabited district, where public opinion is not strong enough to effectually resent it being deposited.'

Thurrock is frequently reported as one of the worst places to live in Britain. It has always acted as a kind of dumping ground for the ills of London, bearing the brunt of smog-producing industry, landfill sites and, latterly, vehicle access to the capital. Perhaps as a result, Thurrock is the least happy and the most toxic area – according to the WHO's findings it has the highest average readings of toxic particles known as PM2.5s in the country. Some of the pollution comes from emissions from vehicles travelling along the M25 and the motorway's adjoining roads, and some from the factories along the Thames. Fly-tipping sites can stretch for miles.

Historically, Spencer said, dumping legislation was always thin on the ground, with records barely kept, aside from ad hoc efforts in filing cabinets. 'The idea was this is the end of the road for the rubbish,' said Spencer. 'We have put it in a hole in the ground, covered it up, and that problem has now gone away. But with climate change, flooding, erosion and heavy rainfall and all the modern environmental issues that we didn't think about [earlier], we realise we haven't put it away. We've just been storing the problem.'

Spencer pointed out the different sources of waste just lying around on the beach. Cadmium leaking from old car batteries. Bottles of unknown medicines. Domestic waste, commercial waste, including many, many different examples of fabric. For ages, she said, there was a big clod of fabric that had long ago been shredded and was coming out of the earth along with little pink cotton reels. She said she always used to imagine the detritus was from a warehouse that had chucked all its bales of rags away, a frayed funeral banner for the demise of the rag trade in east London.

Plastic is already fusing with the ecology of the Thames. 'Something like 75 per cent [of all plastic ever produced] has already gone to landfill. So there is a huge amount of plastic in there that could be released.' Microplastics have been found in human organs and tissue and mammals, fish, pretty much everything, with the potential impact on human health not exactly known.

Spencer started her journey by analysing the toxicity of these kinds of landfill sites and their effect on the surrounding salt marsh habitats at a site on the Medway Estuary on the other side of the Thames. She took what is called a sediment core, which in effect helped her dig into the records of historical pollution. The result was a kind of palimpsest of London's industrial boom. 'You are going back down into history and analysing the chemistry and you can see how the quality of the river changed. The Thames was polluted noticeably from the 1820s/1830s and it reached a big peak in the late 1800s; you can imagine, the Industrial Revolution, lead smelting, and all that kind of thing. Then it sort of tapers off a little bit, and then mid-twentieth century, post-World War II, in big cities like London there would be a huge population growth, [more] industrial growth. You can see the water quality deteriorate and that is recorded in the sediment.'

The Control of Pollution Act in 1974, which placed restrictions on the disposal of toxic waste and radioactive waste, put us on the way to the more discerning waste disposal practices of today. Before that air pollution was the big topic, particularly in these parts, with the pea-souper smogs that crept eastwards from London into the metropolitan Essex areas until the Clean Air Act of the 1950s. It wasn't until the 1970s, however, that environmental regulations really started, when legislation that ensured such improvements as the removal of lead from petrol was brought forward. Among the endless bleakness of this beach of despair, what is heartening about talking to Spencer is the undeniable evidence of legislation – the stark face of human decision-making – working in practice.

With her colleague at QMUL, Dr James H Brand, Spencer created a report of the risk of pollution from historic coastal sites for the Environment Agency, using research into two other former landfills on the Essex side of the Thames Estuary. Leigh Marsh was used as a site for dumping between 1955 and 1967 and Hadleigh Marsh, which was active during the 1980s. Their research is the first of its kind as it looks at the risk of pollution to estuaries or coasts in the event of flooding or erosion. They analysed waste and soil-like material from the landfill and, compared to published sediment quality guidelines, some of the samples were found to have lead concentrations of more than twelve times the recommended level for good ecological health.

Once, on a picnic on a beautiful and hot springtime day on Two Tree Island, a nature reserve at the edge of the estuary, my 3-year-old daughter, Greta, kept asking 'What's that?' whenever she spotted the thick brown bottoms of beer bottles, 1980s Tesco bags, or old shoes – so many shoes – protruding out of the dry ground. It was a surreal detail from a pleasant trip that I might once have laughed off but now, accompanied by my children who will inherit the problems, it felt like a bad dream. Most people think of the sea wall at Hadleigh Marsh as a pleasantly grassy place for a 4-kilometre-long stroll towards the reward of a pint and some cockles at Leigh-on-Sea. And to all intents and purposes it is, or at least was, until Spencer told me that the raised bank of what I presumed was earth and hardcore and other materials was in fact made largely from the things that people had deemed fit to throw away during the boom years of guilt-free consumption.

On the way downhill to the Tilbury tip, Spencer stopped to show me how stark the geological differences created by rubbish were. We gazed south-west towards the stretch of coastal landfill at Tilbury known as Bottle Beach. Spencer pointed out that behind a field used for agriculture there was a long portion of land higher than the marsh. 'That landscape shouldn't look like that,' she said. 'If you'd have gone back 150 years, we would have just been looking at a flat marsh, your kind of Charles Dickens *Great Expectations* salt marsh. It should have just been completely, completely flat.' Spencer said if you drive out of London on the A13 as you head east, you should be able to see the river, as you are driving along the floodplain. 'But you can't, you're seeing a whole landscape of landfill.'

Essex. A place of facelifts and implants and unnatural curves, terminology applying to its post-landfill landscape as much as it does its reality celebrities. The capped-off rubbish hillsides, horizons that let you into the secret there used to be enormous dumps of one kind or another all over this terrain. The hills along the estuary might look like natural formations, but many are in fact the remnants of former dumping grounds. An artificial hill in an old metropolitan Essex area of east London has been known for years as Beckton Alp due to its enormity, despite the fact it was formed from a huge heap of toxic spoil dumped by the old Gas Works. Its most imaginative use was as a dry ski slope, opened in 1989 by Princess Diana.

The erosion of landfill into estuaries is far from being a problem exclusive to Essex but one that applies to plenty of others, such as the Humber that divides East Yorkshire and North Lincolnshire. It's just that Essex happens to be next to England's giant capital, and so its landfills tended to be supersized. Mucking Marsh in Thurrock was one of the largest landfills in western Europe, taking on 660,000 tonnes of rubbish from the dustbins of west London each year, brought downriver on barges every day before dawn. 'It could be seen from space,' said Graham Harwood, a Goldsmiths academic and artist based in Leigh-on-Sea. He and his wife, Matsuko Yokokoji, run the art initiative YoHa, whose work unpicks the Essex estuary's hidden past. I met Harwood as he stood on the cockle shell shingle by Leigh-on-Sea's old town fixing an old rowing boat. He handed me some boots and we walked out onto the mud to the wide channel called the Gut. It was still too full of water when we arrived so we had to wait five minutes, and sit on the rim of his rowing boat. He told me about the tradition of protest in Essex against dumping and ecological disaster: 'No More Oil On Canvey's Soil,' protesters chanted to stop the oil refineries on Canvey in the 1970s. He told me about the retired former dump workers who, like him, are the members of the old craft club here, made up of ex-cocklers, lorry drivers and people who worked at the tips. 'It's not a kind of yacht club, it's more a kind of self-maintenance club . . . old blokes like that have been here as long as the barnacles.'

We walked out onto the mud, which was still at its most sloppy, and followed the tide out. The sun was hiding behind thick clouds. Graham was an artist and academic but after decades on the Essex coast had acquired the slightly grizzly air of the seafarer. He kept acquiring boats, he told me, and seemed addicted to improving his knowledge of doing them up, but frustrated by never having the 'born knowledge' that the Leigh fishing families had.

Harwood told me he was interested in 'the philosophy of waste'. Dumps had a 'magical quality' to them, he said. He wanted to set up public assemblies between the retired tip workers, who know what kinds of toxicity are buried in the landfills, and political stakeholders, young people and activists. He wanted to, he said, 'set up the kinds of dialogues about the haunting of waste in the future. Think, the worst has already happened, so what can we do with this.'

At the heart of Harwood's philosophy is 'the wasteland', an idea also central to Essex's place in the world. 'A kind of Calvinistic idea of improper use from God's point of view. If you have land like these marshes, which are not used, because by God you have to be a steward of the land, you have to improve it, so you have to dam the fucking thing off and farm it.' He told me that when people went to the Americas and found land no one was farming, it was called wasteland. 'Therefore you could go in and kill every fucker there, because they weren't using it appropriately,' he said. 'This idea of waste is so kind of fixed in our culture, and it's so embedded in colonialism as well. And so you can see the way that London has used Essex as a kind of colony . . . sending out vast tracts of shit.' At Pitsea tip they are using a bird hide overlooking the tip that is now rebranded an RSPB wildlife centre, he said 'but is still just a pile of crap. A mountain that has grown and grown and grown.' Essex is crap.

Harwood told me of how DP World, the Dubai-based owners of the mega port just upriver, had been dredging, and there had been huge problems with heavy metals that had been disturbed. The company re-engineered the estuary for much bigger ships. 'They keep dredging the whole time, which destroys all the young fish, so they've lost all the fishing for soles,' he said. 'The cocklers kind of fight it and sometimes get compensation for this and that.'

We walked over the mud and onto a kind of marshland islet that constituted the tip of Two Tree Island as Harwood talked further about his ideas around the marshes as a site of waste but also production. He showed me where sewage and slurry used to be pumped out, and that there were once timber wharves on the Thames that sent the wood sourced from the trees that lined the hills above us years before the houses arrived. We looked at the carcasses of boats embedded in the mud, waiting to disintegrate into the ooze as so many have before, wrecks on top of wrecks on top of wrecks.

After we returned to the shore, Harwood introduced me to a gentleman called Mick with a Captain Bird's Eye beard and an all-year tan. It turned out he hadn't been at sea all his life, but at Pitsea tip, for what felt like a lifetime.

He worked on the water from 17, going out fishing on a boat called *Audacity*. 'There used to be a lot of flounders in there. You could get a bag full easily just with a stick with a hook on the end.' He said the fishing wasn't the same any more and he reckoned it was not so much due to DP World's big port, but the landfill. There were also no crabs for a long time. 'I used to go to the old creek over there and I'd get a bucket full of soft crab,' he said. 'I went up there a couple of year ago, and there was none.'

Pitsea was an old Victorian tip where, Mick said, no one

Mucking landfill site, 2003

ever knew exactly what was being dumped. In the end they
found out the soil in some of the places he worked was often
contaminated with 'arsenic, strychnine, who knows what'. A
lorry driver, Thomas Carroll, died after inhaling lethal fumes
given off by two toxic loads dumped in Pitsea, which made
the press across the UK. 'About fifteen minutes before Mr
Carroll arrived with a 1,500 gallon load of aluminium oxide
in sulphuric acid, another toxic load had been dumped at
the tip,' reported the *Aberdeen Evening Express* in 1975. 'The
mixture of the two gave off hydrogen sulphide – a highly poisonous gas.' According to the *Daily Mirror*, the tip at Pitsea
was nicknamed 'the bin of Britain'. The verdict was acute
asphyxial death, which appeared to have been due to inhaling
vomit due to the poisonous fumes, read a statement by the
South Essex Coroner, Dr Charles Clarke. 'The lining of his
windpipe was red and swollen, obviously damaged by some
poisonous noxious substance,' he told the BBC. Only months
after Carroll's death, the *Mirror* reported that a tanker driver
was 'taken to hospital with a mysterious illness after dumping

a load of chemicals' at the 'poison waste tip' in Pitsea. He had similarly dumped a mix of acids on top of another driver's load of sulphuric acid. Harwood said he has been told by some former drivers at Mucking that they would lock themselves in their cab to avoid the stench of gases that came out of the ground. 'There was no protection for the drivers, nothing. Sometimes they would see tyres melting.'

When undertaker John Harris was tasked with the reburial of the 3,300 skeletons that were discovered in 2015 by the Crossrail tunnellers under the site of the infamous Bedlam hospital at Liverpool Street station, he found there was no room left in London's cemeteries. So, he did what any self-respecting East Ender does when they feel the capital has deserted them – he found a nice spot in Essex to rest his bones.

'There isn't the burial space in London, just like there isn't the housing,' said Harris, the director of T Cribb and Sons, one of the oldest family-run funeral directors in east London. The plot he found for the Bedlam skeletons was in Willow Cemetery on Canvey Island. The new arrival opened a dormant insecurity that was thought to have been consigned to history, and prompted questions from locals: were they bringing the black death to Canvey, as some of the skeletons were found to have died of plague? He even consulted the World Health Organisation and went on the radio to dispel local fears about safety.

London councils also dump the living in Essex. Situated in a no-man's-land between the city and its green-fringed commuter belt, Thurrock had long been earmarked as one possible solution to the city's housing crisis. In 2015, London councils paid private landlords to house more than eighty homeless families in Thurrock, which put a strain on the borough's already precarious homeless problem. 'They just pay more than we can here,' said John Kent, the former Labour leader of Thurrock Council. 'Which has a knock-on effect. So we are now really, really struggling to keep pace with the increasing homelessness.'

The first services to be privatised under Thatcher nation-wide were Southend's bin collection services, on April Fool's Day 1981. The enthusiastic council tore up the service's 100-plus year status in the public realm and handed over a contract to Exclusive Cleaning group, a company owned by the businessman, David Evans, who was also a Tory councillor in St Albans. Evans could not have been more of a do-it-yourself Thatcherite. He set up the business with his wife, Janice, out of their garage. At first the couple did most of the cleaning themselves, but the Southend contract catapulted the business from growing concern to life-changing success. He was the chairman and managing director of Brengreen Holdings with fifteen subsidiary companies and 30,000 employees by 1982, which was sold on for £32m in 1986. He became the MP of the new town constituency of Welwyn Hatfield in 1987.

The council had reportedly been irked by the binmen in Southend's demand of a bonus payment for every new house built that they would service – and this being 1980s Essex, some routes would be full of new houses, and so more expensive for the council.

The council also made the outlandish claim that corruption, such as the falsification of timesheets, influenced the decision to privatise. Evans actually met the binmen himself, accompanied by police officers and dogs – a convenient piece of political theatre that spread the 1980s gospel that unions were inherently violent. 'They were chanting unions in and Evans out,' he said. 'One of them spat in my face and the policeman suggested that we retreated as quickly as possible as they feared for my safety.' *Tribune* reported that all of Southend's refuse workers were made redundant, with most re-hired on worse terms. While on the face of it some people's wages had improved, overall the picture was bleak. 'The council merely went through the motions of considering the union's case because it had a dogmatic commitment to private enterprise,' wrote *Tribune* journalist Nigel Smith. Today, the upshot of privatisation in Southend is a lack of wheelie bins that have left locals having to take black sacks out in the morning before work to avoid foxes tearing at them overnight, filling streets with torn plastic, discarded cat litter and smushed in tea bags in the aftermath of bin day.

Rubbish has been used in an attempt to shore up sea defences for hundreds of years. Brian, our guide on our walk onto Foulness via the Broomway, took us on a detour due to the eroding rubbish from the sea wall there. The practice of using the land east of Tower Bridge to dump noxious industry and waste management is a long one. 'Bovril' boats – so-called due to the rich, brown hue of their pungent cargo brought from the sewage works of east London and dumped at the mouth of the Thames – were an Estuary tradition for more than 110 years, until the practice of sloshing the capital's excrement into the brine was phased out in 1998.

But the matter that London no longer wanted has also been utilised in more productive and creative ways. The RSPB used more than 3m tonnes of material excavated from Crossrail's tunnel digs to raise part of Wallasea Island at the mouth of the Thames by an average of 1.5m, transforming farmland into a coastal marshland haven for egrets and oystercatchers and creating lagoons across 670 hectares in a process of managing realignment in response to the climate crisis.

Spencer sounded hopeful when she said one of the big things that has changed in recent years is that marsh landscapes are now valued. The Thames Estuary and many other Essex marshes are protected Ramsar wetland sites recognised by the global body Unesco. Marshes store carbon, purify water, provide valuable habitat and act as a natural buffer against coastal erosion. 'This [the Tilbury former landfill site] should be natural salt marsh wetlands and it should be removing nitrates and other pollutants from the water.' The Environment Agency would like to turn some of the adjacent farmland back into salt marsh to provide habitat and storage for flood waters with sea levels rising, but the presence of waste is restricting those plans.

Mucking Marsh stopped taking rubbish in 2012, years after it was named a site of special scientific interest in 1991 due to the populations of Shelduck, Grey Plover, Dunlin, Black-tailed Godwit and Redshank who roosted on the salt marsh, and the abundance of sea purslane and sea aster, not to mention rare spiders. (The Essex dumping grounds are close to ecological sites, reflecting the national picture: a third of all coastal historical landfills are located near designated eco-logical sites.) Mucking's conversion was partly financed by almost £3 million in funds from DP World, the company that some in Leigh suspect of ruining their catch, and Enovert, a waste management company that used to use the site for dumping. Another large landfill site at Pitsea is earmarked to be transformed by the RSPB in the next decade.

Similarly, Two Tree Island in Leigh-on-Sea was converted back into public land in the 1970s, but blackberries, apples, pears, damsons, plums and cherries now all grow from the former dump. People also come to swim in the water at Leigh, where there are also wild food foraging clubs. A local chef, John Lawson, has written about how his love for foraging was ignited by sourcing samphire fresh from Two Tree Island. (Professor Spencer was more wary of this – environmental reports for Two Tree Island have identified cyanide on the site and she didn't even want to take samples back to the lab.)

A specific issue with the site Spencer and Brand were studying was the proximity to where the cockney day-tripper favourite 'bivalve molluscs' – or in layman's terms, cockles – were produced. As we carried on walking over Bottle Beach at Tilbury, Spencer kept pointing out lumps of asbestos. 'We know asbestos is harmful if we inhale it, but I started investigating what people knew about consuming asbestos and there is a significant amount of research that suggests that, just as the fibres can work their way into the soft lung tissue, there is also evidence to suggest they can work their way into the tissue of the gut. And then you've got shellfishing at Leigh-on-Sea . . . I don't think anyone's ever really looked for it.' I started to feel queasy thinking of the amount of cockles I had eaten while in Leigh the day before.

Climate change poses the biggest and most unknown threat to upgrading the problem from a manageable burden to a disaster, and the report suggested that the relocation of waste from these types of coastal landfills may be required if environmental pressures prove too great. But it wasn't just the effects of climate change, the tides and the storms, helping erode landfill in Thurrock. It was the effects of curiosity too. Bottle Beach is popular with the mudlarking community, a burgeoning group of amateur historians and curious walkers who attend to shorelines to see what secrets are spilled up by river banks and mudflats all over the world. People come and dig through the rubbish, burrowing holes into the scrub to find trinkets. There were old twentieth-century booze and medicine bottles in lines as if they had been filed for consideration by a digger but didn't make the final cut. Kate said one of her PhD students found a poison bottle still corked and full of liquid. There were certain people Professor Spencer saw regularly 'sitting in a toxic hole' and eating sandwiches after digging like a mole into heavily contaminated earth with no gloves on. '"Well, I'm fine," they'd say. "I've been doing it since I was a kid." But then asbestos takes forty years to take hold.'

The world's populations are only just coming to terms with the problem of landfill and rubbish. The post-war boom in consumer goods in the late twentieth century resulted in enormous amounts of household waste, and we will all leave our own footprint. Coastal erosion, while potentially tragic, could have a positive effect as in making this hidden toxic legacy visible it is allowing people to see the scale of the challenge.

After ten years looking at the landfill problem, Spencer couldn't see too many obvious and workable answers. 'The solution seems to be: "Don't worry about it until something happens." . . . It's shameful. And there's a moral issue – it's no different to throwing your rubbish out of your car window. Your car's clean . . .' Thankfully the issue is slowly picking up ground in the places that count, but with the emphasis on 'slowly'. BBC radio producers were calling. Spencer was on an expert witness panel for a United Nations rapporteur in 2017, a report into the impacts of toxic waste in human health in the UK, but she said she is still waiting for the UK government's Department for Environment, Food & Rural Affairs to comment.

We crossed the threshold from the first landfill to the next, which started accepting rubbish in the 1930s. Kate picked up an old portion of newspaper she found in the landfill, carefully turning the page to find it was from 1936. As we carried on, we started to smell something revolting. The odour was getting more and more potent despite the constant gale that was whipping against us. We speculated what it could be. A toxic mix from the landfill? We noticed a large shape that was shiny yet fibrous, blackened and hardening . . . before realising it was a decomposing seal carcass. A swarm of flies pinged off it, making a cloud as we approached. Later, I read that sea mammal strandings such as this have become linked to legacy pollutants. How unlucky, I thought, to have ended up here.

Mucking In

*

When my friend Adam and I decided to walk from West Ham to Southend, we spent part of the first morning walking against the traffic on the fume-filled A13. Later, we breathed in the sweet, sickly, acrid smell coming from oil depots and factories at Thameside Thurrock, passing under the majestic Queen Elizabeth II bridge which links Essex to Kent before limping to a standstill in Tilbury, where I was walking so tentatively a nun stopped me in the street to ask if I needed help. But on the second day, Essex started to open up and reveal itself. Adam and I were joined by Hayley and another friend Jack, a musician from Leigh-on-Sea who has written intensely dark, beautiful and beguiling songs in part inspired by the marshes we walked over for his band These New Puritans. We set off not long after dawn from East Tilbury station with an OS map showing us the way. Our group had to make a detour as a marked path near Mucking landfill was no longer accessible, so we improvised and headed for what we thought was solid ground across the Thurrock marshland. It was a decision that ended with Hayley plunging into icy water before most of Essex had even eaten their breakfast. We persevered after Hayley changed into a spare pair of trousers. Suddenly we saw a JCB goofily career towards us over the uneven mounds at Mucking. We had thought we were completely isolated, beyond arterial roads and industrial estates that separate proper London from this damp nothingness. The vehicle turned sharply and stopped right in front of us. A bloke in a hard hat told us we had strayed onto the site of an old rubbish dump, Mucking, which was being converted into a nature reserve. It was only then we pondered the levels of toxicity of the freezing water that Hayley fell into.

And yet, we kept coming back. Some years later, once the nature reserve at Mucking had been opened to the public, we planned a visit for my 34th birthday, an excursion that with each step felt like an inauspicious start to my mid-thirties. Blasts of estuarial wind submitted us to a day that felt damned. Air shimmered above large pipes that were pumping out methane gas on the edge of this desolate spot that was once the largest rubbish dump in Europe. Ahead of us, the high ground obscured the fringe of a sky that is usually all-conquering around here, an unnatural hillscape formed from decades of the city's crap. If the profligate and boastful 'loadsamoney' aspect of Essex's accumulation of wealth was the front, then the waste mountains were the back. When your highest points are made of the stuff another part of the country didn't want, I thought to myself, what are you supposed to make of your topography, your wildernesses? How do you engage with it all?

The journey started awkwardly: we had set off from the train station at East Tilbury around lunchtime but ditched an initial desire to follow the Thames as much as possible after encountering a heavily flooded path, instead heading inland, skirting around puddles and pools.

The boggy, sodden ground caused our party to walk gingerly. Some had started to lose momentum in the pelt of wind and rain, which seemed to be getting in everywhere. The occasion had turned into a Herzog-Kinski epic relocated to the Essex marsh and scripted by Mike Leigh. We reached the entrance to the new nature reserve. Our curiosity was stirred, but not by the wildlife: we saw a signpost for a visitors' centre, and made our faintly desperate way towards it. (The centre is run by Essex Wildlife Trust, the county's leading conservation charity, with more than 33,000 members, which manages and protects over 8,200 acres of land.) Yet the walk was a long one over a steady incline made by decades and decades of rubbish. Greta, who was then 15 months, woke up and started to wail. Prompted by Hayley, we all sang to her, which calmed our toddler down long enough for us to resume the mission for cups of hot tea and slabs of bread pudding. These rub-bishscapes of south Essex entwined with our memories the same way microplastics are said to have done with the fibres of our bodies. When Hayley's grandfather Ernest died, his funeral was at Bowers Gifford, one of the highest points of south Essex. As I followed the hearse into the crematorium, the enormous capped mound of rubbish at Pitsea came into view. Most people glide past these vistas on the train without a second glance, but I began to obsess about them. On the train out to meet Professor Spencer, I had marvelled at the Pitsea horizon again, a nonsensical Thames Estuary hillside towering over the mudflats, a Brecon Beacon of waste. The train soon passed Mucking, and more hills of rubbish. It was so big it blocked the enormous cranes at the London Gateway container port from view. Coming to places like Tilbury and Mucking made me feel like I was very much living in the Age of Consequences, of chickens that have come home to roost and now are looking at us with searching eyes. The reckoning in this area of Essex, which of course mirrors the global environmental reckoning, began to remind me of when someone goes to therapy and they suddenly realise they have all these seemingly insurmountable issues that they have never noticed before and are faced with a stark reality: 'Oh God, I've actually got to deal with this now.'

11

Home at Last

'So they went onward, heedless of their own safety'
The Battle of Maldon, from the verse translation by Bill Griffiths

In 2011, a houseboat that had turned into a slightly forlorn TV star washed up on the beach of Westcliff-on-Sea. Each episode of the reality series *Grand Designs* usually followed a slightly maniacal, more often than not male and usually well-off protagonist pitting their project management and building skills against the challenge of erecting an ambitiously sized, ingeniously placed or unusually conceived living space that frequently went over budget. In this episode, however, the tension felt a bit different, perhaps a little sadder. Instead of the usual roll call of hyper-confident and high-salaried visionaries, it was the turn of two social workers, Chris and Sze, who had bitten off more than they could chew, having wanted a bit more space for their two children than their flat in Wanstead, east London, would allow. The *Medway Eco Barge*, so named as it was moored up on the Medway River in Kent, was their grand vision. It would be wholly salvaged and therefore a sustainable undertaking, renovated from recycled timber and corrugated iron. But it still eventually required an £80,000 budget, which proved unaffordable on the wages Chris and Sze were on. Builds on *Grand Designs* always run into all sorts of problems, but this was different; the couple and the show's enthusiastic host, Kevin McCloud, ended up unable to even visit it due to an eviction notice and an ensuing court case. At the end of the episode Chris proclaimed the barge a 'wonder' that 'created itself', despite the fact it remained unfinished. Instead, it was left to the elements and became fair game for anyone who wanted it, reportedly vandalised before becoming unmoored and drifting across the Thames to Essex.

From the upstairs of Chalkwell Hall, a Georgian former stately home that was acquired by the arts organisation Metal in the 2000s, where I am writing this, I can look out in the direction of the beach that Chris and Sze's lost dream washed up on, and out to where the Thames Estuary opens up to the rest of the world to become the North Sea. Gasometers and power stations on the other side of the water vie with enormous cargo ships holding containers stacked like building blocks and filled with consumer goods. Between the landscaped gardens and the thin and glittering layer of water that will soon become an expanse at high tide, is the Chalkwell Park Estate. Neatly roofed and often dormered houses mingle as if at some particularly busy networking drinks in the City, commuter train carriages winding through a gap in proceedings – from Shoeburyness to Fenchurch Street or from Fenchurch Street to Shoeburyness every few minutes. These houses are considered the pinnacle of what you can aspire to when buying property around here. I used to have a friend whose parents were lucky enough to have bought one of them, and the contrast in dimensions compared to my council-built end of terrace, deeper in suburbia, was stark: their enviable lifestyle choices just oozed of decisions made with money in the bank, and properties bought and sold, bought and sold.

The home has become symbolic of Essex. Grayson Perry

A House for Essex in Wrabness, 2018

and Charles Holland's project 'A House for Essex' riffs on this narrative: Essex as a success story for the idea of making a home, from the plotland dreamers who moved out to former farmers' fields between the wars to build their own bunga-lows, to the influx of East Enders, to the new towns of Harlow and Basildon. 'A House for Essex' does funny things to your sense of perspective. In a similar way to other great and sin-gular architectural elements I see as synonymous with Essex, it can feel as if it dominates the Stour Estuary, while at the same time feeling subsumed by its surroundings. Looking back at photographs I took after we stopped in Wrabness to see it, Hayley looks like a tiny Borrower against its Escher-like tessellations and grand, golden arch shaped windows. From the front path the building is a perfectly quaint trian-gular house; but walk around it and view it from its side and the building concertinas out into bigger and bigger sections, as if revealing Essex's hidden depths.

The house's slyly elongated nature hints at the baggage of a life left behind. In preparation, Grayson Perry conjured a fictional backstory that the house was built in tribute not to God or a figurehead or deity of another religion, but to Julie Cope, a fictional Essex everywoman. Julie was born on Canvey (plotlands), moved as a teenager to Basildon (state-funded new town) before heading to South Woodham Ferrers (privately funded new town) as a young woman; she moved to the older Essex of Maldon in middle age, then the Dutch quarter in Colchester, where she was killed in an accident with a takeaway delivery scooter. The home in Wrabness is supposed to have been built by Julie's widowed husband in tribute to her life, choosing a relatively secluded spot almost as far north within the county as it is possible to go without breaching the Stour and sullying Suffolk.

Charles Holland, an architect, teacher and writer who grew up in a village near Essex's county town, Chelmsford, was asked by Alain de Botton's Living Architecture company to take part in the project when he was the director of the now disbanded collaborative group Fashion Architecture Taste (FAT), and he was paired with the Colchester-born artist Grayson Perry (who coincidentally went to the same school in Chelmsford). Holland, De Botton and Perry devised the idea of a secular chapel, a site that would allow them to reflect on Essex. They wondered about where to put it and followed leads for sites for sale. They went to see a bungalow in the sleepy one-time smuggling outpost of Paglesham and a former oyster packing factory in South Fambridge. They visited a woman who had 50 labradors on the Dengie and a house in Maldon on the Blackwater navigation. 'We went to various places but none of them were quite right,' said Holland – until they went to Wrabness. The house's chosen site reflected Essex's nuances and wider conflicts. 'Wrabness is a very ordinary village overlooking this somewhat bleak estuary. It has lots of those qualities of Essex, which aren't exactly beautiful and picturesque.'

The Essex Way – an 81-mile right of way from Epping Forest to the port of Harwich, secured after pressure from the Campaign to Protect Rural England and the Ramblers – passes through Wrabness on its final stretch. The idea of pilgrimage fed into the design of the house, which evokes a similar quality to wooden Russian church architecture, a religious model of building that speaks to Essex's spiritual side, but also its domesticity. Holland told me his immediate inspiration for the building was the Chapel of St Peter-on-the-Wall in Bradwell on the Dengie Peninsula. The Northumbrian missionary St Cedd oversaw the building of St Peter's, the oldest church and perhaps the most sacred site in Essex, in the seventh century. The chapel itself has become a bit of an icon in recent years, a mainstay of Essex Instagram feeds, while retaining its role as a site of spiritual pilgrimage. A trickle of visitors, whether Christian or ramblers, regularly walk the 45-mile trek along St Peter's Way, from Ongar to Bradwell. When people arrive at the chapel they react to the wondrous simplicity of St Peter's, a spartan yet bewitching room that acts like a balm, an injection of old Essex minimalism for those suffering maxed-out lives and a defence against the occasionally battering wind across the flatness.

Situated next to the thriving and inclusive Christian community of Othona, St Peter's is the only surviving element of an Anglo-Saxon presence once dominant on this section of the Essex coast, and it sits on a promontory away from the bungalows and three-beds that line the roads out to the Dengie Peninsula proper. To me, the Dengie is the flat and bewitching heart of Essex, where old meets new, and a sense of wildness buffets against the agricultural industry (one crop is peas that are dried and sent to Japan to be sold as wasabi peas). The Dengie was one of the first places Hayley

St Peter-on-the-Wall, Dengie Peninsula

and I would come to when we started our forays into Essex to escape the wearying overload of the city. Following the River Crouch from South Woodham Ferrers, we quickly entered a countryside usually viewed from air-conditioned vehicles, a maze of public footpaths, through fields of scratchy corn and tunnels made from overhanging branches. Some of the public footpaths suggested the route was not often travelled. We whipped away overgrown stinging nettles, before coming across an abandoned quarry that had evolved into a wild nature reserve. During one particular trip to the Dengie, we walked all day in conditions so relentlessly wet my trousers started to lactate the white soap of the detergent still remnant from their last wash. When we finally made it to Bradwell, it was getting dark. The rain was still pelting down and the nuclear power station was emitting an unworldly glow through the damp gloaming. But we found that when we reached St Peter's, we couldn't go in to seek respite: building works meant the entrance was blocked by a Portaloo.

The only time I visited 'A House for Essex', I trespassed to have a look at it and was told to leave by the keeper. I was with Hayley, her mother, Ann, and Greta and Ernest. We had decided to go to Wrabness on the way back from somewhere, parking at the train station, and walking through the quiet, somehow typically unassuming village to see the house.

For a while we took a respectful look at the house from behind the perimeter fence, choosing not to open the gate with the subtly sized sign forbidding entry, so small that it was easy to miss. But the draw was too strong not to try and get a bit closer, so we opened the gate and marvelled at the details of the house, the thousands of ceramic tiles, some of which featured the three swords of Essex, others the repeated image of a maternal Julie. The building reflected so many conflicting aspects of the Essex story, from sacred to profane, modernist to outlandishly ersatz. Ernest, still in the grey zone between crawling and walking, lolloped about on the grass as Greta thrilled herself peering through the window, until we were collared by the housekeeper who lived in the village, who told us we were trespassing and we should leave.

'A House for Essex', or at least the way I accessed it having not paid the more than £1600 required to stay there for the weekend, represents the end of the idea of the Essex home as an accessible dream. Instead, it came to symbolise the limits of England's affinity with private property. It all reminded me of the time I went to see the petrified oaks at Mundon after I had been intrigued by their blackened and spindly presence in photographs, but was disappointed to realise after I had arrived that there was no way of getting close to the trees as they were on private land. The idea of the private, demarcated and sealed-off is unfortunately not just a hallmark of

Essex but of England, a country that seems to simmer in its
sense of finitude.

Holland said he wasn't that comfortable with any readings that Julie's happiness is tied to material advancement
and the happy event of becoming 'solidly middle class'; her
trajectory was the same as those of Essex man and Essex
girl, from the impoverished East End life to the comforts of
domesticity and an implicit bettering of herself with every
step into the leafier north: 'For me, when I think about the
story I think about it much more in social-geographic and
architectural terms,' said Holland. 'I think about the difference between Basildon and South Woodham Ferrers, I think
about the post-war journey of Essex, the difference between
the mysterious, older, more remote parts and the aspirational
parts. It wasn't necessarily an aspirational journey so much
as a cross-section through very different readings of Essex.'

I thought about how I had met so many real-life Julies
since returning to Essex, people whose lives told a wider
story of the county and its fortunes. I was reminded of how,
before we had children, Hayley and I spent the night in the
Alma, a cosy pub in Harwich, the ancient port town a few
miles east from Wrabness at the end of the Stour. There we
watched a cover band of 60-somethings called DK and the
Mustangs play loose and explosive rock'n'roll that wouldn't
have sounded out of place if it was transmitted to us from
Radio Caroline off the coast not far from here in 1964. The
venue was heaving, the scene betraying the fact that pub
cover bands represent England's actually experienced folk
music these days. A young bloke of not more than 21 wearing
a parka stood in front of the stage, arms aloft, singing along to
every word of Del Shannon's hit 'Runaway', despite it coming
out in 1961, the best part of four decades before he was born.

After the gig, Hayley and I talked to the guitarist, Vernon.
He was born in 1948, the year the NHS was established in the

UK, and grew up in a prefab in Dagenham before he moved to Clacton 30-odd years ago. Clacton was all right, he said, but he wouldn't be seen dead in Frinton. Vernon was a classic fallen Labour man. He said he was elected union representative at May & Baker pharmaceuticals at the age of 18 – the youngest shop steward in the country. As unemployment rose under Thatcher, he started an artist's co-op in Clacton, but he said he was no longer interested in politics. He was fed up with corruption, he said, and with politicians like double-glazing salesmen. Through his life he had worked variously as a taxi driver, a builder, a haulage man, and second-hand shop owner until he retired with 35p to show for it. His union, now, is his band and the people he knows: his community, who he can trust. Here is the tale of English apathy writ small. Among the crumbling, privatised promises and fabricated, mythic realities, people find their own way out. 'Because we all fantasise what we want to be, or where we want to be; what could be or what will never be,' said Vernon. 'And then you realise that reality steps in, and you think, "Bloody shit."'

Essex might have become a success story about the idea of making a home. But in doing so it contributed to making the mere idea of it, for many, as unobtainable as a unicorn ride. The less well-off no longer come to Essex in search of some small, actionable rejection of the received wisdom of their fate, as some of the working-class people who have moved here over the years have. Londoners are still moving to Essex, but often without the agency once afforded to them, and they already own property. Though Essex was part of our roots, it is the story of mine and Hayley's return. In east London, we'd bought a flat at a low deposit after being accepted onto a scheme in which the fact that Hayley is a radiographer for the NHS, and thus designated a key worker, worked in our favour. We were selected and lived in the two-bedroom flat until it started to feel too small around the time we had our second child. So we moved to Southend: the combination of bigger houses for less money, proximity to both our families and a lot of friends who were having children, it being still commutable to London, and near the sea, and the fact we are both fascinated with the eeriness of the abundant marshland walks in the area, all meant it made sense after an initial aversion to 'moving home' was quashed. We exchanged a two-bed flat in Walthamstow for a four-bed a couple of minutes from the sea in Southend, our willingness to pay the suddenly inflated price in its own way contributing to the inflation of house prices in this area. We are very much part of the problem. But is that a healthy way to think about it? Should we be blaming ourselves as individuals, or is there somewhere else to look?

Years of stagnating wages and rising house prices makes it feel as if any sort of social mobility, not just the idea of upward mobility as typified by the loud myth of Essex man, is one that no longer applies to great swaths of the population. Essex man and Essex girl have retired on the appreciating assets they bought in the 1980s, and their kids' best hope is often to borrow the deposit from them, hoping for the 'luck' of inheritance from a dead grandparent. The future is out of their hands. I scrambled around for anyone still imbibing the Essex energy, hooked on the snuff of possibility, chasing the dream. Clearly, people in Essex were still making money: I only had to check the personalised number plates or the full restaurants for that. And yet, even working in the City, the career so tied to the fate of Essex man, no longer had as much of a guarantee attached to it. On the way back from a few pints in London, I started talking to a young City boy who had also had a few and was going back to Essex. In a sense he fitted in with Simon Heffer's caricature perfectly, with his slicked back hair, suit and the type of job that fitted into the Essex man paradigm. Only a few years ago he might have already been well on the way to building his own mini Essex fiefdom, with a house, a car and a couple of children. He was getting off at Benfleet, as he was still living with his mum and dad on Canvey. His generation, he said, were stunted compared to the generation of his parents, who looked down on them and sometimes compared them unfavourably. No one he knew had the money to buy a house.

If one statistic can tell the story of the country in the 2020s, then it is this one: 73 per cent of people between 65 and 74 owned their own home in 2020, compared to less than 5 per cent of under 35s. Since the global economic crash of 2008, house prices have more than doubled while people's pay has largely stayed the same. The result, wrote the sociologist and political economist William Davies, was a ratio of housing wealth to GDP 'above the level seen in Japan before its historic crash in 1991'. Without the fruits of post-war consensus such as council housing to sell off and infrastructural improvements to fall back on, the Thatcher government would not have had the assets to strip and the stable country to play with. Her government was symbolised by the Right to Buy policy and the merciless pivot to financial services and away from the troublesome and failing industries, but at least back then then there was something in it for the upwardly mobile; their dream property was in reach if they just secured an average job and scrimped a bit.

Driving past the souped-up thatched cottages, half-built heritage-conscious gated communities, and boarded-up shops and pubs in Essex, I keep thinking, 'The houses have won.' I have daydreamed more than once that maybe this is how, more than six centuries after they ransacked Essex, the peasants finally beat their ecclesiastical masters or lords of the manor, by making their own castles on the land once denied them, the lucky ones even erecting their own gates and moats. Brexit revealed a thirst for sovereignty that was in many ways an end point of the guiding philosophy of England, a country lacking an alternative to neoliberal consensus despite the torrents of evidence that such faithfulness to the ideological concept has resulted in a deeply fractured society. Essex man's home is indeed his castle: property ownership is higher in Castle Point, south Essex, than anywhere else in the country. The supremacy of sovereignty as a guiding principle has created two choices of a role to stake claim to: the king or the peasant, the master or the servant.

When it comes to Essex, we talk about Right to Buy, but not so much buy-to-let, which was also introduced by the Thatcher government with the Housing Act of 1988. The Act introduced 'assured shorthold tenancies', which gave tenants fewer rights to remain in rental properties. Lenders began offering buy-to-let mortgages in 1996, and there are many experts who believe their popularity caused the market to overheat in the runup to the 2008 crash, when 19 per cent of all purchases were buy-to-let. The academic and writer Anna Minton reported that as a result more than 40 per cent of the housing benefit bill paid by desperate, cash-strapped councils goes into the pockets of private landlords. When buy-to-let boomed in the late 1990s, there were concentrations of such properties reported in Essex – places such as Loughton on the outskirts of London; by 2018, Southend-on-Sea was named the 'UK's top buy-to-let hotspot' in a story in the *Daily Mail*, 'with the average property bringing in £23,280 a year in rent, representing a yield of 6.6 per cent after mortgage costs,' according to mortgage broker Private Finance. The national press cheer-led that 'the only way is Essex' when it came to cashing in on London homes for more space in an area that is still commutable, as well as property investment and buy-to-let. According to a 2019 piece in the *Telegraph*, Southend had the ninth highest house price increase in the country; Thurrock, where house prices rose by more than 70 per cent between 2010 and 2020, was top. Essex's initial characteristic as a place of respite for those in need has suffered as a consequence. Children's homes for East End kids are being set up in unsuitable rental properties in Essex, not because of any desire to take advantage of the convalescing qualities of the open skies and the coastal air outside the city, but because the rents are cheaper. The *Guardian* highlighted in 2022 that the Salvation Army that had set up in Hadleigh to help better the lives of destitute Londoners had become a 'rogue landlord' that for years ignored complaints of 'unforgivable' hazards in rental properties: from floods, to leaks, to rats, to lack of water, to lack of heating. It was especially grim that a company so outwardly proud of its mission since it took poor east Londoners to live on the pioneering farm colony it set up in the late nineteenth century, had been treating its Hadleigh tenants so badly. Everywhere I looked, parts of the mis-sold Essex dream seemed to be warping and bending, warning future generations to not make the same mistakes.

There have been signs that the thread linking the idea of Essex to a distinctively Thatcherite model of 'every Essex man for himself' has been wearing thin in recent years, as Essex grows tired of cuts to public services after perpetual austerity and a permanently combusting Conservative Party. Creative responses to ideas around Essex have come to the fore. The artist Michael Landy was born in the part of Essex that is now considered Greater London. Landy remembered the day the family moved from Hackney, going over the flyover at Blackwall Tunnel in his dad's Morris Minor with his two sisters and their cat, Tinkerbell, in the boot: 'It felt cleaner. You could get to Hainault Forest on your bike.'

Landy started making art by drawing dilapidated buildings on the edges of Ilford. His family was part of a big Irish community around Ilford and Dagenham at the time. 'They mostly worked on the roads, tunnels, railways. Manual labour really – my Dad was a tunnel miner.' His father often travelled the country for work and had an accident in Northumberland when he was 37 that meant he could never work again. 'That's when the cave collapsed on him,' Landy told me.

We entered the posh end of Kingswood Road, as Landy used to think of it, where the properties were detached and featured decorative lions. When we arrived at 62 Kingswood Road, the house he grew up in, he pointed out the pebbledash job his dad had done, which had survived pretty well. Landy made headlines in 2004 when he recreated an exact scale replica of the family home we were looking at, when his mum and dad still lived there, long after he had moved out to set up his artist practice in London proper, and had it displayed in the Tate Britain's Duveen Gallery as the work *Semi-Detached*. He said that reporters came to his parents' doorstep after the work was shown: 'Essex man's home truths put on show,' read the *Daily Telegraph* headline.

He started the process by making a photographic inventory of the house, but was soon drawing and making videos of his mother and father as they went about their lives, effectively becoming artist-in-residence in his childhood home for over a year. His father pottered around, engaged in badly done DIY jobs and going to and from the garden shed, and his mother did housework. 'Nothing really goes on in a house, so the hum of the fridge freezer took on its own relevance,' said Landy. Art fabricators worked to make an exact replica of the family home but they couldn't get the pebbledash right, and so Landy had to commission a firm used to working on real terraced houses to come and do it. 'Art fabricators are supposed to be able to do anything and everything but they couldn't do pebbledashing.'

He recreated the house right down to the blue-tacked front doorbell and the fading Crimestoppers sticker. 'When we showed it at the Tate, Mum was embarrassed by the crumbling paintwork, even though she supplied the net curtains.' His father was an angry man, always trying to come to terms with leaving Ireland and ending up in pointless altercations down the pub in the process, but spending this amount of time documenting him made Landy understand him better. He found the report of his father's accident, which called him a 'total wreck case', but which also detailed what big shoulders he had as he dug underground. 'He loved what he did, if you can love digging underground with a drill.' Reading about his father's physical impairments gave Landy insight into the real pain experienced by his father for the first time, 'all the anger' at being written off at an age when many people these days are still contemplating settling down.

Landy launched himself to wider recognition in 2001 with *Breakdown*, which was part performance art, part new beginning for the artist, setting up a Fordist factory complete with production line in an empty shop in Oxford Street to systematically destroy every single material belonging he owned, which ran to 7,227 items. It was a rejection, in a way, of the Essex dream as promoted by Thatcherism, of buying your way to happiness, but also a reflection on the fate of working-class 'jobs for life'. Perhaps Landy saw that you could not escape the inevitable disappointments of working-class life, of what your body and your soul was put through, simply by surrounding yourself with walls and filling the cavities with trinkets. It was only later that Landy realised that when he made *Breakdown* he had been the same age as his father was when he had his life-changing accident.

The nearby Becontree Estate, one of the first new projects to let Londoners leak into Essex, and certainly the biggest, is a place that has itself undergone its own re-evaluation of late. During the pandemic, Becontree had recorded some positive results about Covid transmission levels compared to the areas around it. 'The estate's low-rise design, with its large open spaces, and individual council houses, meant vulnerable older residents and those shielding were able to isolate more easily and were less exposed,' reported the *Evening Standard*. I spent some time during 2021 walking around Becontree with one of its greatest documenters and champions, the artist Verity-Jane Keefe, while taking part in a writing residency for Living Together, her project that marked 100 years of this monumental estate.

For our last walk together, she took me to see the development's oldest houses on Chitty's Lane, where we commented on the street's unusually high kerbs and the old metal coal chute doors that were still visible on many of the houses. The first residents had arrived a century before our visits. I found an advert from 1923 for the Becontree Literary and Debating Society, which met every Tuesday at 'the Institute, Chittys Lane'. The subjects of debate varied from domestic ('How to plant a garden in Becontree') to societal ('The housing problem'). Group effort is a kind of magic. After a year working with her, I recognised it as a hallmark of Keefe's work, typified by the Becontree group, which started as an open invitation to residents to help shape the course of Living Together. The group met up throughout the pandemic by taking part in doorstep and garden chats, and, when possible, dinners, discussions, screenings, workshops and trips.

The simple act of living can seem an impossible one in the twenty-first century, something that Keefe's work gently queried, implicitly asking why, exactly, does this have to be the case. Her exhibition, *Lived In Architecture: Becontree at*

100 at the Royal Institute of British Architects in London, turned her gallery at RIBA into a Becontree 'best of', and was resplendent with details including a mock Tudor threshold, crazy paving, a plinth and a Doric column. Keefe's project riffed on Right to Buy, not by castigating the people who took part in the policy, but by making a virtue of the aesthetic outcomes of thousands of individual choices. When people bought their houses, they individualised them with columns flanking doors, ivy crawling up the brickwork, satellite dishes, bold extensions and snazzy little palm trees. In the crush of British class assumptions, it sometimes feels as if many would prefer neighbourhoods such as Becontree to agree to an austerity of ambition when it comes to home improvement. Keefe's work suggested the estate's modern bricolage of crazy paving and snazzy columns were evidence that it still had a pulse.

Outside the Costa Coffee in Basildon, on a warm spring day, I marvelled at how the town centre was so alive as a place of congregation. We were in the woozy weeks after the lifting of another Covid lockdown, and I felt overjoyed that this civic space was filled with so much chatter. People, no longer cocooned in their homes, were dressed up, some had had their hair done. A man whose shopping bags hung from him like plump fruit about to fall from the tree listened to the Bangles' 'Eternal Flame' on a portable radio. I suddenly noticed the bench I was sitting on was surrounded by dogs. A woman came over and asked one of the owners, who it seemed she had never met before, if she could stroke theirs. 'Oh, look at the beautiful dog. Hello, baby!' The dog licked her face all over, to her squeals of delight.

It was local election day, and the vote was the Reds' to lose. The Labour leader of Basildon Council, Gavin Callaghan, was seeking a mandate for his masterplan to completely change the town centre from being primarily geared towards shopping, entertainment and civic amenities, to becoming a residential space for thousands of new homes via a series of tower blocks, up to twenty-six storeys, which would be marketed to commuters. Callaghan proudly pegged the future of Basildon to the project; quite simply, in the language of capitalist realism, there would be no alternative.

Some residents begged to differ. One, 35-year-old Jake Hogg, who lived in Pitsea, decided to try to do something about it and formed the Basildon Community Residents' Party, with the explicit aim of taking on the Labour council's vision of a new Basildon. Hogg was born in Basildon hospital in the mid 1980s, when Mark Francois, then a Basildon councillor, and MP David Amess were presiding over a changing of the political guard. Hogg's granddad was from near Durham, the first in his generation not to have to go to the coal pit. Instead, he went to secondary school, served in the army, then became an engineer at Shell and was moved to Shell Haven oil refinery near Canvey, before settling in Basildon. Hogg was not against housebuilding. He had recently gone back to working in the building trade, primarily as a plasterer, after six years working for a homeless charity. He had a bad shoulder injury some years back and had to drop out of the trade for a while, so took a job as a caretaker at a homeless shelter in Thurrock, which just about paid his rent. He was then offered a job in St Mungo's, helping look around Basildon at night to liaise with people without homes, which he said is a growing problem in Essex; he said he could see new developments like the masterplan exacerbating it massively. Land banking – the act of purchasing land and sitting on it as its value appreciates – had helped to squeeze people into shop doorways. 'For years faith groups have wanted to start a homeless shelter in one of these empty shops where they've ripped out all the electrics,' he said. 'But they are told the rates are too much.'

When Basildon wanted to reinvent itself in 2010, it did so not in the town centre, but on the side of the A127. A tongue-in-cheek 'BASILDON' sign that mimicked Hollywood's was erected on the Noak Bridge roundabout, which had never before been compared to the hills above LA. It was installed by the local authority who thought people had forgotten about the new town, and wanted to try and grab the attention of passing trade. It was a typically twenty-first-century solution to the problems of civic decline: showy, headline grabbing, of little worth to the public. The reaction was predictable. 'They've realised Hollywood isn't actually in America at all, it's in Essex,' said comedian Paul Merton on the satirical BBC panel show *Have I Got News For You*, which has been known to punch down as well as up: 'They've got the Basildon "Walk of Fame"; if you've ever paid your council tax in Basildon, they put a star in the pavement.' Meanwhile, genuinely celebrated mid-century buildings such as the recently demolished Freedom House are missed by Basildon. Laura Whiting reminisced about the balcony of the old building and the colonnade. 'The light was gorgeous,' she said. 'A lot of the architects used to go to it and study civic relationships. That's lost now.' Whiting, an architectural designer who also started the local arts organisation Directions Bas, told me she enjoyed the scale of Basildon – how the low-rise shopping blocks still felt accessible and 'domestic'. The vertiginous towers, on the other hand, would do nothing but dominate their surroundings. 'The scale of thinking is bigger, but materiality and quality are lesser.'

The new towns originally represented something other than the blind capitalism of private building, but Basildon's future as a series of land banks and other failures of planning was baked into the way it was built in the first place.

In reality, the town wasn't just a brave new state-led rollout of municipal strength, but could also be described as an ad hoc amalgamation of property-developer efforts and statist interventions in a post-war moment when the ambition to solve issues such as the housing crisis was high, but finances were stretched.

Whiting led me up some steps to look over the town towards its market square. She told me that the buildings that we surveyed, now emptied out for eventual presumed demolition, were designed by architect Lionel H. Frewster & Partners and developed by Ravenseft Properties Ltd, one of Land Securities' subsidiary companies. Land Securities and Ravenseft were set up to exploit the fact that land was never going to be as cheap and easy to acquire as it was after the Second World War. Land Securities started its life in 1944 with three properties in Kensington worth £19,321; by 1951, its assets were worth more than £11 million. 'They just went round the whole country buying up cheap land. They had an umbrella company and then a subsidiary – it was a kind of tax avoidance. They were the biggest builders of the new towns. This idea of speculation, intentional decline, and speculation – that was the first cycle of it, and this is the second.'

The Labour minister Lewis Silkin's original New Towns Act 1946 had stipulated that each new town, when completed, should be handed back to the local authority, but the Conservative government of 1959, to Labour's dismay, decided that the development corporations should stay in place. Then, for Thatcher's government, the selling off of new town assets was just another spoke in the wheel of ideology of privatisation, asset stripping and lower taxation.

When it comes to our shared environments, decline does not happen overnight. It comes slowly, by a thousand cuts, policy reversals and blindsides. In Basildon, it is perfectly easy for the politician or journalist visiting for an afternoon to see 'decline' and want 'solutions' without considering what has happened to produce such a situation in the first place. Decline in Basildon was by no means inevitable. In the new towns, it was always assumed that incentives would be put in place to keep shops thriving in the centre of town. After the development corporations that were meant to ensure these safeguards existed were wound up in the 1980s, a storm of market forces trundled in like the black clouds that sometimes enter the Essex coast, sly and slow at first, but with bursts of rain that built and built. Before you knew it, you were drenched through.

Laura and I looked out at the cinema that's being put together in the wake of Freedom House. She told me that she had been in discussions with the Twentieth Century Society and a charity about putting together a proposal to make the building an arts space. The town didn't need a new cinema; it already had one. Laura said she did all the feasibility studies for it, and it was stacking up. But then the planning got brought forward to do the cinema, and so that was that.

People like Jake and Laura face accusations of Nimbyism, but all they wanted to do was preserve buildings that were well-designed and perfectly functional. Basildon would have benefited from a community-focused hub like an arts centre. A development corporation could have at least facilitated this but, in conditions created primarily by the Conservative Party but often tolerated by Labour, the only chances for change were always unimaginative developer-weighted ideas like the masterplan, knocking down buildings that could have lasted and replacing them with the supersized steel-framed sheds that have become the architecture of our times.

But, while the flag flies somewhat ragged, you can still find a sense of utopianism in Harlow. Nowhere is it more obvious than in the carefully sustained endurance of its public art. An Art Trust was set up in the town in 1953 to ensure the new residents had access to high quality works of art on their doorstep. Henry Moore's *Family Group* sculpture, a stone version of the more celebrated bronze of a mother cradling a child with its father that was made for Stevenage new town, was initially installed in Harlow Town Park on the older side of the town, and today sits behind glass at the new Civic Centre. The survival of public art singles Harlow out as a special place in the ever-growing clusters of settlements around this area of Essex that is squeezed by the M25 and M11 and alleviated by Epping Forest. There are some lovely moments in the residential corners of Harlow. Dr Alina Congreve, a trustee of Harlow Art Trust, took me to see the town's favourite piece of public art here, *Donkey* by the Austrian-born architect Willi Soukop, a little sculpture with a Ronseal name. *Donkey* is an ever so slightly Eeyorish presence, created by Soukop the year he first escaped from the political turmoil of mid-30s Vienna for Dartington in south Devon. Soukop designed the sculpture for children not Harlow to play with, an offer that you can see they have keenly taken up through the years, the ears and back of the work shiny from decades of petting. Harlow's creator Frederick Gibberd was always concerned about the damage caused to the collection by children, but in the case of *Donkey* he felt the resultant polishing added to its interest.

'They really should talk about the new towns in the same way they talk about the NHS,' said Chris Snow, the chair of the trust, as we looked at Barbara Hepworth's sculpture *Contrapuntal Forms*, an abstract-minimalist vision of two figures carved from limestone that has stood outside the Glebelands Estate since it was donated by the Arts Council of Britain after it was originally displayed at the Festival Of Britain. 'We have huge civic pride in the NHS but not the new towns.'

As we traversed through Harlow's tree-lined walkways,

Congreve reminisced about going on a trip to Rotterdam with Laura Whiting, who I had met in Basildon. 'The shopping area, Lijnbaan, is exactly like the town centre in Harlow. Architecturally it is very similar, but it is in beautiful condition: there are lovely shops in it, lots of people, lots of public art.' Harlow by contrast housed a shopping centre that was unloved and underused. 'Lijnbaan shows what it would be like if we were a bit kinder to new towns like Harlow. It's not an inevitable failure of the architecture. It has shops that people want to buy from. I'd like to take some councillors to Rotterdam and to Stuttgart and say, "This is what it could be like: you don't have to knock down the town centre and rebuild it, you could just make it better. There is nothing inherent about the architecture that's wrong or malformed."'

The difference between Harlow and Rotterdam was based around who owned the buildings. She talked about trying to facilitate the display of an Antony Gormley artwork on a roof in Stevenage, a new town built around the same time as Harlow and Basildon: 'Every building they tried to put it on was owned by an offshore trust in the Cayman Islands or Panama.' They eventually chose to locate it on the top of a Pizza Express building because it was the only place they could find the owner of.

Back on the Thames Estuary, in the end, the Basildon Community Residents' Party didn't win any seats. But it did win votes, enough to change the shape of Basildon Council and slow down the masterplan. Gavin Callaghan was no longer able to lead the council, and so it fell to the Conservatives. Unable to steer the masterplan, Callaghan quit the council entirely. One of the party's biggest scalps was Aidan McGurran losing his seat in the ward of Vange. McGurran was a tabloid journalist and made his name as the *Sun*'s 'Lenny Lottery' when the popular weekly game of chance launched in the 90s, before he was poached by Piers Morgan's *Mirror* newspaper (there was a dispute over his trademark costume, a white suit decorated with red balls).

In May 2020, it was reported that, according to the Basildon Conservatives, Callaghan and McGurran had failed to declare a vested interest in the masterplan, when links to the communications company Cratus, which was in line to profit from the regeneration of Basildon, were revealed. (Callaghan and McGurran deny these claims.) Jake shook his head as he told me the story. He remembered Lenny Lottery well, as his nan was obsessed with playing the National Lottery in its early heyday, which made the idea of his re-emergence in Basildon all the stranger. There seemed something so perfect about it: Basildon was the place with the highest proportion of *Sun* readers per person at the newspaper's height in the early 90s, and here was one of its old faces trying to push through a wholesale regeneration of the town centre in place of the original new town masterplan without properly consulting the residents. Basildon is not the only area of the UK to see left-wing community-conscious residents celebrating local Labour council losses, and it can't be explained away by rabid factionalism. Up and down the country are stories of Labour backing unpopular developments that exclude the poorest.

All around Essex, singular symbols such as the 'House for Essex' or St Peter's look out to the water's edge. In Maldon, there is a statue commemorating the fallen Anglo-Saxon warrior Byrhtnoth (the Earldorman of Essex, speculated to be the premier nobleman in England), depicting him with his shield and his sword, ready to do battle with the invading Vikings. Byrhtnoth was a lone voice in rejecting the costly policy of appeasement of the Vikings favoured by King Aethelred. The army of Scandinavian warriors landed on Northey Island and were stranded by the tide. When the tide receded, they could not get their army across the narrow causeway, when Byrhtnoth is said to have helped them on to land to where they could fight fairly with the defending English army.

Much of what we know about the battle is taken from the early English poem recorded at Ely Cathedral. 'The Battle of Maldon' feels a particularly apt poem for Essex, because it is fragmented, with the beginning and the end of the work missing. The scholar and poet Bill Griffiths wrote that the lyrical depiction of the ensuing Battle of Maldon, which happened in August AD 991, was a political poem as much as it was historical or heroic. After Byrhtnot – who, the statue's description suggests, was 68 at the time of battle – is killed, the poem becomes a story of collective faith and endurance in a shared cause, even without the guidance of a leader. Some men flee after Byrhtnoth's death, but two brothers, Oswald and Eadwold, persuade the rest of the surviving men to stand firm:

> Brothers, encouraged the battlers,
> Told their friends this phrase
> That now when it mattered most they must make the effort,
> unsparingly use their swords.

The sense of solidarity evoked by the Battle of Maldon may well have been pure fantasy or wishful thinking from the writer of the poem. But then so much of the new political thought and utopian visions that gave rise to action like the new towns and the NHS was once a wishful, fantastical pipe dream that in the end became an admittedly flawed but nevertheless improved material reality. The thought of these men at the end of the millennium before last effecting a purposeful solidarity on the salt marsh at Maldon began to connect with so much of the Essex that I had learned about.

I travelled to the edge of Harlow to an area I'd never been

to before. On the drive there, I had to slow down as I passed a boy driving a pony and trap. Despite being built in the 1980s, this end of town looked a bit more run down than some of the more sought-after post-war areas. I was visiting a veteran housing campaigner called Mick Patrick. Observing Covid rules, we talked at the doorstep. Patrick's father was from Holloway in north London. He had worked on the railways and was considered a key worker, so he was offered a house in newly built Harlow. Mick had always lived in council housing. 'The ideology of council housing was to give people a home. Now, in some areas, we've got two out of five with private landlords. The housing waiting list is now called the "housing needs register", to make [social] housing a last resort rather than a right.'

To live in England today is to live under capitalistic forces not unlike the Vikings demanding their ransom. Patrick said in the mid-70s you could put your name down for a house and get a choice of three in a street. Today, many young people face a future of private rents, sofa surfing, short-term Airbnbs, staying with their parents, or homelessness. The houses being built are unaffordable, and of some of the lowest spec in Europe.

Patrick told me how, some years ago, he was part of a successful campaign for Harlow to retain its council housing, which was under threat from a stock transfer by the Tory government, ending up with a parliament visit. He suggested that residents were only now realising the consequences of the long-term Tory cuts and the necessity of a boost in council housing. 'You ain't got to speak to many people for too long until they can see the need.' He and his fellow campaigners in Harlow had been pressuring the council to start building council housing again, and now they are: sixteen in fact. It wasn't much, but it was a start. 'It just transforms people's lives,' Patrick said. He left me to go to a meeting with a local union branch, Essex Unite. I thanked him and said goodbye. I began to feel quite moved at the work this man and others like him had to put in to achieve the relatively small gain of sixteen council houses. But every gain counts. I turned back towards the house as I walked away and told him to keep fighting. 'I will,' he said. 'And my son after me.'

Epilogue

Runwell

I headed out into the storm, my face pinched by the tightened hood of my coat. It was dusk, the so-called 'golden hour', which has become a sacred moment in the online local life of Southend, purple-orange estuary sunsets shared across social media. But golden it wasn't. I peered through the gap in my hood towards the doomy mouth of the river, the driving saline rain and wind penetrating like a gale through an old Essex barn. I headed purposefully towards the estuary, climbing over the concrete sea wall and onto the sand before descending to the seaweed, rocks and oyster shells revealed by the absent tide. Dunlin on the lookout for worms bounced across the wet shoreline, but everything else seemed to have gone, rubbed out by the weather as if someone downloaded a reverse Instagram filter that turned pretty pictures of dusk into a sky too monstrous for JMW Turner.

The next day coastal and marshy Essex was overtaken by a persistent mist, enveloping it completely. But as I approached Runwell in our silver Ford Fiesta, the road turned west to reveal a sudden burst of beautiful sunset. The clouds had cleared, leaving blue sky and white streaks and the last of the great orange sun. I had come to Runwell, a place equidistant from Chelmsford and Southend, to meet the Devil. A friend had told me the quite possibly apocryphal story of a local curate by the name of Rainaldus, who had practised the 'Black Arts' within the grounds of St Mary's Church. One morning, the story goes, while conducting a service with his flock, Rainaldus was confronted by the Devil, who made a grab for the startled priest. Fleeing in terror, the curate escaped through the south door, while the Devil, unable to pass through the sanctified portals, vented his spleen by burning his mark into the old oak door. After a while, the congregation, having also escaped when the pursuit began, came creeping back. They searched in vain for their wayward curate but all they ever found was a foul-smelling puddle of green liquid bubbling away by the south porch. In the middle of this pool lay a small, flint stone resembling a human head, which, legend has it, was later mounted on the south wall near where Rainaldus had held the mass, bearing the Latin inscription *Stipendium peccati mors est* (The wages of sin is Death). I had heard the claw marks still reside on the church door.

I parked the car down a quiet residential street, with a brook flowing fast beside it following the weekend's rainfall. I saw the church and headed towards it. As if in a cliched scene about someone stopping to check out a spooky church in a village they don't know all that well, I realised I was under the fixed gaze of a local man, staring at me unabashed. I crossed the road to say hello, but he just seemed to look straight through me. I walked back across the road towards the church and entered the graveyard. I turned towards the south door where the Devil was meant to have left his claw marks, and wondered if I might be able to see them myself before the dusk grew bolder and the moon took charge. Before I reached the south door something startled me – there was a body in the Devil's doorway.

The temperature was freezing but the person was alive, wrapped up and sleeping. I didn't wake them. You shouldn't wake a person sleeping peacefully, no matter what general difficulty they may be in. They had shelter here.

Not knowing what to do, I read a gravestone of a local woman who had died in December 1851.

My flesh shall slumber in the ground
Till the last trumpet shall sound
Then bust the chains with sweet surprise
And in my saviour's image rise

I looked up to see an aeroplane catching the sunbeams that had already deserted the land. My mind started to fix on the din of the road. Runwell was once a small village but Ramuz's plotlands boom saw to that. The most popular teller of the Rainaldus story was John Edward Bazille-Corbin, the rector of St Mary's from 1923 to 1961, who wrote a book full of antiquary and portent about the village, which was partly a lament for the decay of rural Essex and conveyed the author's alarm at how the 1924 population had trebled by the time he was writing his new edition in 1942. 'Till some twenty years ago, the district was entirely rural,' he wrote. 'Today there are very few true Essex country-folk residing in it. Runwell's present population is for the most part comprised of former town dwellers, chiefly Londoners, emigrants at a recent date from north and east London.' The sudden movement of all these urbanised desires into rural Essex alarmed Bazille-Corbin, who wrote of old country houses that would have been in the family for years now changing hands from cockney to cockney at a rate of knots.

The selling off of parcels of landed estates oversaw the destruction of a whole way of life sacred to the antiquarian rector (Oxford alumnus, qualified barrister, high Tory who after serving for the Royal Artillery in the First World War taught classics in Guernsey). As rector, he occupied an unusual position: that of being a free Catholic Church of England pastor of the San Luigi Orders, the Catholicate of the West, which wanted to revive Catholicism, while also being devoted to ritualism and fringe occult tales such as that of Rainaldus.

Runwell is a name that looms large over memories of my childhood, adolescence and first years of hedonism. People would 'end up in Runwell', people who, I recall the unkind saying from back then, 'couldn't handle' the chemically enhanced club life of being young in Essex at the turn of the millennium. Runwell Mental Hospital was built on former manorial land, once known as the Runwell Hall Estate, which was compulsorily purchased by the local authorities of East Ham and Southend in 1933 – the metropolitan and the seaside Essex boroughs joining forces to build the hospital following the migration of so many residents of the former to the latter. The hospital appeared like a series of gleaming white structures connected by concrete roads and roundabouts. Units were built on a slight slope, sheltered from the east, north and west by trees, while also being generously spaced, allowing ample sunlight to the grounds and buildings. 'In this way, it is hoped that an atmosphere may be engendered of light and airy buildings without obtrusive restraint and with a freedom from the institutional feeling,' wrote the East Ham medical officer in 1937. There were wide verandas with large solaria and airy rooms with French windows to enable the patients to feel that they were in a sanatorium rather than a grim institution. The hospital, which has now been converted as part of a large luxury housing estate, eventually became home to the largest brain archive in the world, 800 brains stored haphazardly in an old air raid shelter and including those of patients who had suffered from schizophrenia, Alzheimer's, Parkinson's disease, multiple sclerosis and amyotrophic lateral sclerosis. The archive was overseen by Dr Clive Bruton, a specialist in psychiatric disease, apparently the classic 'outsider who got results'. In the archive of the Essex Record Office one afternoon, I couldn't stop looking at a picture of Bruton holding one of the Runwell brains as if it was a prize marrow. Bruton was a pioneering presence when it came to modernising opinion around schizophrenia and epilepsy, and his studies into boxing – there were lots of boxer brains in jars at Runwell, too – resulted in matches being reduced in length from fifteen rounds to twelve, head-gear being made compulsory in amateur matches, and the banning of the sport from schools.

Runwell was so named after the Running Well, a spring-fed natural water source at the highest spot in the parish, where evidence of ragstone and limestone betrayed a possible pagan pre-Christian chapel. Bazille-Corbin quoted Professor Eilert Ekwall, the Swedish scholar of the English language, who linked the first syllable of Runwell to the old English 'run', meaning mystery or secret, suggesting the well itself was a secret, sacred site 'closely connected with the mystery of some religious observance'. Bazille-Corbin wrote that a pre-Christian cult of devotion to the 'Lady of the Well' subsequently arose around the site. He wrote that when Christian missionaries travelled to the area in the sixth century, they set up camp, building a hut for worship with an altar of flint and sunbaked bricks. There was apparently also a convent of nuns here in the twelfth century who would greet the visitors who came to the Running Well, by this time seeking not simply to quench their thirst, but to utilise the healing qualities of the water. According to Bazille-Corbin: 'Some came intending to bathe their injuries or diseased limbs in the water of the well, hoping this – and assuredly, if their faith, love and penitence were not feigned, they were not always disappointed – to cure their ailments and relieve their pain. Many a pilgrim would bring with him a bottle and fill it at the spring so as to convey to the sick at home, some of its healthy water.'

Not a great deal of evidence is provided to back up Bazille-Corbin's claims, but it didn't really matter. His was an officiation of stories handed down the generations and told to a man who had become simultaneously obsessed with the apparent power and legacy of the well, while remaining in full knowledge that it could all have been made up: 'Yet the little chapel can never have been of any size, and both it and the Holy Well were relatively unimportant. Their very existence is nowhere directly recorded in any known official document.'

The mystery of the Running Well is one that has provoked much speculation among occult and antiquarian writers – a mysterious, unknowable and incongruous place tucked away in a county that everyone thinks they know. Bazille-Corbin's self-published tome shares qualities with the zine or scrapbook at times, all hand-drawn maps and esoteric editing. Antiquarians sought the sacred and the hidden to provide a kernel of authenticity against the dread and trauma of the wholesale development such as that witnessed at Runwell: 'We are thus taken back to a very remote period where, through the mists of tradition or fable, we require to feel out towards the beginning of its long past history.'

But the Running Well represented something more utilitarian than all that. Natural wells were scarce in Essex, wrote Bazille-Corbin, and for years the well was apparently the only source of pure drinking water in the area. Consider the magic of this clean water source against the Essex of pestilent marshland and polluted and over-industrialised rivers, what a miracle it must have felt to travellers, whether passing through or making pilgrimage. I drove back home a different way, through country lanes and the quiet streets of residential Runwell and into the edgeland of East Hanningfield, near the reservoir that provides our own drinking water. I took a detour and turned left down a grimly muted road called Workhouse Lane, the infamous corner of a misunderstood county that not even the Essex Boys' greatest obsessives would be able to find. I felt compelled to park the Fiesta and search for the spot where Tony Tucker and co were killed in their Range Rover. The murder of these three Essex characters represented something more than the death of three wannabe gangsters. They represented Essex as despoiled and devilish and wanting more than it could handle. On the drive to Runwell I had thought about how odd it was that these two sacred sites of Essex – one violent and modern but still mysterious, the other ancient and full of magic – were situated in quiet spots just a short drive from the A130 and a few minutes away from one another. I used to think Essex was characterised by these kinds of hidden places, from its idols excavated during the building of new roads to the magical stories of cunning men handed down through generations, but now I think it might instead be the place where England is finally seen, where it refuses to hide. It's all laid out, on show like the throngs of people in Southend and the homes and the cars attached to them, and the way the mud and the marsh are exposed by the extremity of the tide.

I returned to Runwell with Hayley on a beautiful winter's day, on a mission to find the Running Well. Ice was thawing and the colour of the grass was popping against the touch of the bright sun. We found an opening in the hedge and our suspicions we might be on the right track were confirmed when I looked over at the green and slightly sloped farmer's field to see a lightly worn desire path towards a grand, old oak tree.

By the tree was a dank muddy puddle. Was that it, the Running Well, a sodden pit now overgrown under brambles? Dispirited, I looked again at the directions on my phone and realised we were in the wrong place. We crossed to the next field, hung a left and ducked into a clearing.

There it was. The first thing we noticed was the light reflecting off it. Someone had put ropes up to help visitors climb down the steep banks. I looked down at the clear water and realised it was constantly vibrating. Was that just the sound of a restless Essex, or the energy at its heart? I climbed a set of steps to crouch by the water. I'd spent so long in the company of despoiled Essex, infected Essex, poisoned, toxic and landfilled Essex, but here was something else. A natural spring with water so clear and so cold I could do nothing else but cup handfuls of it into my mouth to drink the clarity of its nondescript, not-there flavour. This water source that pre-dated the Anglo-Saxon county name felt like Essex's hidden monument, a little, life-giving well in a nook between three fields that had drawn people towards it for centuries. We left for the light and the path home. As we walked back over the sloping hill, our boots kept getting stuck in the claggy ground. We stopped to look at a discarded Victorian medicine receptacle that upon closer inspection was an empty bottle of Disaronno amaretto liqueur, before we stamped the clay from our boots, got into the Fiesta, and headed for the A130.

Bibliography

The following is a selection of sources that have been useful in writing *The Invention of Essex*. If a source has been used across multiple chapters, it is listed in the chapter in which it was first used. Newspapers and magazines not given here are listed in the main text.

Prologue
Mark Brown, 'Britain's equivalent to Tutankhamun found in Southend-on-Sea', theGuardian.com, 8 May 2019.
JB Priestley, *English Journey*, London, William Heinemann Ltd, 1934.

1. Marsh, Maligned
William Addison, *Essex Heyday*, London, JM Dent & Sons, 1949.
Sabine Baring-Gould, *Further Reminiscences, 1864–1894*, London, John Lane, 1925.
Sabine Baring-Gould, *Mehalah: A Story of the Salt Marshes*, London, Smith, Elder & Co, 1880.
James Brome, *Travels Over England, Scotland, and Wales*, London, Rob. Gosling, 1707.
Randal Bingley, *Fobbing: Life and Landscape*, Stanford-le-Hope, Lejins Publishing, 1997.
Bickford H.C. Dickinson, *Sabine Baring-Gould: Squarson, Writer & Folklorist*, Newton Abbott, David & Charles, 1970.
Joan Didion, 'The Art of Non-fiction', from *The Paris Review Interviews Volume 1*, Edinburgh, Canongate, 2007.
Hilda Grieve, *The Great Tide*, Essex Record Office, 1959.
Simon Heffer, 'Mrs Thatcher's Bruiser', *Sunday Telegraph*, October 1990.
Ray Leigh and Brent Wood (Richard Littlejohn and Mitch Symonds), *The Essex Girl Joke Book*, London, Corgi, 1989.

Donald Maxwell, *Unknown Essex*, London, John Lane, 1925.

Arthur Morrison, *Cunning Murrell*, New York, Doubleday, 1900.

Piers Morgan, 'What do you get if you cross two Essex girls with New Kids? Sex all night' *Sun*, November 1991.

Heather Nunn and Anita Biressi, *Class and Contemporary British Culture*, London, Palgrave Macmillan, 2013.

Sarah Perry, *The Essex Serpent*, London, Serpent's Tail, 2016.

Nikolaus Pevsner, *The Buildings of England: Essex*, London, Penguin, 1954.

Keith Thomas, *Religion and the Decline of Magic*, London, Penguin Books, 2003.

Herbert W Tompkins, *Marsh Country Rambles*, London, Chatto & Windus, 1904.

C Henry Warren, *Essex*, London, Robert Hale Ltd, 1950.

J. Woodfall Ebsworth (ed), *Choyce Drollery: Songs and Sonnets, Being A Collection of Divers Excellent Pieces of Poetry, of Several Eminent Authors*, Boston, Robert Roberts, Strait Bar-Gate, 1661.

Ken Worpole and Jason Orton, *New English Landscape*, London, Field Station, 2013.

Ian Yearsley, *The Islands of Essex*, Romford, Ian Henry Publications, 1994.

2. Under the Water's Spell

Margery Allingham, *The Oaken Heart*, London, Michael Joseph, 1941.

THC Bartrop, 'Malaria, Mosquitoes and the Essex Marshes', *Essex Naturalist*, Volume 31, 1962, pages 35–51.

Philip Benton, *The History of Rochford Hundred*, Rochford, A. Harrington, 1867.

Daniel Defoe, *A Tour Thro' the Whole Island of Great Britain*, London, first published 1724–26, Penguin, 1971.

Mary Dobson, 'Marsh Fever – the geography of malaria in England', *Journal of Historical Geography*, Volume 6, 1980, pages 357–389.

Lucia Dove, *Vloed*, Wivenhoe, Dunlin Press, 2021.

Neville M. Goodman, 'A Case Of Malaria Arising In This Country', *British Medical Journal*, Volume 2, No. 3286, Dec. 22, 1923, page 1205.

'DEATH OF JOHN HARRIOTT, ESQ', *The Weekly Entertainer: or, Agreeable and instructive repository*, 3 Feb 1817.

John Harriott, *Struggles Through Life, Exemplified in the Various Travels*

and *Adventures in Europe, Asia, Africa, and America*, London,
Longman, Hurst, Rees, and Orme, 1807 / 1808.

John Hunter, *Essex Landscape*, Essex Record Office, 1999.

TW Keeble, 'A Cure for the Ague: The Contribution of Robert Talbor
(1642–81)', *Journal of the Royal Society of Medicine*, Volume 90, Issue
5, pages 285–290.

Robert Macfarlane, *The Old Ways*, London, Hamish Hamilton, 2012.

Robert Talbor, *Pyretologia: a rational account of the cause & cure of
agues, with their signes, diagnostick & prognostick*, London, For R.
Robinson, 1672.

3. 'These Children of Nature'

Walter Besant, *East London*, London, Chatto & Windus, 1903.

John William Burrows, *Southend on Sea and District Historical Notes*,
Southend, John H Burrows, 1909.

David Churchill, 'Living in a Leisure Town: Residential Reactions to
the Growth of Popular Tourism in Southend, 1870–1890', *Urban
History*, Volume 41, 1, Cambridge, Cambridge University, Press,
2014.

Yvonne Cloud, *Beside the Seaside*, London, John Lane The Bodley
Head, 1938.

Ken Crowe, 'The arrival of Mr and Mrs London at Southend': A Zoom
lecture given Wednesday 10 May 2021.

Gregory Dart, *Metropolitan Art and Literature, 1810–1840: Cockney
Adventures*, Cambridge, Cambridge University Press, 2012.

Donald Glennie, *Our Town: an Encyclopaedia of Southend-on-Sea and
District*, Southend-on-Sea, Civic Publications, 1947.

William Hazlitt, *The Plain Speaker: Opinions on Books, Men, and
Things: in Two Volumes, Volume 1*, Henry Colburn, London, New
Burlington-Street, 1826.

Robert Arthur Jones, 'New Name for Southend', a letter to the
Southend Standard and Essex Weekly Advertiser, 24 December 1907.

John Keats, *The Poetical Works of John Keats*, Oxford, Oxford
University Press, 1902.

Henry Mayhew, *London Labour and the London Poor*, London, Penguin
Classics, 1985.

Keith Purvis, 'Southend-on-Sea 1891 to 1911: The Emergence of a
Commuter Town?', Open University MA Thesis, 2020.

EW Shepherd, *The Story of Southend Pier and Its Associations*,
    Hertfordshire, Egon Publishers, 1979.
Paul Theroux, *The Kingdom by the Sea*, London, Hamish Hamilton,
    1983.
Jim Worsdale, *Southend at War*, self-published, 1988.

4. A Curious Frontier
John Edward Bazille-Corbin, *Runwell St. Mary*, typescript, 1942.
SL Bensusan and H Cranmer-Byng, *Essex Plays*, Colchester, Benham,
    1933.
SL Bensusan, *Back of Beyond: A Countryman's Pre-War Commonplace
    Book*, London, Blandford Press, 1945.
John Booker, *Essex and Industrial Revolution*, Essex Record Office,
    1974.
AFJ Brown, *Prosperity and Poverty: Rural Essex, 1700–1815*, Essex
    Record Office, 1996.
Jim Clifford, *West Ham and the River Lea*, Vancouver, UBC Press, 2017.
Gillian Darley, *Excellent Essex*, London, Old Street Publishing Ltd,
    2019.
EH Hunt and SJ Pam, 'Essex Agriculture in the Golden Age', 1850-73,
    The Agricultural History Review, pages 160–177.
Norma Jennings, Nellie Sims and George Saddington, *From Country
    to Cockney: Romford Market Within Living Memory*, Redden Court
    Enterprises, Romford, 1996.
Todd Kuchta, *Semi-Detached Empire: Suburbia and the Colonization of
    Britain, 1880 to the Present*, Charlottesville, University of Virginia
    Press, 2010.
Thomas P. Linehan, *East London for Mosley: The British Union of
    Fascists in East London and South-West Essex, 1933-40*, London,
    Routledge, 1997.
Hugh Llewellyn-Smith, 'New Survey of London Life and Labour',
    Journal of the Royal Statistical Society, Volume 92, No. 4, 1929, pages
    530–558.
Sidney Low, 'The Rise Of The Suburbs', *The Contemporary Review*,
    October 1891.
Joe Morgan, *Eastenders Don't Cry*, South Woodham Ferrers, New
    Author Publications Ltd, 1994.
Henry Morley, 'Londoners Over the Border' *Household Words*,

12 September 1857, Volume 16, Issue 390 (accessed: https://djo.org.
    uk/household-words/volume-xvi/page-241.html)

Carolynn Roncaglia, 'Claudius' Houseboat', *Greece & Rome*, Volume
    66 , Issue 1, The Classical Association, April 2019 , pp. 61–70.

Colin Ward, *Arcadia for All*, Nottingham, Five Leaves Publications,
    2004.

Jennifer Westwood and Jacqueline Simpson, *Haunted England: The
    Penguin Book of Ghosts*, London, Penguin, 2010.

Sarah Wise, *The Blackest Streets: The Life and Death of a Victorian
    Slum*, London, Bodley Head, 2008.

Ted Woodgate, *Brothers, Be United, And You Will Be Strong: The Farm
    Workers Union in the Basildon Area, 1872–94*, self-published in
    Billericay, 2022.

5. The Better Life

Anon, 'From AN ARCHITECT'S Commonplace Book', *The Architects'
    Journal*, (Archive : 1929–2005), Volume 108, 23 December 1948, Art
    & Architecture Archive, page 569.

Reyner Banham, *A City Crowned with Green*, BBC, 1964.

Bernard Braine, 'New Town, Basildon (freeholders)', *Hansard*, 15 May
    1950.

John Carey (ed), *The Faber Book of Utopias*, London, Faber and Faber,
    1999.

'Osea – Back To Basics: from *The Daily Graphic*, 1 February, 1904',
    Penny Farthing: the Newsletter of Maldon District Museum
    Association, Issue 28, Spring 2002.

Gillian Darley, *Factory*, London, Reaktion Books, 2003.

Hayley Dixon and Joe Hill (ed), *Radical Essex*, Southend-on-Sea, Focal
    Point Gallery, 2018.

Ben Dowell, 'Father of C4's Sarah Mulvey claims treatment centre let
    her down', https://www.theguardian.com/media/2012/may/22/
    father-c4-sarah-mulvey-treatment-centre, 22 May 2012.

John Frankland, *South Woodham Ferrers: A Pictorial History*,
    Chichester, Phillmore & Co Ltd, 1992.

Henry George, *Progress and Poverty*, Everyman's Library edition,
    London, JM Dent & Sons, 1911 (first published by D. Appleton and.
    Company, 1880).

Marcus Granath, *Searching for the Promised Land*, Bexleyheath,
    GoldStar Books, 2004.

Victor Gray, *A New World in Essex: The Rise and Fall of the Purleigh Brotherhood Colony, 1896–1903*, Wivenhoe, Campanula Books, 2019.

Dennis Hayes and Alan Hudson, *Basildon: The Mood of the Nation*, London, Demos, 2001.

Owen Hatherley, *Red Metropolis*, London, Repeater Books, 2020.

Verity-Jane Keefe, *Living Together (100 years of the Becontree Estate) [art project]*, <www.livingtogether.org.uk>, 2021.

Jonathan Meades/Francis Hanly, *The Joy of Essex*, BBC Four, 2013.

Arthur Mee, *The King's England: Essex*, London, Hodder and Stoughton, 1966.

William Morris, *News from Nowhere*, London, Reeves and Turner, 1891.

Nikolaus Pevsner, *The Englishness of English Art*, London, Peregrine Books, 1964.

Vivienne Salmon, *The Harveys: A Farming Family in Thundersley*, Hadleigh & Faraway Places, The Hadleigh & Thundersley Community Archive, 2021.

CI Smith, *New Town Utopia* [film], Cult Modern, 2018.

Lord Taylor and Sidney Chave, *Mental Health and Environment*, London, Longmans, 1964.

Norman Tebbit, *Upwardly Mobile*, London, Futura Publications, 1989.

Guy Thorne, *The Great Acceptance: The Life Story of FN Charrington*, London, Hodder and Stoughton, 1913.

Colin Ward, 'Letters: Housing the Nation: Replies To Crosland', *Architects' Journal*, (Archive : 1929–2005) Volume 160, Issue 46, 13 November 1974, Art & Architecture Archive, page 1141.

Colin Ward, *New Town, Home Town: The Lessons Of Experience*, London, Calouste Gulbenkian Foundation, 1993.

Colin Ward and Dennis Hardy, 'The Non-Plan Plot', *Architects' Journal*, Volume 180, Issue 51, 19 December 1984, pages 35–43.

Ken Worpole, *No Matter How Many Skies Have Fallen*, Dorset, Little Toller, 2021.

6. We Play for Real

Hervey Benham, *The Smugglers' Century*, Essex Record Office, 1986.

Huw Benyon, *Working for Ford*, London, Allen Lane, 1973.

Will Birch, *No Sleep Till Canvey Island*, London, Virgin Books, 2003.

Anthony Clavane, *A Yorkshire Tragedy: The Rise and Fall of a Sporting Powerhouse*, London, Riverrun, 2016.

Ford's Dagenham Dream, BBC Four, 2009.

Bibliography

Elliot Gibbons, *Southend's Twilight Worlds*, Southend-on-Sea, The Old Waterworks, 2022.

Will Gilbey/Andrew Loveday, *Rise of the Footsoldier: Marbella*, Carnaby International, 2019.

Zoe Howe, *Lee Brilleaux: Rock'n'Roll Gentleman*, Edinburgh, Polygon, 2015.

Wilko Johnson and Zoe Howe, *Looking Back at Me*, London, Cadiz Music, 2012.

Peter Kane, 'Police quiz for soccer boss', *Daily Mirror*, 24 October 1984.

Billy Kenber, 'Gang boss said he could "take out" Leah Betts drug suppliers', *The Times*, 20 February 2017.

Bernard O'Mahoney, *Essex Boys: A Terrifying Exposé of the British Drugs Scene*, Edinburgh, Mainstream Publishing Company, 2000.

International Centre for the History of Crime, Policing and Justice: 1987: Crime increase Eastern Division, accessed via <open.ac.uk/Arts/history-from-police-archives/RB1/Pt4/pt4TL198690.html>

Room 101, BBC2, 2002.

Ian Sinclair, *London Orbital*, London, Penguin, 2001.

Ray Stone and Ant Gavin Smits, *A Driven Life, Anton Johnson: Adventurer and Entrepreneur*, self-published, 2021.

Luke Turner, 'The return of pop perverts Nitzer Ebb', https://www.theguardian.com/music/2019/jan/03/the-return-of-pop-perverts-nitzer-ebb-if-people-arent-looking-at-the-stage-it-still-can-be-sexual, 3 January 2019.

7. Doing Very Well

David Amess, *Against All Odds*, Conservative Party pamphlet, 1992.

Bryan Appleyard, 'Blair's voters in Versace: Essex man and woman are in the money, yet the feel-good factor is leading them to choose Labour', *The Independent*, 1 May 1996.

Juliet Barker, *England, Arise: The People, The King & The Great Revolt of 1381*, London, Abacas, 2015.

Andy Beckett, *When the Lights Went Out*, London, Faber and Faber, 2009.

Andy Beckett, *Promised You a Miracle*, London, Penguin, 2016.

Philip Carden, *Steel Times*, Volume 199, Issue 4, April 1971.

Laurence Cawley, 'Margaret Thatcher funeral attended by "Essex Man"', <www.bbc.co.uk/news>, 2013.

David Crouch, *Essex Man and Woman: A Search for Reality*, Essex, Essex Chronicle, 1992.

'Iain Dale speaks to Sir David Amess', *Ian Dale All Talk*, LBC, May 2021.

RB Dobson (ed), *The Peasants' Revolt of 1381*, London, The Macmillan Press, 1970.

Paul Field, Robin Bunce, Leila Hassan & Margaret Peacock (eds), *Here To Stay, Here To Fight: A Race Today Anthology*, London Pluto Press, 2019.

John H Goldthorpe, David Lockwood, Frank Bechhofer & Jennifer Platt, *The Affluent Worker*, Cambridge, Cambridge University Press, 1968.

Paul Harrison, *Inside the Inner City*, London, Penguin, 1985.

Rachel Hartley, *No Mean City: A Guide to the Economic City of London*, London, Queen Anne Press, 1967.

Rodney Hilton, *Bond Men Made Free: Medieval Peasant Movements and the English Rising of 1381*, London, University Paperback / Methuen & Co, 1977.

George Jones and Robert Shrimsley, 'Essex man turns on Tories, Blair hails victory in Basildon', *Daily Telegraph*, 3 May 1996.

Joe Kennedy, *Authentocrats*, London, Repeater Books, 2018.

Barrie Keeffe/John Mackenzie, *The Long Good Friday*, Black Lion Films / Calendar Productions / HandMade Films, 1980.

Mike Leigh, *Meantime*, Channel 4, 1983.

Mike Leigh, *Play For Today: Abigail's Party*, BBC, 1977.

Laurence Marks and Maurice Gran/Tony Dow, *Birds of a Feather* series 1, BBC, 1989.

James Meek, 'Robin Hood in a Time of Austerity', *London Review of Books*, Volume 38, No. 4, 18 February 2016, pages 3–8.

William Morris, *A Dream of John Ball and A King's Lesson*, London, Kelmscott, 1892.

Tony Norfield, *The City: London and the Global Power of Finance*, London, Verso, 2016.

Thomas Paine, *Rights of Man*, London, JS Jordan, 1792.

Andrew Pierce, 'Profile – Andy Coulson', *Daily Telegraph*, 1 Jun 2007.

Jonathan Raban, *Soft City*, London, Hamish Hamilton, 1974.

'Social Changes In Britain', *Television Mail*, Volume 7, Issue 21, 11 January 1963, page 13.

Bibliography

8. Reality Bites

'VIEWS AND REVIEWS: marginalia: DEDHAM VALE IN DANGER', *The Architectural Review*, Volume 137, Issue 819; 1 May 1965, Art & Architecture Archive page 329.

'Editorial', *Essex Review*, Volume 1, Issue 1, January 1892.

Gemma Collins interviewed on Sky News, 25 October 2016.

James Corden and Ruth Jones / Christine Gernon, *Gavin and Stacey*, series 1, BBC.

EH Gombrich, *Art And Illusion: A Study in the Psychology of Pictorial Representation*, Phaidon, 1977.

Ian La Frenais and Dick Clement / Jonathan Gash, *Lovejoy*, BBC, 1986–1994.

Lovejoy filming locations map, google.com/maps.

James Mowatt, 'Essex: Class Mythopoeia' [dissertation], Birkbeck, 2020.

The Only Way Is Essex, ITV, 2010–2022.

Leslie Parris, Ian Fleming-Williams and Conal Shields, *Constable: Paintings, Watercolours & Drawings*, The Tate Gallery, 1976.

Richard Pendlebury, 'After an Ordinary Essex Girl Trounces The Big Brother Celebrities . . . Chantelle, This Eliza Doolittle of Our Age', *Daily Mail*, 30 January 2006.

EP Thompson, *The Making of the English Working Class*, London, Penguin, 1991 reprint.

Patrick Wright, *On Living in An Old Country*, London, Verso, 1985.

9. Unstoppable, Immovable

Atomic Weapons Research Establishment Foulness Island, 1947 Explosives Storage Area, Historic England listing, <historicengland.org.uk/listing/the-list/list-entry/1411759o>.

JA Baker, *The Peregrine: The Hill of Summer & Diaries: The Complete Works of J. A. Baker*, London, William Collins, 2011.

Raw news footage of Barling Bomber aftermath, *Thames News*, 25 August 1988.

Sandra Barwick, 'In Essex, something is burning', *The Independent*, 7 May 1994.

James Canton, *Out of Essex*, Oxford Signal Books, 2013.

Kelly Close, *Last Whites of the East End*, BBC, 2016.

Joseph Conrad, *Heart of Darkness*, London, Penguin Classics, 2007 (first published 1899).

Joseph Conrad, *A Mirror of the Sea & A Personal Record*, London, Wordsworth Editions, 2008.

David Eversley, 'A balance of social priorities', *Built Environment*, July 1973.

Frederick G T Farenden, *Running a village pub under MOD rules on Foulness Island*, Foulness Island, Farenden Publishing, 2003.

Matthew Flintham, 'The Shoeburyness Complex: Military space and the problem of the civilian body', Chris Pearson, Peter Coates and Tim Coates (eds.), *Militarized landscapes: from Gettysburg to Salisbury Plain*, London, Continuum, 2009, pages 81–94.

Neil Hanson, *The Custom of the Sea*, London, Doubleday, 1999.

Warren Harper (curator) and Gabriella Hirst (artist), *How to Make a Bomb* [gallery show], Southend-on-Sea, The Old Waterworks / Focal Point Gallery, 2021.

Elsa James, *Forgotten Black Essex* [gallery show], Southend-on-Sea, Metal, 2018.

Elsa James, *Othered in a Region That Has Been Historically Othered* [gallery show], Southend-on-Sea, Focal Point Gallery, 2022.

Prof Judith Okely, 'Letter to the *Guardian*: Gypsy life in Essex is brushed over', https://www.theguardian.com/uk-news/2019/jul/01/gypsy-life-in-essex-is-brushed-over, 1 July 2019.

ONS, 'Subnational estimates of dwellings and households by tenure, England: 2020', <ons.gov.uk/peoplepopulationandcommunity>, 31 January 2022.

Samuel Purchas, *Purchas, His Pilgrimage*, Printed by William Stansby for Henrie Fetherstone, accessed via https://www.google.co.uk/books/edition/Purchas_His_Pilgrimage_Or_Relations_of_t/jkZpAAAAcAAJ?hl=en&gbpv=0, 1626 (first published 1614),.

Samuel Purchas, *Purchas, His Pilgrimes*, Printed by William Stansby for Henrie Fetherstone, accessed via https://www.google.co.uk/books/edition/Purchas_his_pilgrimes/ojSN5RNaVNkC?hl=en&gbpv=0, 1625.

The Reunion, The Dale Farm Evictions, BBC Radio 4, 2022.

Sukhdev Sandhu, *London Calling*, London, Harper Perennial, 2004.

Daniel Trilling, *Bloody Nasty People*, London, Verso, 2012.

Tim Walker, 'Barling Bomber report', *Observer*, 28 August 1988.

10. Mucking In

Dr James H Brand and Prof Kate Spencer, 'Assessing the risk of pollution from historic coastal landfills', Queen Mary University, 2017.

Lizzie Davies, '"It's one big cesspit here": Thurrock, the country's capital of misery', https://www.theguardian.com/lifeandstyle/2012/jul/25/thurrock-capital-misery, 25 July 2012.

Chris Durlacher, *The Secret Life of Rubbish*, BBC Four, 2012.

Lee Jackson, *Dirty Old London*, Connecticut and London, Yale University Press, 2014.

Rachel Lichtenstein, *Estuary*, London, Hamish Hamilton, 2016.

David Nash, 'Fish Rescued From the Rubbish', *Angling Times*, 9 December, 1971.

Lizzie Presser, 'London's homelessness crisis is spilling into the home counties', https://www.theguardian.com/society/2015/sep/30/london-homelessness-crisis-home-counties-councils, 30 September 2015.

Justin Rowlatt, 'Toxic air puts six million at risk of lung damage', bbc.co.uk/news, 11 February 2021.

11. **Home at Last**

William Davies, 'Bloody Furious: review of Generation Left by Keir Milburn', *LRB*, 20 February 2020.

Grand Designs, Channel 4, 2011.

Bill Griffiths (ed and trans), *The Battle of Maldon*, Cambridgeshire, Anglo-Saxon Books, 1991.

Verity-Jane Keefe, *Lived In Architecture: Becontree at 100* [gallery show], London, RIBA, 2021.

Michael Landy, *Welcome to Essex* [gallery show], Colchester, FirstSite, 2021.

Michael Landy, *Semi-Detached* [gallery show], London, Tate, 2004.

Anna Minton, *Big Capital*, London, Penguin, 2018.

Dominic Rushe, '"Essex Boys" case of traders accused of manipulating markets heads for trial', https://www.theguardian.com/business/2022/apr/13/essex-boys-oil-price-manipulation-trial, 13 April 2022.

Epilogue: Runwell

Derek Johnson, *Essex Curiosities*, Buckinghamshire, Spurbooks Ltd, 1973.

'Opening Of Runwell Hospital' booklet, June 1937.

Index

Page numbers in *italics* denotes a photo

Index

Basildon 21, 106, 107–10,
111–13, *113*, 120, 137–8, 160, 178,
179–80, 262, 276–80, 282–3
  Amess as MP for 178–9, 180
  decline in 279–80
  demolishment of Freedom
    House 278
  demolishment of plotlands
    to make way for 108–9
  home ownership 154
  and homeless 277–8
  house building 277
  inequality in 179–80
  isolation of first cockneys
    coming to 112–13
  local elections 276–7, 282
  and Moyet 142
  town centre masterplan 277,
    280, 282, 283
  votes for Thatcher 178
Basildon Community
  Residents' Party 277, 282
Basildon Council 282
Basildon Development
  Corporation (BDC) 108–9,
  113, 172
Basildon Echo 169
Basildon man 178
Bata estate (East Tilbury) 86–8
Bata Shoe Company 86–7, *87*
Bata, Tomáš 86–7
'Battle of Maldon, The' (poem)
  284
Bawden, Edward 82
Bazalgette, Joseph 73
Bazille-Corbin, John 76,
  289–90, 291, 292
Beadle, Thomas 38
Bear, William E 42

Beckett, Andy 172
Beckett, Thomas 193
Beckton Alp 247
Becontree 109–10, 112, 158
Becontree Estate (Chadwell
  Heath) 102–5, *103*, 275–6
Becontree Literary and
  Debating Society 275
Bedlam hospital, reburial of
  skeletons found under site
  of 251
Benfleet 105
Benton, Philip 30, 38
Berendsen, Daniella 194
Berkshire 19
Besant, Walter 55–7, 65–6
  East London 65
Betjeman, John 51, 60
Bettis, Yasmin 196–9
Betts, Leah 126, 131
Big Brother 192
bigotry 163, 225
Billericay District Council 107
bin collection services 252–3
  privatisation of 252
Bingley, Randal 8, 147
Birds of a Feather (TV
  programme) 174–5
Black Death 148, 149
black people 226–30
  landing of *Windrush* at
    Tilbury 227–9, *228*
  racism against 226–7, 229
Blackwater Estuary 8, 34, 64–5,
  205
Blackwater River 18, 26, 67
Blair, Tony 181
Blythe, Ronald 157
BNP 233

Index

Chalkwell Hall 261
Chalkwell Park Estate 261
Chappel Viaduct 64
Charrington, Frederick 84, 85
Chelmsford 156–7
Chigwell 117, 174
children's homes 272
Childs, Amy 193, 194
City of London 166–8
  deregulation of (1986) 167
  development of under
    Thatcher 167
  and Essex man 165–6, 167–8
  growth of 167
Clacton 53
Clacton Butlins 53
Clark, Perry 74–5
Clarke, Vince 137–8, 141
class 19, 20–1, 22
classlessness 157, 157–8
Claudius, Emperor 69
clay soil 42
Clean Air Act 245
Cliff pub (Southend) 138
Clifford, Jim 72, 73
climate change 255
coastal erosion 43, 254, 256
cockles 60
cockney 57–8
Coggeshall 57, 94
Colchester 69, 186
Cole, Eric 86
Coleridge, Samuel Taylor
  'Kubla Khan' 208
Coles, Darren 122–3
Collins, Gemma 195, 202
commuter/commuting 156–8
Conder, Terry 25
Congreve, Dr Alina 281, 282

Conrad, Joseph
  Heart of Darkness 223
  The Mirror of the Sea 223
Conservative Party 22, 23, 160,
  179, 272
  and Essex man 164, 168
  and home ownership 153–4
  see also Thatcher, Margaret
Constable, John 183–8, 202–3
  The Hay Wain 185
  The Vale of Dedham 230
consumerism 24, 158, 160
Control of Pollution Act (1974)
  245
Cooper, Sir Richard Powell
  61–2
Cope, Julie (fictional Essex
  woman) 263, 267
Corden, James 189
Costello, Elvis 142–3
costermongers (barrow boys)
  56
Cotswolds 11, 41
Coulson, Andy 23, 169–70
council housing 285
  Becontree Estate 102–3, *103*
  see also Right to Buy policy
Country Life magazine 10–11
Courcy, Anne de 175
Cowley family 114–15
Cranmer-Byng, H 65
Creekmouth 43–4
Creekmouth Preservation
  Society 43–4
crime 130
Critchley, Julian
  Westminster Blues 152
Crittall, Francis Henry 89
Crittall Windows 89, 90

Index

Index

Index

Index

Right to Buy policy 99, 154,
    155, 167, 179, 270, 271, 276
Thatcherism 164, 170, 176, 181,
    274
The Only Way Is Essex see
    Towie
Theroux, Paul 62
These New Puritans 257
Thomas, Keith
    *Religion and the Decline of
    Magic* 14
Thompson, EP 184
Thresh, Dr 186–7
Thunderer, HMS 71
Thundersley 91
Thurrock 146–7, 220, 221–2,
    224, 225
    house price increase 272
    housing of homeless families
        in by London councils
        251–2
    landfills 247
    pollution 243
Thurrock Council, and
    pollution of South
    Ockendon pits 241
Thurrock suspension bridge 64
tides 9, 27, 28, 43, 47, 79
Tilbury 223–5, 226
    Amazon fulfilment centre
        222–3
    coastal landfill (Bottle
        Beach) 246, 255
    decline of 224
    history 223
    landing of the *Windrush*
        227–8, 228
    racist attacks 227
Tilbury Band 224–5

Tilbury Docks 223–4
Tilbury Fort 39
Tollesbury 8, 9, 64, 67
Tollesbury cannibals 205
Tompkins, Herbert W
    Marsh Country Rambles 15
Top of the Pops 141–2
Tower Hamlets Mission 84
Towie (The Only Way is Essex)
    21–2, 198–200, 201, 202
trade unions 170–2, 224
travellers 230
    and Dale Farm Travellers
        stand-off (2011) 230–1
Trilling, Daniel
    Bloody Nasty People 233
Trinovantes 69
Tucker, Tony 126, 127, 130, 133,
    293
Turner, Luke 139
Two Tree Island 246, 254
Two Tree Island tip 249
Tyler, Wat 149, 151

U
Ukip 225, 233
unions *see* trade unions

V
Van Dyke, Dick 57
Varty, Robert 97
Vermuyden, Cornelius 34
Vesey-Fitzgerald, Brian 19
Victorian era 51, 56, 67, 70, 71–5
Vikings 283
Volkswagen 175

W
Wallasea Island 32, 253

Acknowledgements

I signed the contract to write *The Invention of Essex* the week before the first Covid lockdown began in March 2020; it was a leap of faith into the unknown in more ways than one. I had been trying to get a book on Essex off the ground for a few years without much luck until Cecily Gayford, who edited this book, took a chance on me. She emailed me out of the blue to suggest I turn an article I had written for the *Guardian*'s Long Read desk, which was published that day, into a book. Since then, Cecily has been a steady, kind, tactful and strong presence, even when faced with the relentless winds of Covid and the complications of life. I was blessed by not one but two editors while writing this book. Shan Vahidy, who was brought in by Cecily to work closely with me on the final drafts, deserves particular praise for helping me fine tune some of the shaggier bits of the text (and cut out the really unkempt sections all together).

I'd especially like to thank David Wolf, Jonathan Shainin and Clare Longrigg on the *Guardian*'s Long Read desk for having faith in the idea of a long-form story on Essex; letting me write at length enough to realise it might make a good book after all. So many editors at the *Guardian* have indulged other ideas about Essex I pitched to them, many of which have ended up in this book, from hanging out with *Towie* wannabes in Brentwood to talking about moving skeletons to Canvey in a Beckton funeral parlour: cheers especially to Kate Abbott, Nancy Groves and Chris Michael for your faith. *Guardian* colleagues have also provided wise counsel, in particular Andy Beckett and Aditya Chakrabortty, who I badgered for advice during the intense middle of the process when I couldn't see the wood for the trees. Thanks to others who have commissioned me to write about Essex, which sometimes resulted in work that I have drawn upon: Kit Caless and Gary Budden at Influx Press; Suze Olbrich at *Somesuch Stories*; Tom Jeffreys at *The*

Learned Pig; Sukhdev Sandhu; John Doran at *The Quietus*; and at *Vice*, Max Daly and former editors Eleanor Morgan and Kev Kharas.

Ken Worpole, the godfather of utopian Essex, is a man who deserves my constant thanks for being an inspiration ever since I heard his first talk at Snape in Suffolk; and Gillian Darley, too, has been a great encouragement and is so full of energy for learning about the county. Big love must be bestowed upon Verity-Jane Keefe for showing me around her muse, the Becontree Estate, sharing her deep knowledge of the place as she led me on drifts around it after she asked me to take part in a writing residency to respond to her centenary project, Living Together – during which some of the work on Becontree in this book was first developed. Cheers to Christine Townley for sitting down with me to talk about Essex's flood defence infrastructure and much else. Thank you Aaron Shrimpton, Dave Murray and Maz Murray for the Basildon chat; Jonny Keyworth for showing me Harlow; Bronia Stewart for taking me out in Brentwood. Thanks to Peter Griffiths for sharing stories of Great Wakering and the flood, and to David Eldridge for talking class and Romford. I can't thank most of the people interviewed for this book here, but I am grateful to each person who talked to me. Ted Woodgate – thanks so much for sharing your knowledge of south Essex farming unions with me, and for connecting me to Stan Newens. Justin Hopper, cheers for telling me what's what in Dedham. Thanks to Flavian Capes and Tilly Shiner for letting me into the secrets of marsh life; and to Jim Clifford for expertly defining how important West Ham is to the Essex story at large. I owe Kate Spencer a debt of gratitude for showing me round the rubbish beaches of Thurrock, and Eloise Hawser for introducing us, and being a figure of energy and encouragement in the background of this book, particularly after I dropped an early draft on her. The same goes for Emma Edmondson, my neighbour and collaborator – thanks for the walks and the talks. As ever I must thank my dear pal Luke Turner for the constant online and IRL chats that reflected a mutual appreciation of the crapness of writing life under lockdown – nice one m8. And to Jennifer Lucy Allen, a rock (or perhaps a foghorn) in the storm who offered me practical tips at the prod of a WhatsApp message.

Mum and Dad, Margaret and Kevin Burrows – thank you for sharing your stories with me and supporting me. Thanks, too, to my sister, Sophie. I owe gratitude to Uncle Mick for helping me find the old Thundersley bungalow. Hayley's family, too: thanks to her mother

Acknowledgements

Ann Hatton and her father Cliff Hatton for their enthusiasm in talking about growing up in Essex, and her grandparents Ernest and Hannelore Singer – rest in peace, Cliff, Ernest and Hannelore. Massive thanks are also due to some of my oldest friends. Will Mudie and Paul Reynolds – AKA the Sift Lords – at Essex Clearances quite literally brought to my door some fine Essex research material that might have otherwise been destined for landfill. To have such serendipitous access to books published by the Essex Record Office and others while the archives were closed felt like magic. Cheers to good pal Justyna Burzynska for helping so much with my online research. I am grateful to Doug Cheeseman for lending his archive of Essex books, transported to my door in supermarket bags for life. Thanks to my old mucker Sarah Wayman, who shared her workings and musings on queer Essex with me, and listened, read and offered advice. Cheers loads to Adam Kinsey and Shona Handley for joining in with the Essex walks depicted in this book, since we started them in the 2000s (Newham Folk Archive forever!). Thanks to Jack and George Barnett for offering new ways to look at Essex through their musical work in These New Puritans (and ta, Jack, for coming on that epic walk in 2012; hope your legs have recovered). I am also hugely grateful to Sophie Sleigh-Johnson, for her uncanny articulations of Essex marshland, for sharing her theories and for getting me hooked on the idea of trying to find the Running Well. Blessings and gratitude to Canvey's Sue, Dave and Sacha Clark. And thanks to pals who have put up with me and listened during the redrafting process: Rebecca Gillieron, Rich Chapman, Vi Varah, Matt Battle, María Angélica Madero, Tom Holloway, Dom Bailey, the O'Sheas and the Knocks and the rest of you.

Thanks to Elsa James who has dragged Essex's public discourse where it needed to be taken, for sharing her family's experience of being Black in Essex and for becoming a good friend. Two Southend institutions deserve credit for supporting me in my work on Essex: the Focal Point Gallery, in particular past and present faces Hayley Dixon, Joe Hill, Holly Firmin, James Ravinet and the former director Andrew Hunt. Metal, based in Chalkwell Hall, offered me a writing residency alongside English Pen at a perfect time for me to formulate my ideas on Essex and housing: thank you Andrea Cunningham, Paige Ockendon, Adjowa Afful and Hannah Clarke.

The people who deserve most thanks in the pages of this book are the ones who share the same living space as me. My children, Greta and

Ernest – thank you for being patient with me as I marched in and out of the writing room, for coming with me on days out to weird old corners of Essex and for giving me great distractions when working on a draft was getting a bit much. To my wife, Hayley Hatton, I owe pretty much everything; thanks for being there, my love and my friend.

Picture Credits